Cyber Law in Sweden

Cyber Law in Sweden

Third Edition

Christine Storr

This book was originally published as a monograph in the International Encyclopaedia of Laws/Cyber Law.

Founding Editor: Roger Blanpain
General Editor: Frank Hendrickx
Volume Editor: Jos Dumortier, Pieter Gryffroy, Ruben Roex & Yung Shin Van Der Sype

Wolters Kluwer

Published by:
Kluwer Law International B.V.
PO Box 316
2400 AH Alphen aan den Rijn
The Netherlands
E-mail: international-sales@wolterskluwer.com
Website: lrus.wolterskluwer.com

Sold and distributed by:
Wolters Kluwer Legal & Regulatory U.S.
7201 McKinney Circle
Frederick, MD 21704
United States of America
E-mail: customer.service@wolterskluwer.com

ISBN 978-94-035-3841-9

e-Book: ISBN 978-94-035-3842-6
web-PDF: ISBN 978-94-035-3843-3

The Author

Christine Storr (previously Kirchberger) (editor of this monograph and main author)

Christine Storr earned her Law degree from the University of Vienna in 1997. After working as a trainee with the European Parliament and at two district courts in Austria, she obtained a Master's degree in Law and Information Technology from the University of Stockholm in 2000.

Christine joined the Law Department at Stockholm University in 2001 as a lecturer. She has been teaching law students as well as computer scientists and media professionals, both in Stockholm and other Swedish universities as well as at King's College in London. Within cyber law, her main focus areas are data protection, electronic commerce, and marketing law. She also teaches and publishes articles on legal information retrieval and legal informatics in general.

Christine is writing her doctoral thesis 'Legal Information as a Tool' in which she focuses on legal information retrieval, the concept of legal information within the framework of the doctrine of legal sources and also examines the information-seeking behaviour of lawyers.

Christine is the main editor of this monograph and has written the General Introduction as well as the parts on Electronic Transactions (Part IV), Privacy Protection (Part VI), and the Conclusion (Part VIII). She can be found as @iinek on Twitter and at iinek.net. Together with Pam Storr she founded legalgeekgirls.com.

The Author

Co-authors

Pam Storr (assistant editor and co-author)

Pam Storr earned her Law degree from the University of Durham, England in 2006. She has LLM degrees from Stockholm University in the fields of Law & Information Technology and Intellectual Property Law, along with a Swedish Law degree.

Pam is a lecturer and legal consultant within the areas of IT law, intellectual property law and media law. She teaches law students, computer scientists and designers, among others, at a number of Swedish universities. Pam's main areas of interest within cyber law are intellectual property rights, privacy, security and the legal impact of new technologies.

Pam is the assistant editor of this monograph and has written the parts on Intellectual Property and Regulation of the ICT Market (Part I Chapters 3 and 4; updates Chapters 1 and 2, and Part II). She can be found as @pamstorr on Twitter and at legalgeekgirls.com.

Ulf Isaksson (Part V)

Ulf Isaksson, partner of the law firm Danowsky & Partners, has a Law degree from Uppsala University (1990) and an LLM from the University of Amsterdam (1993). He began his professional career as a law clerk in the Stockholm District Court (1990–1992). In 1993, he joined Danowsky & Partners, a Swedish law firm focused on corporate and commercial law and dispute resolution. The firm is considered as one of the leading Swedish law firms within media and intellectual property rights.

Ulf has represented publishers and other companies and organizations in the media industry, both as counsel and as litigator. He has been assigned by the Swedish Bar Association to comment on proposed legislation regarding copyright and media. He is also the author of several articles, mainly in the field of media and intellectual property. He is a guest lecturer in the field of media law at the University of Stockholm.

Co-authors

Part V of this monograph was written together with Karl Hägg who is an associate at the law firm Danowsky & Partners. Karl Hägg has a Law degree from Uppsala University (2010). He has also studied for one year at the Department of Media and Communications at the same university. He had an internship at Danowsky & Partners during the fall of 2009 and joined the firm directly after his graduation. Karl also has experience as a company lawyer during the later part of his student days.

Johan Kahn (Part III)

Johan Kahn has nearly twenty years of experience in advising clients on digital legal issues such as technology services, outsourcing and data protection. He is a partner with the Swedish specialist law firm Kahn Pedersen. Johan has published a large number of other publications and is frequently invited to speak at legal conferences, both in Sweden and internationally.

Part III in this volume was written together with Daniel Lundqvist who is a partner at Advokatfirman Kahn Pedersen. Daniel Lundqvist has more than ten years of experience in providing legal advice in connection with complex services agreements, IT contracts, sourcing and data protection.

Henrik Nilsson (original versions of Part I Chapters 1 and 2)

Henrik Nilsson is an Advokat at Gärde Wesslau law firm in Stockholm, Sweden. He has practised Telecommunications Law since 1997 and is a frequent contributor to legal and business journals on these issues.

Henrik Nilsson advises clients on regulatory and commercial issues with a focus on the IT and telecom industries and acts on behalf of clients before government agencies and authorities, in Sweden and internationally such as with European Union (EU) organizations. He has previously worked for the Swedish Competition Authority and the Swedish Post and Telecom Agency as well as international and domestic law firms. Henrik is ranked for IT & telecommunications law by Chambers & Partners 2014 and Legal500 2014.

Per Nordenson (Part I Chapter 5)

Per Nordenson has a Law degree from the University of Stockholm and worked at the Stockholm District Court for two years after graduating. He worked at Advokatfirman Frie and subsequently at Advokatfirman Cederquist until 2004 as a partner. He founded Nordenson Advokatbyrå in 2004 and specializes in litigation and arbitration, telecommunications and IT, including IP-related and advertising matters, mergers and acquisitions, distribution and agency matters, real estate and tenant law.

Per Nordenson is a member of the Swedish Bar Association and IBA and has a broad experience of advising in business law, particularly as counsel in domestic and international litigation, including arbitration and dispute resolution. During the past five to six years, he acted as counsel for clients in a large number of cases and matters under the frameworks for regulation of telecommunications within the EU. He has also been lecturing on Procedural Law at, among others, the University of Stockholm.

Erik O. Wennerström (Part VII)

Erik O. Wennerström has a Master's degree in Law from the University of Uppsala in Sweden. In 1990, he joined the Ministry for Foreign Affairs of Sweden and served with its diplomatic service, until he joined the European Commission in 1996, to work *inter alia* with issues related to judicial cooperation in criminal law. For the Commission, he drafted, for example, the Framework Decision on Fraud and Counterfeiting of Non-cash Means of Payment, later adopted and made part of the EU acquis, and was instrumental in areas encompassing measures against cybercrime. Returning to Sweden, he joined the Ministry of Justice in time for the first Swedish EU Presidency in 2001. He has negotiated and rendered legal advice in the fields of Police Cooperation, Judicial Cooperation, Telecommunications Law, and Information Exchange to the Swedish Government and the cooperation mechanisms under the EU. He has given lectures at several European universities and is the author of numerous articles and books. After obtaining his Doctor's degree in Law from his alma mater in 2007, he returned to the Ministry for Foreign Affairs, where he worked as the Principal Legal Adviser on International Law. After a number of years as the Director General of the Swedish National Council for Crime Prevention (*Brottsförebyggande rådet – Brå*), Erik is now a judge at the European Court of Human Rights.

Co-authors

Table of Contents

List of Abbreviations

ADR	Alternative Dispute Resolution
B2B	Business-to-Business
B2C	Business-to-Consumer
BEREC	Body of European Regulators for Electronic Communications
CEF	Connecting Europe Facility
CEN	European Committee for Standardization
CENELEC	European Committee for Electrotechnical Standardization
CGEA	Community General Export Authorization
CJEU	Court of Justice of the European Union
DIGG	Agency for Digital Government (*Myndigheten för digital förvaltning*)
DOS	Denial-of-Service
ECB	European Central Bank
ECC	Export Control Council
EDI	Electronic Data Interchange
EDIFACT	Electronic Data Interchange for Administration, Commerce and Transport
EDPB	European Data Protection Board
EEA	European Economic Area
EPC	European Patent Convention
EPO	European Patent Office
ESV	Swedish National Financial Management Authority (*Ekonomistyrningsverket*)
ETS	European Treaty Series
ETSI	European Telecommunications Standards Institute
EU	European Union
FI	Financial Inspection Board (*Finansinspektionen*)
FMV	Defence Materiel Administration (*Försvarets materielverk*)
GDP	Gross Domestic Product
GDPR	General Data Protection Regulation

List of Abbreviations

HFD	*Högsta förvaltningsdomstolens årsbok*
IAB	Swedish Interactive Advertising Bureau
ICT	Information Communication Technology
IEC	International Electrotechnical Commission
ISO	International Organization for Standardization
ISP	Internet/Information Service Provider
LoAs	Levels of Assurance
MSB	Swedish Civil Contingencies Agency (*Myndigheten för samhällsskydd och beredskap*)
NEA	Swedish Alliance for Electronic Business (*Nätverket för Elektroniska Affärer*)
NJA	*Nytt Juridiskt Arkiv*
NSB	Swedish National Standardization Body
PEPPOL	Pan-European Public Procurement On-Line
PSD	Payment Services Directive
PSTN	Public Switched Telephone Network
PTS	Swedish Post and Telecom Agency (*Post- och telestyrelsen*)
SaaS	Software-as-a Service
SALAR	Swedish Association of Local Authorities and Regions (*see SKL for Swedish*)
SEPA	Single Euro Payments Area
SFS	Swedish Code of Statutes (*Svensk Författningssamling*)
SIS	Swedish Institute for Standards
SKL	*Sveriges Kommuner och Landsting* (see SALAR for the English abbreviation)
SMP	Significant Market Power
SNPAC	Swedish Number Portability Administrative Center
SOU	Swedish Government Official Reports (*Statens Offentliga Utredningar*)
SSR	Swedish Standards Council (*Sveriges Standardiseringsråd*)
TFEU	Treaty on the Functioning of the European Union
TRIPS	Trade-Related Aspects of Intellectual Property Rights
UMTS	Universal Mobile Telecommunications System
UN	United Nations
USO	Universal Service Obligation
VAT	Value Added Tax
WACs	Website Authentication Certificates
WCT	WIPO Copyright Treaty
WIPO	World Intellectual Property Organization

General Introduction

Chapter 1. General Background of the Country

§1. Geography and Demographics

1. With its 450,000 km^2, Sweden is the third-largest country in Western Europe. In between Denmark and Germany in the south, the Atlantic Ocean/Nordic Sea and Norway in the west, the Baltic Sea in the east and the Polar Circle in the north, Sweden is mainly covered by forest (52%), water (9%), and agricultural land (8%).

2. The total population of about 10 million is spread mainly in communities with more than 2,000 residents. The three largest cities – Stockholm (the capital), Gothenburg, and Malmö – house together 3.8 million people, the population of Stockholm being the largest with 2.2 million. While the southern part, especially the area in between the cities Stockholm, Gothenburg, and Malmö, as well as the Baltic coastline north of Stockholm, are the most densely populated areas, the northern part, Norrland, is rather sparsely populated.

3. Sweden is a rather homogenous country, with about 12% of Swedish residents being foreign born. There are two minority groups of native inhabitants, the Finnish-speaking group in the northeast, along the Finnish border (about 30,000) and the Sami (Lapp) population of about 15,000. The Sami also live in other nearby northern areas such as Norway, Finland, and Russia and are about 60,000 in total.

The national language is Swedish, a Germanic language. Other minority languages include Sami (Lapp), Finnish, Meänkieli (Tornedalen Finnish), Yiddish, and Romani Chib.

§2. Economics

4. From a historical point of view, the country's rich natural resources, including forests, ore deposits, and hydroelectric power, have been the basis of Sweden's industrial economy. Today, Sweden's economy is export oriented, as exports of goods and services amount to almost half of the Gross Domestic Product (GDP).

One-third of Sweden's exported goods are vehicles and machines, while pharmaceuticals and chemicals amount to 13%. The European Union (EU) is Sweden's most important export market.[1]

5. Sweden's GDP amounted to SEK 471,000 (ca EUR 46,500) per capita in 2018, which is a 2.3% increase since the year before. The Gross National Income in 2018 was SEK 478,000 (ca EUR 47,200) per capita.[2] The inflation rate (CPI with a fixed interest rate – CPIF) was 1.8% in March 2019.[3] Income tax and social security contributions are high compared internationally, and Sweden had one of the highest employment rates in the EU with 81.8% in 2018.[4] Innovation has also been one of the focus in the past years, as Sweden tops the Innovation Union Scoreboard, an index published by the European Commission.[5]

§3. Administrative Structure

I. General Democratic Framework

6. Sweden is a constitutional monarchy with a democratically elected parliament. While the monarch nowadays mainly has representative duties, the one-chamber Parliament (*Riksdagen*) is the main legislative power and approves the prime minister who appoints the Government (*Regeringen*) consisting of about ten ministries. According to the constitution, '[t]he Government governs the Realm', which mainly consists of drafting the national budget (which is approved later by the parliament), submitting legislative bills, administering justice, and heading government agencies.

The distribution of political power is one of separation of function, not separation of power, as expressed in the constitution:[6]

> Chapter 1. Basic principles of the form of government
> Art. 1. All public power in Sweden proceeds from the people.
> Art. 4. The Riksdag is the foremost representative of the people.

7. The Parliament comprises 349 members in its single chamber.[7] Elections are generally held every four years.[8] Commonly, elections for counties and municipalities are held on the same day. Every Swedish citizen who is at least 18 years old can vote in all three elections. Non-Swedish citizens who are citizens of either another EU Member State or a Nordic country and registered in Sweden at the time

1. *See* Sweden.se, sweden.se/business/, 13 Apr. 2019.
2. Statistics Sweden, *National Accounts, quarterly and annual estimates*, www.scb.se/NR0103-en, 13 Apr. 2019.
3. Statistics Sweden, *Consumer Price Index (CPI)*, www.scb.se/PR0101-en, 13 Apr. 2019.
4. Eurostat, *Key figures on Europe: Statistics visualised – 2018 edition*, p. 23.
5. ec.europa.eu/growth/industry/innovation/facts-figures/scoreboards_en, 13 Apr. 2019.
6. Laura Carlson, *The Fundamentals of Swedish Law* (Lund: Studentlitteratur AB, 2019), 25.
7. Chapter 3 Art. 1 Instrument of Government (*regeringsform (RF)*).
8. Chapter 3 Art. 3 Instrument of Government.

of election can vote in their county and municipality.[9] In order to achieve seats in the parliament, a party has to reach at least 4% of the votes cast nationally.[10]

8. The Swedish public administration features three levels of government: national, regional, and local. On a regional level, Sweden is divided into twenty-one counties with county councils (*landsting*), while on a local level, Sweden is governed by 290 municipalities (*kommuner*). The counties' areas of responsibilities range from medical care to regional traffic and transit planning, while municipalities are responsible for services such as housing, roads, schools, childcare, and fire protection.

The importance of local government is expressed in Chapter 1 Article 1 of the Instrument of Government: Swedish democracy 'shall be realized through a representative and parliamentary polity and through local self-government'. Chapter 1 section 2 of the Swedish Local Government Act (*kommunallag (2017:725)*) furthermore states:

> Sweden is divided into municipalities and county councils. These attend to the matters indicated in this Act or in special regulations, proceeding on principles of democracy and local self-government.

Each of the twenty-one counties (*län*) is headed by a county administrative board (*länsstyrelse*) which in its turn is led by a governor (*landshövding*).[11] The county administrative board is part of the local administration and deals with questions such as healthcare and regional transportation. County councils (*landsting*), however, with their county council assemblies (*landstingsfullmäktige*) are elected at the regional level.[12]

Municipalities are led by a municipal assembly (*kommunalfullmäktige*), who are elected locally, and who in turn appoint the municipal council (*kommunstyrelse*).

In general, there is no hierarchical exercise of powers between municipalities, counties, and regions, as they all have different areas of responsibility. In some cases, however, the Parliament or any national authority may set requirements that local authorities must follow.[13]

II. Public Agencies

9. In addition to public administration, there are around 400 public authorities with specific areas of competence in Sweden.[14] They are commonly independent and have the authority – delegated by the Government – to issue regulations within

9. Carlson, 30.
10. Chapter 3 Art. 7 Instrument of Government.
11. *See* www.lansstyrelsen.se/, 5 Apr. 2014.
12. Chapter 1 Art. 7 Instrument of Government: 'Sweden has municipalities and county councils. The decision-making power in these local authorities is exercised by elected assemblies.'
13. For example, regarding national standards for education. *See* Carlson, 33.
14. Swedish Ministry of Finance, *Styra och ställa – förslag till en effektivare statsförvaltning*, SOU 2008:118 (Stockholm: Finansdepartementet, 2006 års förvaltningskommitté, 2008), 9.

their area of responsibility.[15] A lot of day-to-day administrative work is carried out by these small or large public authorities, and they are also able to decide in specific cases regarding private subjects vis-à-vis public authorities.

10. Two specific agencies that should be mentioned here are the Parliamentary Ombudsmen (*Justitieombudsmannen*/JO) and the Chancellor of Justice (*Justitiekanslern*/JK). The Parliamentary Ombudsmen[16] are elected by the Swedish Parliament and supervise courts of law and other public authorities as well as the public officials they employ in their application of the law. The Chancellor of Justice,[17] though appointed by the Government, is an independent institution. The duties include:

- representing the State in trials and other legal disputes;
- receiving complaints and claims for damages directed to the State;
- supervising the governmental authorities and the civil servants;
- ensuring freedom of the press and other media, and acting as the only public prosecutor in cases regarding offences against the freedom of the press and other media; and
- protecting privacy in different fields.

11. Other agencies of particular interest within the Information Communication Technology (ICT) sector are the Swedish Post and Telecom Agency (*Post- och telestyrelsen* – PTS), the Swedish Consumer Agency (*Konsumentverket*) and the Swedish Civil Contingencies Agency (*Myndigheten för samhällsskydd och beredskap* – MSB) with regards to information security.

The Swedish PTS[18] is the supervisory authority with regards to electronic communications[19] and also monitors the postal sector in Sweden. PTS issues regulations within the electronic communications sector, supervises communications operators and informs the general public on issues regarding Internet security and consumer rights with regards to communication services. It reports to the Ministry of Enterprise, Energy, and Communications and is headed by a board appointed by the Government.[20]

PTS is partly funded through charges imposed on operators and undertakings for licences subject to PTS' supervision and is also involved in initiatives such as Surf Calmly (*Surfa Lugnt*).[21]

---

15. Chapter 8 Art. 11 Instrument of Government: 'Where, under the present Chapter, the Riksdag authorizes the Government to adopt provisions in a particular matter, the Riksdag may authorize the Government in such context to delegate the power to adopt regulations in the matter to an administrative authority or a local authority.'
16. The first was appointed in 1810. www.jo.se.
17. The Chancellor of Justice is not appointed for a specific term, but until retirement. The function was first introduced by King Charles XII in 1713. *See* www.jk.se.
18. www.pts.se.
19. The term 'electronic communications' includes telephony, the Internet and radio.
20. Swedish Post and Telecom Agency (PTS), 'Introducing the Swedish Post and Telecom Agency (PTS)', www.pts.se/upload/Ovrigt/Om-PTS/infomaterial/pts-broschyr-eng-08.pdf, accessed 5 Apr. 2014.
21. www.surfalugnt.se.

The Swedish Consumer Agency (*Konsumentverket*)[22] is responsible for ensuring consumer interests and is headed by the Consumer Ombudsman (*Konsumentombudsman*/KO) who can pursue consumer interests by legal action in the courts.

The MSB[23] supervises and issues guidelines concerning civil protection, public safety, emergency management and civil defence.[24] Within information security, MSB, *inter alia*, administers the national strategy and action plan, supports and coordinates societal information security and is responsible for a Swedish national service tasked with the prevention and management IT incidents (CERT- SE).[25]

III. General Court Administration

12. Chapter 11 Instrument of Government regulates the courts. According to Article 2, courts are independent of other arms of government, and their decisions cannot be influenced by the Parliament or any other public authority.[26]

The Swedish judicial system is built upon two pillars, the general courts and the administrative courts. In addition, there exist specialized courts with specific jurisdiction, such as the Patent and Market Court and the Patent and Market Court of Appeal for matters of intellectual property law, competition law and marketing law.[27] They all fall under the administration of the Ministry of Justice and its agency, the National Court Administration (*Domstolsverket*).[28]

The general courts consist of the district courts (*Tingsrätt*), Courts of Appeal (*Hovrätt*), and the Supreme Court (*Högsta domstolen*); the general administrative courts comprise county administrative courts (*Förvaltningsrätt*),[29] Administrative Courts of Appeal (*Kammarrätt*), and the Supreme Administrative Court (*Högsta förvaltningsdomstolen*).[30]

§4. Legal System

13. From a historical perspective, the Swedish legal system has been influenced mainly by German law. However, since Sweden joined the EU in 1995, harmonization on a European level has been prevailing.[31]

22. www.konsumentverket.se.
23. www.msb.se.
24. www.msb.se/en/About-MSB/, accessed 15 Apr. 2019.
25. www.msb.se/en/Prevention/Information-security/, accessed 15 Apr. 2019.
26. Chapter 11 Art. 2 Instrument of Government: 'No public authority, including the Riksdag, may determine how a court of law shall adjudicate an individual case or otherwise apply a rule of law in a particular case.'
27. They replaced the Market Court (*Marknadsdomstolen*) and the Court of Patent Appeals (*Patentbesvärsrätten*) in September 2016. *See* www.domstol.se/Funktioner/English/The-Swedish-courts/Patent-and-Market-Courts/, accessed 15 Apr. 2019.
28. www.domstol.se.
29. Earlier called *Länsrätt* in Swedish.
30. Earlier called *Regeringsrätten* in Swedish.
31. *See* Carlson, 35–36.

Like many other jurisdictions, the Swedish legal system is divided into private and public law, the latter including areas such as constitutional, administrative, procedural and criminal law, and the former including family law as well as the law of obligations and property.

14. The Swedish doctrine of legal sources is based upon a hierarchy of legal material, where legislative preparatory works have more importance than in other European countries. The following sources are commonly recognized in Sweden:[32]

(1) The Constitution consisting of four fundamental laws: the Instrument of Government (*regeringsform/RF*), the Act of Succession (*successionsordning*), the Freedom of the Press Act (*tryckfrihetsförordning/TF*), and the Fundamental Law on Freedom of Expression (*yttrandefrihetsgrundlag/YGL*).[33]
(2) Legislation, including parliamentary acts (*lagar*), government ordinances (*förordningar*), as well as agency regulations (*föreskrifter*).
(3) Legislative preparatory works (*förarbeten*) including governmental bills (*proposition*) as well as other governmental reports preceding the Governmental Bill, such as Swedish Government Official Reports (*Statens Offentliga Utredningar* – SOU) and Ministry Publications Series (Ds).[34]
(4) Case law, mainly including decisions by the highest courts such as the Supreme Court (*Högsta domstolen*) for civil and criminal matters, the Supreme Administrative Court (*Högsta förvaltningsdomstolen*) for administrative law, as well as some specialized courts such as the Patent and Market Court of Appeal (*Patent- och marknadsöverdomstolen*) for matters within intellectual property, marketing and competition law, and the Labour Court (*Arbetsdomstolen*) for labour law related matters. To some extent decisions by the appellate courts can also have value as a legal source.
(5) Custom.
(6) Legal scholarship (*doktrin*).

15. Swedish Parliamentary Acts and Government Ordinances are published in the Swedish *Code of Statutes* (*Svensk Författningssamling*) or SFS.[35] Each Act or Ordinance receives a unique SFS number, which consists of the year it is published and a chronological number, for example, 1998:204.[36] A statute will always keep its original SFS number, even if the law is amended. Using the SFS number of a law is a common way to refer to legislation in Sweden.

Public agencies in Sweden are in general independent and have a rather important function in the legal system, not only from an administrative but also from a

32. Ulf Bernitz et al., *Finna rätt: juristens källmaterial och arbetsmetoder* (Stockholm: Norstedts Juridik, 2008), 28 et seq.
33. As in many other jurisdictions, constitutional law takes precedence over regular laws; hence, the hierarchy is not surprising in that respect.
34. An overview of the legislative process can be found at www.riksdagen.se/en/How-the-Riksdag-works/, 15 Apr. 2019.
35. Since 1 Apr. 2018 the official journal is published electronically online at, svenskforfattningssamling.se.
36. The SFS number of the previously in force Personal Data Act (*personuppgiftslag*).

legislative point of view. Within their area of competence,[37] agencies, such as the Swedish Tax Agency (*Skatteverket*) and the PTS, can issue binding regulations.[38]

16. Legislative preparatory works have a rather important status in Sweden as a legal source. Specifically, the Government Bill (*proposition*) as well as the governmental reports preceding the Governmental Bill, which include the SOU[39] and Ministry Publications Series (Ds),[40] often complement the rather abstract statutes by providing interpretation as well as examples of application of the law.

17. Though there is no strict obligation for courts to follow case law, such as the *stare decisis* in English law, typically, the lower courts follow decisions by the higher courts. There are two highest courts in Sweden, the Supreme Court (*Högsta domstolen*) for civil and criminal matters and the Supreme Administrative Court (*Högsta förvaltningsdomstolen*) for administrative law. In addition, specialized courts exist within certain fields of law, for example, the Patent and Market Court of Appeal.

These courts publish their decisions in official series. Judgments by the Supreme Court are published in the series *Nytt Juridiskt Arkiv* (NJA) and are referred to by year of publication followed by volume, page number, for example, NJA 2005 s. 361. The Supreme Administrative Court publishes its decision in the series *Högsta förvaltningsdomstolens årsbok* (HFD).[41] Cases are referred to by year of decision and reference number, for example, RÅ 2001 ref. 35.

37. Commonly delegated by the Government who in turn is authorized by a statutory provision enacted by the Parliament.
38. A list of some of these agencies and their regulations can be found at, www.lagrummet.se/rattsinformation/forfattningar/.
39. Statens offentliga utredningar (SOU).
40. Departementsserien (Ds).
41. Previously *Regeringsrättens årsbok* (RÅ).

Chapter 2. Telecommunications Infrastructure

§1. General Infrastructure

18. Sweden has one of the most developed telecommunication markets in the world. The infrastructure is increasingly focused on the mobile market, while the number of fixed-line communications slowly declines. The market for mobile services has reached a penetration rate of more than 100% which is the result of consumers holding multiple subscriptions, commonly one for private and one for business purposes.[42] In June 2018, there were 14.2 million mobile phone subscriptions.[43]

The Swedish telecommunications market was liberalized in 1993 and did become very competitive as a result. At the moment, several operators provide mobile services. Four of them – Telia Company, Tele2, Telenor (previously Vodafone), and Hi3G (Tre/3) – own 96% of the mobile subscriptions market.[44]

Six different frequencies are being used for mobile telephony and mobile broadband services: 450 MHz, 800 MHz, 900 MHz, 1,800 MHz, 2100 MHz, and 2,600 MHz. The mobile network operators cooperate in creating and maintaining the infrastructure; the cooperation can differ depending on the frequency.[45]

In 2014, there were around 45,000 base stations in Sweden, spread over 15,000 unique antenna masts. 2G and 3G voice networks covered 84% of the geographic area and more than 99% of the population area of Sweden; 1 Mbps data networks (3G) covered 39% of the geographic area and 99% of the population area of Sweden; 10 Mbps data networks (3G) covered 24% of the geographic area and 95% of the population area of Sweden; 10 Mbps data networks (4G) covered 42% of the geographic area and 98% of the population area of Sweden. The lowest coverage was for 30 Mbps data networks (4G), which covered 2% of the geographic area and 61% of the population area of Sweden.[46]

19. Sweden, unlike other European countries, did not auction licences for the Universal Mobile Telecommunications System (UMTS)[47] services. Instead, the licences were awarded after an application procedure where financial capacity, technical, and economic feasibility as well as access to relevant expert knowledge and experience were taken into account. In December 2000, PTS allotted UMTS licences to Europolitan, Hi3G (Tre/3), Orange, and Tele2. These licences were later changed and now include Hi3G (Tre/3), Telenor (previously Vodafone), and TeliaSonera/Tele2 (SULAB).[48]

---

42. Economist Intelligence Unit, *Telecoms and Technology Report Sweden*, November 2009.
43. Swedish Post and Telecom Agency (PTS), *Svensk telekommarknad första halvåret 2018*, report nr 18-7901, 13 Nov. 2018.
44. *Ibid.*, 5.
45. The report Swedish Post and Telecom Agency (PTS), 'Rapport av uppdrag att samla in statistik om tillgången till mobila kommunikationsnät', PTS-ER-2014:11, 12–13, shows the different operators who own the networks.
46. *Ibid.*, 20, 28–38.
47. Universal Mobile Telecommunications System.
48. *See* www.pts.se/sv/Telefoni/Mobil-telefoni/Mobiltelesystem/, accessed 5 Apr. 2014.

The operators are allocated certain radio frequencies[49] and the licences include a condition that obliges the mobile operators to provide certain UMTS coverage throughout Sweden in accordance with their original applications. The definition of coverage concerns the amount of citizens that have to be able to access the UMTS network, not a certain amount of masts or financial investment. In accordance with PTS regulations, the companies were allowed to cooperate with regard to 70% of the radio infrastructure and up to 100% with regard to the masts.[50]

In 2010, PTS announced the winners of the auction for the fourth-generation (4G) frequencies, which will allow access speeds of more than 100 Mbits/second. In total, 758 municipal and two national licences were awarded.[51] Among them, TeliaSonera received a licence[52] for fifteen years at a cost of SEK 563 million.[53]

§2. Broadband

20. Access to broadband is provided either through wired networks – such as fixed telephone, cable television or fibre-based networks – or by wireless means. The fixed telephone network covers 98% of households and 95% of businesses,[54] while wireless 3G networks reached 99% of the population in Sweden in 2009. In 2019, only around 450 households and companies did *not* have access to 10 Mbit/s connection via cable or mobile networks.[55] Cable networks and fibre-based networks are mainly available in urban areas.[56]

Providing access to broadband for households and businesses has been one of the goals of the Swedish Government.[57] While the infrastructure for broadband is mainly provided by private operators and public sector players, services for individuals and businesses are primarily offered by private operators.

§3. Operators

21. TeliaSonera is the largest telecommunications operator in Sweden and has held a virtual monopoly on traditional Public Switched Telephone Network (PSTN)

49. 2 × 15 MHz radiofrequencies in the 1920–1980 MHz band together with the 2110–2170 MHz band, as well as 5 MHz in the 1900–1920 MHz band.
50. *See* Swedish Post and Telecom Agency (PTS), 'Faktablad – 3G i Sverige', PTS-F-2005:5, 1 June 2006, in Swedish at, www.pts.se/globalassets/startpage/dokument/icke-legala-dokument/faktablad/radio/3g_i_sverige.pdf.
51. Economist Intelligence Unit, *Telecoms and Technology Report Sweden*, November 2009.
52. The license concerns four frequency blocks totalling 2 × 20 MHz in the 2.6 GHz band.
53. *See* Press Release by TeliaSonera, 'TeliaSonera to build 4G – next generation mobile network', 18 Nov. 2008.
54. xDSL technology is used for broadband connection.
55. Swedish Post and Telecom Agency (PTS), 'Telefoni, grundläggande internet och kopparnätsavvecklingen', PTS-ER-2019:10, 2019-03-28, 18–19.
56. Swedish Ministry of Enterprise, Energy and Communications, 'Broadband Strategy for Sweden', 6 Nov. 2009, www.regeringen.se/sb/d/2025/a/134980, 9–10.
57. According to the Broadband Strategy Sweden, 90% of all households and businesses shall have access to broadband at a minimum speed of 100 Mbps, by 2020.

subscriptions. With the rise of IP-telephony, the number of subscriptions will decline over time, possibly due to lower costs for the consumer.[58]

The second-largest operator for telecommunications as well as mobile services is Tele2, the company was formed in 1993 and offers fixed-line and mobile telephony (Comviq), as well as data network and Internet services.[59]

Telenor, a Norwegian company, is currently the third-largest telecommunications operator in Sweden. It acquired Vodafone's Swedish mobile operation in January 2006, and while it provides fixed-line telecommunications in Norway, it focuses on mobile and broadband services in Sweden.[60]

Rather unique for the Swedish telecom market with regards to operators are around 200 city networks (*stadsnät*) that locally provide broadband through fibre networks. Often, these network providers are cities or municipalities, who offer the connections as open networks, which enable other market players to offer their services on top of the city network.[61]

Sweden's telecommunications industry in general is dominated by Ericsson, a manufacturer of wireless telecommunication equipment and provider of related services to mobile and fixed network operators worldwide. Ericsson is followed by TeliaSonera which is the second-largest company based on net sales and employees.[62]

58. Economist Intelligence Unit, *Telecoms and Technology Report Sweden*, November 2009. *See also* Swedish Competition Authority (*Konkurrensverket*), Konkurrensen i Sverige 2018, Rapport 2018:1, February 2018.
59. *Ibid.*
60. *Ibid.*
61. More information can be found in Swedish at the organization representing the city networks, ssnf.org.
62. Economist Intelligence Unit, *Telecoms and Technology Report Sweden*, November 2009.

Chapter 3. The Information and Communications Technology Market

§1. Fixed Communications Market

22. In June 2018, there were 2.4 million fixed telephone subscriptions in Sweden, compared to 4.0 million in 2013 and 5.2 million in 2009. Out of the 2.4 million, around 1.0 million were PSTN-based (compared to 2.45 million in 2013) and 1.4 million based on IP (compared to 1.48 in 2013 and 860,000 in 2009). IP-telephony is mainly based on xDSL and fibre or fibre LAN.[63]

From these subscriptions, 3.0 billion outgoing traffic minutes were registered during the first half of 2018, compared to 6.9 in 2013 and 11.5 billion in 2009.[64]

Looking at the market share in June 2018, the former state monopoly Telia Company had 53.4%, followed by the operators Comhem (which is a cable TV operator; 12.7%), Telenor (6.1%) and Tele2 (5.2%).[65]

In 2017, 41% of the population in Sweden had a fixed telephone subscription in their home, which means more households do *not* have a fixed telephone subscription compared to the households that do.[66] The number of fixed telephone subscriptions was 69% in 2013[67] and 84% in 2009.[68]

§2. Mobile Communication Market

23. After steadily growing for several years, subscriptions (and active prepaid cards) for mobile voice services and mobile data services reached 14.2 million in June 2018 (compared to 14.0 million in June 2013). Out of these, 77% were contract subscriptions (compared to around 60% in 2008) and the rest prepaid cards. A total of 1.9 million mobile subscriptions were used solely for voice services.[69]

Mobile broadband subscriptions as a stand-alone service (i.e., only mobile packet data and no voice traffic, e.g., dongle, plug-in card) amounted to 1.7 million in 2018 (compared to 2.1 million in 2013), while the number for subscriptions as an add-on

63. Swedish Post and Telecom Agency (PTS), 'The Swedish Telecommunications Market, First half year 2013'; Swedish Post and Telecom Agency (PTS), 'Svensk telekommarknad första halvåret 2018', report nr 18-7901, 13 Nov. 2018.
64. Swedish Post and Telecom Agency (PTS), 'The Swedish Telecommunications Market, First half year 2013'; Swedish Post and Telecom Agency (PTS), 'Svensk telekommarknad första halvåret 2018', report nr 18-7901, 13 Nov. 2018.
65. Swedish Post and Telecom Agency (PTS), 'Svensk telekommarknad första halvåret 2018', report nr 18-7901, 13 Nov. 2018.
66. Swedish Post and Telecom Agency (PTS), 'Svenskarnas användning av telefoni och internet, PTS individundersökning 2017', statistik.pts.se/individundersoekning/dokument/.
67. Swedish Post and Telecom Agency (PTS), 'Svenskarnas användning av telefoni och internet, PTS individundersökning 2017'.
68. Swedish Post and Telecom Agency (PTS), 'Survey of Individuals 2009, Use of telephony and the Internet by Swedes', PTS-ER-2009:28.
69. Swedish Post and Telecom Agency (PTS), 'Svensk telekommarknad första halvåret 2018', report nr 18-7901, 13 Nov. 2018.

service (i.e., a few GB of data per month is included in regular subscription) was 10.6 million (compared to 5.4 million in 2013).[70]

In June 2018, 9.1 million subscriptions used services in 4G (LTE) networks, compared to 811,000 in 2013 and 83,000 in 2012.[71] As several operators have launched Voice over LTE, subscribers could use 4G for phone calls, which amounted to 3.3 billion voice minutes (20% of all voice traffic).

The number of outgoing voice minutes from mobile telephones amounted to 16.9 billion minutes in the first half of 2018 (compared to 12.6 billion in 2013 and 9.6 billion in 2009). On average, mobile phone calls lasted 3.3 minutes and on average 68 calls were made per customer and per month. During the same period in 2018, around 4.0 billion text messages (SMS) were sent from mobile telephones (7.5 in 2013 and 6.8 in 2009), averaging 53 text messages per customer per month (105 in 2013 and 112 in 2009). These 4.0 billion text messages do not include messages transmitted via other services such as iMessage, WhatsApp, or chat functions in apps.[72]

24. The mobile communication market is dominated by the network-owning operators Telia Company, Tele2, HI3G (Tre/3) and Telenor; the largest operator being TeliaSonera with a market share of 36.1% followed by Tele2/Comviq (27.8%), Telenor (18.9%), and HI3G (Tre/3) with 13.6%.

With a population of around 10 million and 14.2 million subscriptions for mobile voice and mobile data services, more than 100% of the Swedish population uses mobile services. Ninety-eight per cent use their mobile phone for private purposes. More or less all subscribers use their phones for calls and almost 90% use their phone to surf the Internet.[73]

§3. Internet Access Market

25. The Swedish market for active Internet subscriptions reached 10.7 million in June 2013,[74] compared to 4.4 million in June 2009. In 2018 the total number of fixed broadband connections was 3.9 million, compared to 3.1 million in 2013. Mobile broadband subscriptions as a stand-alone service amounted to 1.7 million in 2018 (compared to 2.1 million in 2013), while the number for subscriptions as an add-on service was 10.6 million (compared to 5.4 million in 2013).[75]

70. *Ibid.*
71. *Ibid.*
72. *Ibid.*
73. PTS, 'Svenskarnas användning av telefoni och internet', 2017.
74. PTS, 'The Swedish Telecommunications Market, First half year 2013'.
75. *Ibid.*

26. Fibre and fibre LAN[76] saw the biggest increase in fixed broadband and amounted to 64% of the market in 2018.[77]

The transmission speed for broadband services is often higher for downloaded data than for uploaded data. The number of subscriptions with a high transmission rate capacity has been increasing in the past years, reaching 2.7 million subscriptions with a download speed of 100 Mbps or more in June 2018 (compared to 840,000 in 2013). The most common download speed for fixed broadband was 100–250 Mbps in June 2018.[78]

Data traffic in the mobile networks increased to 493 petabytes in the first half of 2018, which was an increase of 30% compared to the same period in 2017. During the first half of 2013 the amount was 124,700 terabytes and in 2009 11,664 terabytes. The average data used in private subscriptions (as add-on service) was 6.4 GB per month, which was an increase of 52%. The average data used in mobile broadband subscriptions was 17.5 GB per month.[79] The average use per month in the first half of 2013 was 6.6 GB for stand-alone services, and 1.2 GB for mobile broadband as an add-on service.[80]

27. The market share is rather equal when it comes to fixed broadband. In June 2018 Telia Company held 33.2%, Telenor 17.4%, Com Hem 21.3%, Bahnhof 6.9% and Bredband 2 6%.[81]

More than 90% of the population in Sweden between the age of 16 and 60 uses the Internet every day, while 93% use the Internet at home.[82]

§4. Other Related Markets

28. In June 2018, the total number of digital paid television subscriptions on the Swedish market was 2.9 million (compared to 5.3 million in 2013). Almost half (1.1 million) of the subscriptions are distributed by fibre, while 2.3 million use analogue cable television. Five operators (Com Hem, Boxer, Telenor, Telia Company and Viasat) hold 96.2% of the market share.[83] Other ways of viewing television (apart from traditional television), such as video-on-demand services,[84] have not been included in the statistics but have an impact on the traditional television subscriptions.[85]

---

76. Internet access is reached via a property network, that is, a LAN (local network) usually based on Ethernet technology. The property network (commonly via optic fibre cables or copper-based cables) in its turn is linked to a public fibre network, for example, an area network.
77. PTS, 'Svensk telekommarknad första halvåret 2018'.
78. *Ibid.*
79. *Ibid.*
80. *Ibid.*
81. *Ibid.*
82. PTS, 'Svenskarnas användning av telefoni och internet', 2017.
83. PTS, 'Svensk telekommarknad första halvåret 2018'.
84. In Sweden both Netflix (netflix.com) and HBO Nordic (hbonordic.com) are offered.
85. PTS, 'The Swedish Telecommunications Market, First half year 2013'.

29. A market that has been very common in the past years are bundled services, where two or more services are combined as one offer with a packaged price. Most commonly, this includes telephony (fixed and/or mobile), television, and Internet access. Overall, there were 2.2 million bundled subscriptions in Sweden in June 2018 (compared to 1.7 million in 2013), with Telia Company, Com Hem and Telenor holding 89% of the market.

30. In 2013, Statistics Sweden presented the results of a survey on the use of IT by enterprises. According to the report, 98% of enterprises use computers, and nearly all of them have access to the Internet. Around 95% of larger Swedish companies (more than 250 employees) offer their employees mobile devices, including mobile broadband. Sixty-nine per cent of larger companies in Sweden use social networks, such as Facebook and LinkedIn.[86]

In total, Swedish companies purchased computer equipment for SEK 10.7 billion and telecommunications equipment for SEK 7.3 billion in 2013.[87]

A survey by Statistics Sweden in November 2018 showed that around 57% of companies with at least ten employees used some form of cloud service in 2018. The most common type of cloud service concerned file storage, followed by e-mail. Within the ICT sector 84% of companies used cloud services in 2018.[88]

The use of big data analytics was still rather low in 2018. Ten per cent of Swedish enterprises with at least ten employees reported analysing big data, compared to 12% in the whole EU.[89]

86. Statistics Sweden (SCB), 'Use of ICT in Swedish Enterprises 2013 (*Företagens användning av it 2013*'), www.scb.se/Statistik/_Publikationer/NV0116_2013A01_BR_IT02BR1401.pdf.
87. *Ibid.*
88. Statistics Sweden (SCB), 'Use of ICT in Swedish Enterprises, 2018 (*It-användning i företag, 2018*)', www.scb.se/hitta-statistik/statistik-efter-amne/naringsverksamhet/naringslivets-struktur/it-anvandning-i-foretag/pong/statistiknyhet/it-anvandning-i-foretag-2018/.
89. Eurostat, 'Digital economy and society statistics – enterprises', ec.europa.eu/eurostat/statistics-explained/index.php/Digital_economy_and_society_statistics_-_enterprises#Enterprises_analysing_big_data, accessed 15 Jan. 2020.

Chapter 4. E-Commerce: Facts and Figures

§1. Internet Use

31. Sweden has a very good ranking as an IT-nation and was listed at the top of the World Economic Forum's Networked Readiness Index in 2012 and was ranked third in 2013[90] and 2016.[91] The index measures how well a country utilizes the benefits of ICT to promote work and entrepreneurship and covers 139 countries.[92]

In a survey from 2018, it was found that 93% of the Swedish population have access to a computer at home, compared to 90% in 2013. Ninety-eight per cent of the Swedish population has access to the Internet, compared to 89% in 2013. Fifty-two per cent use their mobile phone to connect to the Internet several times a day, compared to 34% using a computer and 16% use a tablet.[93]

Ninety per cent use the Internet on a daily basis (compared to 62% in 2009 and 52% in 2007), 68% check email, 63% use social networks (53% in total use Facebook, 38% are on Instagram), 61% search on Google, 51% use chats, 45% listen to music (38% use Spotify), 37% read newspapers and 28% watch YouTube, while 19% watch Netflix.[94]

Fifty per cent of the Swedish population have smart gadgets using Internet of Things technology in their home, such as watches, fridges and cars, and around 35% have 1–5 different things.[95]

Almost 83% of the population use social media; 76% are members of Facebook, 60% members of Instagram, 38% use Snapchat, 22% Twitter, 30% LinkedIn and 10% Reddit. Snapchat and Instagram are most popular in the age group up to 26 years.[96]

§2. E-commerce

32. During the period January to March 2016, a total of 60% of individuals in Sweden, aged 16–85,[97] bought or ordered goods or services over the Internet, for their private use. Two-thirds of people who used e-commerce between April 2015 and March 2016 bought goods or services from Swedish companies, almost 25% ordered services or goods from other EU countries and 16% ordered from countries

---

90. World Economic Forum, 'Global Information Technology Report 2013', www.weforum.org/reports/global-information-technology-report-2013.
91. World Economic Forum, 'Global Information Technology Report 2016', www.weforum.org/reports/the-global-information-technology-report-2016.
92. SE (the) Internet Infrastructure Foundation, 'Swedes and the Internet 2018', 2018.svenskarnaochinternet.se/the-swedes-and-the-internet-2018-summary/.
93. *Ibid.*
94. *Ibid.*
95. *Ibid.*
96. *Ibid.*
97. This amounts to around 4.5 million people.

outside the EU. The most common types of goods or services were clothes and sports products, as well as travel tickets and tickets for events.[98]

Sweden is the largest e-commerce market in the Nordic countries with SEK 42.6 billion value of online purchases. Of a total of SEK 104.3 billion online purchases during the first half of 2018 within the Nordic countries, i.e., Sweden, Norway, Denmark and Finland, domestic Nordic commerce amounted to SEK 86.2 billion while purchases from abroad reached SEK around 18.1 billion. The latter took place mainly from the UK, China, Germany or the US.[99]

Though purchases made in a physical shop still amount to 65% in Sweden, purchases made online via the computer are 17% and via the mobile 10%. This number can be compared to Finland, where only 47% concern physical shops, 31% computers and 10% mobile phones.[100]

Of the online purchases made in the first quarter of 2019, 38% entailed clothes or shoes, 34% beauty or healthcare, 24% books or media, 20% electronics, 13% groceries, 11% furniture and 10% sports or leisure.[101]

33. In 2016, 21% of the turnover of Swedish companies with at least ten employees came from e-commerce. These companies are mostly active within the field of logistics (38%), manufacturing (29%) and retail (29%).[102]

The payment market in Sweden has been digitalized constantly over the past years. The amount of cash in circulation in Sweden has halved since 2007. In 2018, only 13% paid for their most recent purchase in cash, compared to 39% in 2010. Paying by card is most common, although payments by mobile phone (Swish) are increasing rapidly. Swish is a service that was launched in late 2012 and builds on a settlement platform (*Betalningar i realtid*) which is jointly owned by banks, with support from the Swedish national bank, the Riksbank. The number of Swish payments (millions of payments per year) made by mobile phone (in real time) has increased from 0 in 2012 to 400 million in 2018.[103]

98. Statistics Sweden (SCB), 'Use of Computers and the Internet by Private Persons in 2016' (*Privatpersoners användning av datorer och internet 2016*), available as pdf at, www.scb.se/contentassets/3e727f0d3a434dc482dd3f79529d0ef5/le0108_2016a01_br_it01br1601.pdf.

99. PostNord, E-commerce in the Nordics 2018 review, www.postnord.com/en/media/publications/e-commerce.

100. *Ibid.*

101. PostNord i samarbete med Svensk Digital Handel och AB Handelns Utredningsinstitut (HUI), 'e-barometern, 2019 årsrapport, p. 5, www.hui.se/statistik-rapporter/index-och-barometrar/e-barometern.

102. Statistics Sweden (SCB), 'E-handel allt viktigare för svenska företag', 23 May 2017, www.scb.se/hitta-statistik/artiklar/2017/E-handel-allt-viktigare-for-svenska-foretag/.

103. Sveriges riksbank, 'Payments in Sweden 2019' (2019), riksbank.se/payments-in-sweden-2019.

Chapter 5. E-government Initiatives

34. E-government has been one of the focus areas for the Swedish Government for a long time. In 1998, the Swedish Government assigned the ICT Commission (*IT-kommissionen*)[104] as an Advisory Board in the field of Information Technology. Its task was to analyse the impact of ICT on the Swedish society and to promote the dissemination of information about the new opportunities in the information society.

Its mandate ended in May 2003 and some other committees and groupings continued some of its work. Among them were the Swedish Agency for Public Management (*Statskontoret*), 24/7 Agency Delegation (*24-timmarsdelegationen*) and E-Commission (*E-nämnden*).[105] The latter merged into Verva (The Swedish Administrative Development Agency)[106] in 2006.

35. Verva was assigned to stimulate the use of public e-services and the employment of the Swedish eID (*e-legitimation*). It published several reports on these issues and contributed greatly to the development and implementation of new e-government applications, *inter alia*, through funding of new e-services. In January 2009, the authority was closed and its different departments were incorporated into the Government Offices of Sweden (*Regeringskansliet*), the Legal, Financial and Administrative Services Agency (*Kammarkollegiet*)[107] and the Delegation for e-government (*Delegation för e-förvaltning*).

36. In January 2008, the Government presented its Action Plan for e-government[108] that mentions four focus areas – regulation, technology and standards, common IT support, and contact with citizens – which should be implemented by 2010. Part of the Action Plan was a conference on e-government during the Swedish EU Presidency in 2009.[109] The Action Plan specifically emphasizes the importance of electronic identification in order to sustain the trust and dialogue between government, citizens, and businesses.

37. In this context, a delegation for e-government (*Delegation för e-förvaltning*)[110] was formed, consisting of representatives from sixteen key public authorities in Sweden.[111] As one of its first tasks, in September 2009, the delegation presented a strategy for public authorities regarding the possible improvement of

104. An archived version of the website is available at, www.itkommissionen.se/index-2.html.
105. Some of the reports can still be found at, www.edelegationen.se/Publikationer/Innan-E-delegationen-bildades/, 5 Apr. 2014.
106. Verket för Förvaltningsutveckling.
107. www.kammarkollegiet.se/kammarkollegiet.
108. *Handlingsplan för eFörvaltning, Nya grunder för IT-baserad verksamhetsutveckling i offentlig förvaltning*, www.regeringen.se/content/1/c6/09/65/12/4ffd1319.pdf, accessed 5 Apr. 2014.
109. The fifth Ministerial e-government Meeting and Conference was held in Malmö, Sweden, www.egov2009.se/.
110. www.edelegationen.se/.
111. A list with the representatives is available at www.edelegationen.se/In-English/About-the-Delegation/Members-and-experts/, accessed 5 Apr. 2014.

their e-government efforts.[112] The strategy was based on the idea that better technical and legal conditions will facilitate the development of coordinated e-services by public agencies.

The tasks of the e-Government Delegation were extended and its main tasks were to work with e-government, social media and reuse of public sector information. The delegation was also tasked with investigating IT standards within the healthcare sector. Some of its projects included My Messages (*Mina Meddelanden*),[113] a public service that allows individuals or companies to receive messages from public authorities electronically instead of on paper; and e-Archive (*e-Arkiv*) and e-registration system (*e-Diarium*)[114] dealing with digital filing by public authorities.[115] In 2015, the delegation's mandate ended. The authorities participating in the delegation started the eSam initiative to continue the work of the e-Government Delegation on a voluntary basis.[116]

In September 2018, a new authority was created, the Agency for Digital Government (*Myndigheten för digital förvaltning – DIGG*).[117] The authority is responsible for issues such as public sector digitalization, national digital services, e-invoicing in the public sector and digital accessibility.

38. The Swedish Association of Local Authorities and Regions (SALAR) (*Sveriges Kommuner och Landsting (SKL)*)[118] has always had a strong role within e-government questions. In 2019 SALAR published a strategy document for innovation in a digital time.[119] The document states that digitalization is not a goal in itself but the goals for public authorities should be high-quality healthcare and education, efficient and sustainable urban development and a service-minded and accessible public administration. The strategy focuses on four main areas: organization and leadership, architecture and security, access to information and digital infrastructure, and coherent digital service.

112. The e-Government Delegation, 'Strategy for the Government Agencies Work on E-government', Summary of SOU 2009:86, www.edelegationen.se/In-English/Reports/Third-generation-eGovernment/.
113. *See* more in Swedish at, www.edelegationen.se/Nationella-utvecklingsinsatser/Forvaltningsgemensamma-tjanster/Mina-meddelanden/, accessed 5 Apr. 2014.
114. *Ibid.*
115. Some of its reports are available in English at, www.edelegationen.se/In-English/Reports/, accessed 5 Apr. 2014.
116. www.esamverka.se/.
117. www.digg.se/about-us.
118. skl.se/tjanster/englishpages.411.html, accessed 15 Jan. 2020.
119. Sveriges Kommuner och Landsting (SKL), 'Utveckling i en digital tid, en strategi för grundläggande förutsättningar', 2019, skl.se/naringslivarbetedigitalisering/digitalisering/strategifordigitalutveckling.6728.html.

Part I. Regulation of the ICT Market

Chapter 1. Regulatory Framework of the Telecommunications Sector

§1. Background and Overview

39. An important milestone in the liberalization of the Swedish telecommunications sector was the introduction in 1993 of the Telecommunications Act (*Telelag (1993:597)*) and the Radio Communications Act (*Lag (1993:599) om radiokommunikation*). These two Acts were the result of the development of private interests in the telecommunications market, seeking to compete with the Government-owned incumbent as much as a part of Sweden's alignment with the then European Community.[120] When the Government adopted the proposal introducing the legislation to the Parliament in March 1993, Sweden had tentatively applied for membership of the Community, but the national referendum approving the application had not yet been held. The legislative bill explained that the proposed regulations sought to adapt Swedish law to existing EU law and a possible European Economic Area (EEA) Agreement.

40. These two Acts were replaced through the implementation of the 2002 EU Regulatory Framework for electronic communications.

The EU regulatory framework consists of five main Directives, two Regulations and several Decisions:

- Directive 2002/21/EC of the European Parliament and of the Council of 7 March 2002 on a Common Regulatory Framework for Electronic Communications Networks and Services, as amended by the Better Regulation Directive 2009/140/EC of 25 November 2009 (hereinafter 'Framework Directive').
- Directive 2002/20/EC of the European Parliament and of the Council of 7 March 2002 on the Authorization of Electronic Communications Networks and Services, as amended by the Better Regulation Directive 2009/140/EC of 25 November 2009 (hereinafter 'Authorization Directive').

120. Government Bill (*Proposition*) 1992/93:200, 'Regeringens proposition om en telelag och en förändrad verksamhetsform för Televerket, m.m.', 69.

- Directive 2002/19/EC of the European Parliament and of the Council of 7 March 2002 on Access to, and Interconnection of, Electronic Communications Networks and Associated Facilities, as amended by the Better Regulation Directive 2009/140/EC of 25 November 2009 (hereinafter 'Access Directive').
- Directive 2002/22/EC of the European Parliament and of the Council of 7 March 2002 Universal Service and User's Rights relating to Electronic Communications Networks and Services, as amended by the Citizens' Rights Directive 2009/136/EC of 25 November 2009 (hereinafter 'Universal Services Directive'), and Regulation (EU) 2015/2120 of the European Parliament and of the Council of 25 November 2015 laying down measures concerning open Internet access.
- Directive 2002/58/EC of the European Parliament and of the Council of 12 July 2002 concerning the Processing of Personal Data and the Protection of Privacy in the Electronic Communications Sector, as amended by the Citizens' Rights Directive 2009/136/EC of 25 November 2009 (hereinafter 'Directive on Privacy and Electronic Communications').
- Regulation (EC) No. 1211/2009 of the European Parliament and of the Council of 25 November 2009 establishing the Body of European Regulators for Electronic Communications (BEREC) and the Office, repealed and replaced by Regulation (EU) 2018/1971 of the European Parliament and of the Council of 11 December 2018 establishing the BEREC and the Agency for Support for BEREC (BEREC Office).
- Regulation (EU) No. 531/2012 of the European Parliament and of the Council of 13 June 2012 on roaming on public mobile communications networks within the Union, as amended by Regulation (EU) 2015/2120 of the European Parliament and of the Council of 25 November 2015 laying down measures concerning open Internet access.

Directive (EU) 2018/1972 of the European Parliament and of the Council of 11 December 2018 establishing the European Electronic Communications Code recasts and replaces the first three directives and their subsequent amendments: the Framework Directive, the Authorization Directive and the Access Directive.[121] The EU Regulatory Framework was transposed into Swedish law in 2003, primarily through the Electronic Communications Act (*lag (2003:389) om elektronisk kommunikation*).[122] A special transitional law was also enacted, the Act on the Introduction of the Electronic Communications Act (*lag (2003:390) om införande av lagen (2003:389) om elektronisk kommunikation*).[123] Telecommunications equipment is regulated separately through the Radio Equipment Act (*radioutrustningslag (2016:392)*). There is also specific legislation regulating the activities of the Swedish country top-level domain.se: the National Top-Level Domains for Sweden on the Internet Act (*lag (2006:24) om nationella toppdomäner för Sverige på Internet*).[124]

121. Directive 2018/1972 is to be transposed into Member States' laws by 21 December 2020.
122. Government Bill (*Proposition*) 2002/03:110, 'Lag om elektronisk kommunikation, m.m.'.
123. *Ibid.*
124. *See* Part II Ch. 6 *infra*, paras 215 et seq.

The Ordinances supplementing the Acts in the area of telecommunications are:

- Ordinance on Electronic Communication (*förordning (2003:396) om elektronisk kommunikation*).
- Ordinance on the Introduction of the Electronic Communications Act (*förordning (2003:397) om införande av lagen (2003:389) om elektronisk kommunikation*).
- Ordinance on National Top-Level Domains for Sweden on the Internet (*förordning (2006:25) om nationella toppdomäner för Sverige på Internet*).
- Ordinance on Radio Equipment (*radioutrustningsförordning (2016:394)*).

The above-mentioned Swedish laws and ordinances have been subject to frequent amendments.

41. The national regulatory authority, the Swedish PTS, has adopted a number of binding Regulations (*föreskrifter*) and soft-law General Advice (*allmänna råd*). The Regulations and General Advice are published in the PTS Collected Regulations (*PTS Författningssamling*, PTSFS).

§2. Scope of the Law

42. The scope of the Electronic Communications Act is set out in its Chapter 1 section 4. The Act applies to electronic communications networks and communications services with associated facilities and services together with other radio use. The terms 'electronic communications network', 'electronic communications services' and 'associated facilities' are defined in Chapter 1 section 7 and follow those given in Article 2 of the Framework Directive. Thus, the Electronic Communications Act applies to transmission systems, to switching or routing equipment, and to other resources as long as they permit the conveyance of signals. The type of information or the means used in the conveyance are irrelevant.

According to Chapter 1 section 7 of the Electronic Communications Act, an 'electronic communications network' is a system for transfer and, in appropriate cases, equipment for connection or routing, passive network elements and other resources that allow the transmission of signals, via wire or radio waves, by optical means or via other electromagnetic transmission media, irrespective of the kind of information transferred. As in the Framework Directive, the definition is function-oriented and technologically neutral, except in requiring the use of electromagnetism. An 'electronic communications service' is defined as a service that is normally provided for payment, and which wholly or mainly comprises the transmission of signals within electronic communications networks. The term 'service' implies that the function is provided to other parties; transmission purely for the transmitter's own use therefore falls outside of the definition. Payment to the service provider need not be in cash but a purely beneficial service, for example, as only provided for charity falls outside of the scope.[125] An 'associated facility' is defined as an

125. Government Bill (Proposition) 2002/03:110, 358. An example could be a company which only provides the service for its own in-house use but also to external users without charge, *pro bono*.

apparatus, function or something else related to an electronic communications service or an electronic communications network, and which facilitates, supports or can support that service, or the provision of services via that network or service. Very few regulations of the Electronic Communications Act are directly applicable to associated facilities.

43. Chapter 1 section 4 states explicitly that the Act is not applicable to content that is transferred in electronic communications networks with the aid of electronic communications services. The intention behind this exception is to exempt the provision of services that do not wholly or mainly consist in the transferring of signals from the application of the Act. Primary examples of such services are the provision of content in radio and television programmes and via the Internet.[126] Chapter 1 section 6 points to the Radio and Television Act (*radio-och TV-lag (2010:696)*) and its provisions concerning broadcasting of sound radio and television programmes that are intended for the public and intended to be received with technical aids. Section 6 also points out that there are provisions concerning radio equipment in the Radio Equipment Act (*radioutrustningslagen (2016:392)*).

44. It follows from Chapter 1 section 5 that the provisions of the Act do not replace regulations for consideration under other legislation. Decisions based on the Electronic Communications Act do not replace decisions required by, for example, right of way in the Utility Easements Act (*ledningsrättslag (1973:1144)*) or the Expropriations Act (*expropriationslag (1972:719)*). It should also be noted that, as regulated in Chapter 10 section 17(1) Code of Judicial Procedure, a court may not preside over a dispute that shall be settled by another authority, court or arbitrator.

The preparatory work to the Electronic Communications Act grants some guidance to this question of scope.[127] According to this guidance, disputes that concern purely contractual issues should be heard by a civil court, even when the issue results from an obligation of the Electronic Communications Act. Disputes regarding obligations such as to provide interconnection or to apply a cost-oriented price would, however, be referred to the supervisory authority. The grounds cited by a plaintiff will typically decide the competent forum. Where an action or a complaint is primarily based on the Electronic Communications Act, the supervisory authority is typically the forum of first instance. Decisions by the authority can be appealed to the Administrative Court.

§3. Policy Objectives and Regulatory Principles

45. The initial sections of the Electronic Communications Act set out the policy objectives and regulatory principles of the Act, closely mirroring the catalogue in Article 8 Framework Directive.

Chapter 1 section 1 states that the provisions of the Act aim to ensure that private individuals, legal entities, and public authorities have access to secure and efficient

126. Government Bill (Proposition) 2002/03:110, 355 et seq.
127. *Ibid.*, 117 et seq.

electronic communications, and the greatest possible benefit regarding the range of electronic communications services and their price and quality. This is primarily to be achieved through the promotion of competition and international harmonization within the sector. The section states that universal services are always to be available, on equivalent terms throughout Sweden, at affordable prices. When applying the Act, particular regard is to be given to the importance of electronic communications for freedom of expression and freedom of information.

Measures taken in accordance with the Act, in accordance with Chapter 1 section 2, may not go beyond what is reasonable and should be proportional having regard to the Act's objective and the interests specified in section 1.

The PTS is the supervisory authority, as stated in section 2 Ordinance on Electronic Communications. PTS is to, in accordance with Chapter 1 section 3 of the Act, receive complaints, consider applications, decide on obligations, examine questions, deal with matters, and exercise supervision under the Act and any subsequent regulations.

§4. The National Regulatory Authorities

46. Administrative authorities such as PTS receive formal instructions from the relevant Government department on goals, priorities and tasks. For PTS, the relevant Government department is the Ministry of Infrastructure, a new ministry formed in April 2019, which took over some of the issues that previously were handled by the Ministry of Enterprise and Innovation, the Ministry of Finance and the Ministry of the Environment.[128] Once a matter has been lodged before an authority such as PTS, for example, a dispute between telecom operators on interconnection requirements, the Government is constitutionally prohibited from directing the outcome of the matter.

47. The Ministry of Infrastructure, as other Ministries, focuses on its roles as policymaker and supervisor of the public authorities under its responsibility. While suggestions for new legislation may originate from the Parliament, public authorities, and other public or private bodies, the Ministry commissions committees to draft legislative proposals and then, after a public consultation, drafts the legislative bills that are tabled in the Parliament. The Ministry negotiates the budget for PTS, approves the fee structure for telecommunications operators and actively supervises PTS' execution of its regulatory obligations. While the Ministry formally represents Sweden in international fora (most importantly the EU institutions and intergovernmental organizations such as the International Telecommunication Union, the Internet Corporation for Assigned Names and Numbers, and the World Summit on the Information Society), its functionaries are often accompanied and advised by experts from PTS or other relevant authorities.

128. PTS was, prior to April 2019, part of the Ministry of Enterprise and Innovation.

48. The national regulatory authority, PTS, was created as *Telestyrelsen* in 1992 as part of the reorganization of the Telecom Administration (*Televerket*) from a government authority to an incorporated limited liability company.[129] *Telestyrelsen* took over the activities of the Government Telecom Council (*Statens telenämnd*) and the Radiospectrum Administration (*Frekvensförvaltningen*).[130] The *Telestyrelsen* became PTS in 1994 when the regulatory functions of the Swedish Post were added to its mandate.

The PTS Director General is appointed by the Government for a term of six years (renewable). While decisions are taken by the Director General and are issued under her or his name, important decisions are reviewed by the PTS Board. The Board shall according to section 15 Ordinance Instructing the PTS (*Förordning (2007:951) med instruktion för PTS*) consist of between five and ten persons. For the term of 1 July 2017–30 June 2020, the Board consists of nine persons, one of whom is the Director General.[131]

49. The functions of PTS are set out in detail in section 1 of the Ordinance Instructing the PTS. The Ordinance designates PTS as the public authority with overarching responsibility for the area of electronic communication. The authority is to work to achieve the goals of information society policy and the objectives set out in the Electronic Communications Act. It is tasked with describing and analysing developments and results in its area of responsibility and to report back to the Government. It is PTS' duty to note and analyse problems within the area, and where necessary, take appropriate action or suggest solutions. PTS shall also ensure that regulations and routines are cost efficient and easy to apply for both citizens and businesses.[132]

50. PTS is charged with promoting the efficient functioning of the electronic communications market from a consumer, regional development, and competition point of view.[133] The main duties of PTS are to establish and supervise the specific obligations of the operators, to promote competition in the audio-visual services market, and to resolve conflicts between operators. The most important tasks of PTS under the Electronic Communications Act are those related to competition in the market and in relation to allocation and supervision of the radio spectrum. PTS is the national regulatory authority in charge of defining the relevant markets, carrying out analysis with the purpose of determining whether a relevant market is effectively competitive, declaring that an operator has a Significant Market Power (SMP), and imposing sector-specific obligations on that operator.

129. Government Bill (Proposition) 1992/93:200, 48 et seq.
130. The Government Telecom Council was formed in 1989 and was charged with the task of issuing regulation for equipment that was to be connected to Telecom Administration facilities, to follow developments in technical standardization bodies and to advise the Government on telecommunications, technical and market developments. The Radiospectrum Administration, originally a department of the Telecom Administration, was responsible for the allocation of radio frequencies.
131. *See* www.pts.se/en/about-pts/organisation/management-and-board/, accessed 23 Sep. 2019.
132. Section 1a Instruction Ordinance.
133. Section 11 Instruction Ordinance.

Section 4 of the Instruction Ordinance contains a catalogue of PTS' obligations. It shall:

- promote access to secure and efficient electronic communications, including ensuring the availability of universal service, and the supply of a broad selection of electronic communication services;
- promote expansion of and monitor access to broadband and mobile coverage in all parts of the country;
- ensure efficient use of radio communication and other radio usage;
- ensure efficient use of numbers in the national numbering plan;
- promote effective competition;
- monitor the development of prices and services;
- conduct information activities aimed at consumers;
- monitor developments in the security of electronic communications and the emergence of any environmental and health risks;
- take decisions on permits and obligations, determine and analyse markets, and exercise supervision in accordance with the Electronic Communications Act;
- issue regulations in accordance with the Ordinance on Electronic Communication;
- draw up and publish plans for frequency distribution;
- provide information on frequency use to the European Communications Office's Frequency Information System;
- carry out supervision in accordance with the Radio Equipment Act, the Act on Supplementary Provisions to the EU Regulation on Electronic Identification (*Lag (2016:561) med kompletterande bestämmelser till EU:s förordning om elektronisk identifiering*), the Top Level Domains Act, the Act on Measures for the Development of Broadband Networks (*Lag (2016:534) om åtgärder för utbyggnad av bredbandsnät*) and the Act on Information Security for Critical Societal and Digital Services (*Lag (2018:1174) om informationssäkerhet för samhällsviktiga och digitala tjänster*); promote robust electronic communications and increased crisis management capabilities and reduce the risk of disruptions including by procuring reinforcement measures;
- promote network and information security with regard to electronic communications, and advise public authorities and private parties on network security.

51. PTS' enforcement of its supervisory duties is facilitated by far-reaching inspection rights and rights to demand information from operators and other market actors. It also has the authority to impose sanctions on operators, mainly with regard to the infringement of its instructions and resolutions as well as in matters related to notifications, numbering and operators' information duties.

PTS is mainly funded through fees on telecommunication operators and through the general government budget.[134]

---

134. *See* further Fact Sheet About PTS, www.pts.se/globalassets/startpage/dokument/icke-legala-dokument/faktablad/ovrigt/eng-om-pts-okt-2018-2.pdf, accessed 23 Sep. 2019.

§5. Provisions of Electronic Communications: Requirements and Conditions

52. The provision of electronic communication networks and services in Sweden is subject to a general authorization, following Article 3 Authorization Directive.[135] Chapter 2 of the Electronic Communications Act sets out the requirement to notify the supervisory authority, PTS, of an intention to provide public communications networks that are normally provided for remuneration or publicly available electronic communications services.

There are no restrictions on who may provide networks or services, such as requiring certain nationality or legal form. There is no obligation to notify of self-provision of networks and services.

PTS has published guidance as to which types of networks and services require notification.[136] The notification form recognizes radio-based access networks, other access networks and other communication networks as public communication networks; fixed call services, fixed IP-based call services, mobile call services, Internet services and other public electronic communication services as public electronic communications services. The notification form is very short at only one page, focusing on collecting the contact details of the operator and providing a short description of the operations that will be conducted. The notifying operator is also required to submit a Certificate of Incorporation.

53. There have been a few cases where the question of notification has been contentious. PTS on 5 November 2008 required Telemar Scandinavia AB to notify PTS of its provision of mobile satellite-based services using the satellite networks Inmarsat, Iridium, Globalstar, and Thuraya.[137] This decision was upheld in appeal to the administrative courts.[138]

In another case, PTS on 2 July 2009 required Skype Communications to submit a notification of its provision of its services branded as Skypeln, SkypeOut, and Skype To Go.[139]

54. The Electronic Communications Act is short on explicit rights for operators in comparison to obligations. Rights to access to capacity from the national numbering plans (most importantly the E.164 plan) and to radio spectrum require separate permissions.[140]

---

135. In other words, there is a freedom to provide such networks and services; an undertaking can only be prevented from doing so where necessary, in accordance with EU law.
136. Swedish Post and Telecom Agency (PTS), 'Guidance for notification of operations', 3 Nov. 2010, www.pts.se/contentassets/1a00430240da4c61aa984754740cd5ab/guidelines-for-notification-of-operators.pdf. *See* further, www.pts.se/en/english-b/telephony/vc/, accessed 23 Sep. 2019.
137. Decision by Swedish Post and Telecom Agency (PTS) of 5 Nov. 2008, No. 08-9691. *See also.*
138. *See* PTS Report PTS-ER-2009:26 on the supervisory role of PTS, '*Tillsyn vid PTS. En beskrivning*', 31 Aug. 2009, 16, pts.se/globalassets/startpage/dokument/icke-legala-dokument/rapporter/2009/09-26-tillsyn-2009.pdf.
139. Decision by Swedish Post and Telecom Agency (PTS) of 2 Jul. 2009, No. 06-14224.
140. *See* Ch. 3 ss 1 (radio spectrum) and 19 (numbering capacity) Electronic Communications Act.

55. The main obligations attached to the general authorization are the following:

- to be subject to a notification procedure as well as to a decision issued by the competent national or regional authority for the use of numbers, radio frequencies and rights of way;
- to negotiate interconnection when requested by other operators of publicly available networks in order to ensure the provision and interoperability of services;
- to comply with universal service obligations (USOs);
- when allocated a number or a range of numbers, not to discriminate against other providers of electronic communications services with regard to the number sequences used to give access to their services;
- to use numbering resources effectively and efficiently, and to comply with number portability requirements;
- when supplying public telephone networks or publicly available telephone services, to route calls to the national, European and international numbering ranges, in the terms specified in the applicable plans;
- to comply with the applicable technical specifications and requirements;
- to guarantee the confidentiality of communications (although enabling the legal interception of the communications by national competent authorities), personal data and privacy protection rules as well as the rights of the users of the service;
- to comply with environmental and town and country planning requirements as well as with the requirements and conditions linked with the granting of, access to, or use of public or private land, or linked with the co-location and facility sharing;
- to comply with the regulation established for the use of frequencies especially when related to its effective and efficient use or to the establishment of measures regarding the limitation of exposure of the general public to electromagnetic fields caused by electronic communications networks;
- to pay the applicable fees;
- to allow and facilitate the carrying out of inspections by the competent national regulatory authorities.

Finally, operators shall provide all the information required by the competent regulatory authority, PTS.[141] PTS is entitled, for the purpose of supervision, to gain access to areas, premises and other space, though not personal residences, where operations subject to the Electronic Communications Act are conducted.[142]

56. The supervisory authority is entitled to seek enforcement via the Enforcement Authority of decisions that relate to measures under the Electronic Communications Act.[143]

141. Chapter 7 s. 3 Electronic Communications Act.
142. Chapter 7 s. 2(1) Electronic Communications Act.
143. Chapter 7 s. 2(2) Electronic Communications Act.

57. Information disclosed to PTS in the course of an investigation or other supervisory activity is protected by secrecy legislation. The Public Access to Information and Secrecy Act (*offentlighets- och sekretesslag (2009:400)*) stipulates secrecy for information held by a supervisory authority which regulates production, trade, transport, and other industrial or commercial activities, if it may be presumed that a private subject would be negatively affected if the information is disclosed, provided that the Government has adopted regulations to this effect.[144] Such specific regulation regarding secrecy for information held by PTS has been issued.[145]

58. The Electronic Communications Act does not explicitly address modifications to the obligations attached to the General Authorization.

59. Following the introduction of the 2002 EU Regulatory Framework, special or exclusive rights are in present times generally rare. The Swedish telecom market has been exposed to competition since the early 1990s. As a result, there are no regulations in the Electronic Communications Act regarding entities with special or exclusive rights.

60. The European Commission opened a case against Sweden in 2007 for failing to correctly implement Article 2 Directive 2002/77/EC of 16 September 2002 on competition in the markets for electronic communications networks and services.[146] Government requirements related to grants of TV broadcasting licences in effect ensured a monopoly for access control services to the state-owned company Boxer Access AB. Following changes to the digital terrestrial television broadcasting licences by the Government, the Commission withdrew its case.

61. The Swedish state holds a 38.4% ownership share of the telecom incumbent Telia Company,[147] but does not control Telia's operations. There are also some 150 municipally owned or controlled broadband networks.[148] These municipal networks typically (but not completely) restrict their operations to providing a network infrastructure, with commercial market entities providing communication services to users utilizing the public networks. From the point of view of the Electronic Communications Act, these municipal networks are treated the same as networks and operations owned and operated by private companies. Following changes to the Competition Act (*Konkurrenslag (2008:579)*), the Swedish Competition Authority (*Konkurrensverket*)[149] has been allowed to intercede against commercial sales activities by publicly owned entities when these distort or restrict competition on

144. Chapter 30 s. 23 Public Access to Information and Secrecy Act.
145. Section 9 Ordinance on Public Information and Secrecy (*offentlighets- och sekretessförordning (2009:641)*) and point 99 Appendix to the Ordinance.
146. Case C-419/07, *Commission of the European Communities v. Kingdom of Sweden*.
147. As of 30 Jun. 2019, *see* www.teliacompany.com/en/investors/share-related-information/share holdings/, accessed 24 Sep. 2019.
148. Swedish Post and Telecom Agency (PTS), 'Good Functionality and Technical Security in Municipally Owned Networks', PTS-ER-2010:2.
149. www.konkurrensverket.se/.

the market, or are likely to do so.[150] A number of decisions have been issued by the Market Court in recent years, although not in relation to electronic networks and services.[151]

§6. Access and Interconnection

62. Chapter 4 of the Electronic Communications Act is titled 'Interconnection and Other Forms of Access'. Interconnection (*'samtrafik'*) is defined as the physical and logical connection of public communications networks to enable users to communicate with each other or to access services provided in the networks.[152] The Act does not provide a definition of 'access', as the concept is not exhaustively defined in the Access Directive,[153] and the legislator wanted to leave the demarcation open.[154] The definition in the Access Directive therefore serves as a useful starting point in applying the Electronic Communications Act.

63. There are few general rules in the Electronic Communications Act regarding interconnection. Chapter 4 section 1 states that an operator of a public communications network is under a duty to negotiate on interconnection with a party that provides or intends to provide public electronic communications services. There is a general secrecy obligation in Chapter 4 section 2 that forbids negotiating parties from improperly forwarding or utilizing information they have become aware of or gained access to concerning another company's business or operating circumstances in the course of negotiations regarding interconnections.

The obligation to negotiate on interconnection is not the same as an obligation to actually reach an agreement. However, an interconnection can be imposed where communication between end users is prevented or threatened; in accordance with Chapter 4 section 3 a party that controls access to end users can be ordered to, in return for fair market reward, conduct interconnection or implement other necessary measures. 'Fair' market reward implies limits to what an interconnecting operator may charge.[155]

Operators may not be ordered to apply different conditions for equivalent services, as this would breach the equal treatment requirement in Article 3(2) Access Directive; this principle is also explicitly stated in Chapter 4 section 13 Electronic Communications Act. An obligation that relates to access has to be linked to the services that are actually provided, unless otherwise prescribed by conditions determined in accordance with a decision to grant a radio licence.[156]

---

150. Chapter 3 ss 27–32 Competition Act.
151. *See* for example MD 2014:1 on refusal to grant access to a fire training area, MD 2015:12 on conducting gym and spa activities, MD 2015:17 on providing products and services for audio-visual teaching material, and MD 2016:3 on the sale of land and construction contracts.
152. Chapter 1 s. 7 Electronic Communications Act.
153. Article 2(2) a.
154. Government Bill (*Proposition*) 2002/03:110, 166.
155. *Ibid.*, 195 et seq.
156. Chapter 4 s. 13(2) Electronic Communications Act.

More detailed or far-reaching obligations than those listed above may only be imposed on operators who have been found to hold SMP in a particular market in the course of the regulatory market analysis.[157]

64. In practice, the absence of a general obligation of interconnection and access becomes near academic. As is set out in its SMP decisions, PTS has held the view that all operators that control access to their subscribers in the form of call termination have. PTS has on a number of occasions issued decisions directed at operators, large and small, obliging them to accept every reasonable request for interconnection from present or intended providers of electronic communication services. These decisions are nominally subject to continuing review but can be expected to be in force for approximately five years.[158] In 2016, PTS concluded that the market for fixed telephony services no longer needed to be regulated as the market was moving towards effective competition as a result of, for example, the availability of fibre and IP services.[159]

65. An operator which PTS has found to have SMP may be ordered to satisfy reasonable requirements on access to and the use of the network and associated facilities with the aim of providing electronic communications services, as stated in Chapter 4 section 8 Electronic Communications Act. Such an obligation, in accordance with this section, may relate to the operator providing access to specified parts of the network and associated facilities, extending access already granted, offering specified services for resale, granting access to technical interfaces, protocol or other key technology necessary for interoperability, offering co-location or other opportunities for joint use of associated facilities, offering specified services to ensure interoperability, offering access to operational support systems or programme systems required to guarantee sound competition, or conducting interconnection or implementing measures for networks or associated facilities to be connected.

In imposing these obligations, PTS is required, in accordance with Chapter 4 section 10, to take account of:

- technical and financial strength for the use and installation of alternative network parts or associated facilities, having regard to market developments and the nature and kind of interconnection and other forms or access;
- available capacity;

157. For more information on the definition of SMP in Swedish law, *see* Part V Chapter 2.

158. PTS publishes an thorough overview of its SMP decisions, in Swedish, at, pts.se/sv/bransch/internet/konkurrensreglering-smp/; the market reviews for 2012-2015 are found at, pts.se/sv/bransch/internet/konkurrensreglering-smp/smp-beslut-2012-2015/, the reviews for 2015-2017 at, pts.se/sv/bransch/internet/konkurrensreglering-smp/smp-beslut-2015-2017/, and on-going reviews at pts.se/sv/bransch/internet/konkurrensreglering-smp/smp-beslut-2015-2017/, accessed 24 Sep. 2019. Information in English is also available (although not as updated) at, www.pts.se/en/english-b/internet/smp---market-reviews/.

159. *See* further PTS decision Dnr. 15-4799, 14 Dec. 2016, pts.se/globalassets/startpage/dokument/legala-dokument/beslut/2016/telefoni/fasta-telefonitjanster/beslut-fasta-telefonitjanster-20161214-final.pdf.

– the risks that a new investment involves for the owner of the network or associated facilities;
– the need to protect long-term competition;
– the intellectual property rights involved;
– interest in cross-border services within the EEA.

66. An SMP operator may be ordered to publicize specific details concerning accounting, technical specifications, network characteristics, conditions for provision and use of services, pricing, or other circumstances needed for transparency on matters relating to interconnection and other forms of access.[160] Such an order is to include a notice concerning what information is to be provided, how detailed it should be and the way in which it is to be publicized.[161] The operator may also be ordered to change an item of information if necessary to adhere to an obligation.[162]

67. An SMP operator may be ordered to apply non-discriminatory conditions in its operations.[163] Such an obligation is in particular to ensure that the operator in similar circumstances applies equivalent terms in relation to others who provide equivalent services, and the services and the information the operator offers to others are provided on the same conditions and of the same quality as the operator's own services.

68. An SMP operator may be ordered to separately account and report specified operations related to interconnection and other forms of access.[164] Such an obligation may refer to an operator applying open pricing or to provide an authority with its accounts, including details of revenues.

69. Where an access obligation is imposed on an SMP operator that consists of access to the network between a main distribution frame or a similar interconnection point and a subscriber's fixed network termination point, and if the network comprises a 'twin cable of metal', the operator is also obliged to publish a reference offer for this specific access, often referred to as the local loop. Only Telia has had a local loop obligation imposed on it.[165] The pricing for such access has been a point of contention, specifically what can be deemed a cost-oriented price for access.[166]

A decision may be combined with a sanction in the form of a set administrative fine, which PTS can ask a court to execute if the decision is respected.

160. Chapter 4 s. 5(1) Electronic Communications Act.
161. Chapter 4 s. 5(2) Electronic Communications Act.
162. Chapter 4 s. 5(3) Electronic Communications Act.
163. Chapter 4 s. 6 Electronic Communications Act.
164. Chapter 4 s. 7 Electronic Communications Act.
165. Decision by PTS of 24 Nov. 2004, No. 04-6948/23.
166. *See* Decision of the Stockholm Administrative Court of 9 May 2016, No. 31074-14 (the case was appealed but leave was not granted by the Stockholm Court of Appeal, *see* decision of 8 Nov. 2016, No. 3760-16).

70. In 2008 provisions imposing a functional separation of the metal-based access network were added to the Electronic Communications Act.[167] By forcing the operator to transfer network assets and facilities to a separate corporate organization, independent from its services operations, the aim is for the operator to treat all service providers utilizing its network without discrimination and in a transparent manner.[168] The criteria for imposing functional separation are strict; only an operator obliged to provide local loop and bit-stream access can be an addressee of this obligation, and only under exceptional circumstances.[169] The only possible recipient of a separation order is the incumbent, Telia.

An operator may decide to carry out such a separation of its own accord in order to guarantee non-discrimination and transparency. This self-imposed transfer can be accepted by the regulator where exceptional circumstances exist, and while this voluntary separation lasts, an order imposing a functional separation may not be issued.[170]

§7. Numbering

71. As Recital 20 of the Framework Directive explains, 'Access to numbering resources on the basis of transparent, objective, and non-discriminatory criteria is essential for undertakings to compete in the electronic communications sector.'

PTS determines the national numbering plans for electronic communications and issues regulations concerning the plans and their use. The plans shall be designed so that electronic communications networks and electronic communications services can be reached in an equivalent way.[171]

72. A party that conducts operations subject to a notification obligation in accordance with Chapter 2 section 1 Electronic Communications Act, or provides electronic communications services in interconnection with a party that conducts such operations, is liable to comply with the approved numbering plans.[172]

A party that provides a public telephony service shall be capable of dealing with all calls to the European Telephony Numbering Space 3883.[173] PTS is required to keep the national numbering plans publicly available, insofar as there are no secrecy concerns.[174] The numbering plans are available at the PTS website.[175]

167. *See* Government Bill 2007/08:73, '*Funktionell separation för bättre bredbandskonkurrens*'.
168. Chapter 4 s. 12 a-b Electronic Communications Act.
169. Chapter 4 s. 12 a Electronic Communications Act.
170. Chapter 4 s. 12 c Electronic Communications Act.
171. Chapter 3 s. 15 Electronic Communications Act and ss 10, 16, and 17 Ordinance on Electronic Communications.
172. Chapter 3 s. 16 Electronic Communications Act.
173. Chapter 3 s. 17. This implements Art. 27(2) Universal Services Directive.
174. Chapter 3 s.18 Electronic Communications Act.
175. The numbering plan is available in English at, www.pts.se/globalassets/startpage/dokument/bransch/telefoni/nummerplan/the-swedish-numbering-plan-for-telephony-accordning-to-itu---2018-07-04.pdf, accessed 25 Sep. 2019.

73. The allocation of numbers from a national numbering plan requires a licence.[176] Licences are given for a series of numbers or individual numbers, such as numbers from the 118 series which are allocated for directory services. PTS is authorized to issue regulations concerning the principles for allocation of numbers.[177]

74. A party that has been allocated a number series may not discriminate against others who provide electronic communications services as regards which numbers allow access to services in the networks.[178]

75. A licence to use numbers may be combined with conditions concerning:[179]

(1) the kind of service for which the number is to be used;
(2) the actual and efficient use of the number;
(3) a reasonable term of validity with reservations for possible changes in the national numbering plan;
(4) undertakings made in conjunction with licences granted for numbers of substantial economic value; and
(5) obligations in accordance with applicable international agreements regarding the use of numbers.

Examples of conditions are the requirement to provide free calls for numbers in the 020 series, the requirement to provide directory services for numbers in the 118 series and the requirement to provide public health information for numbers in the 1177 series.

Requirements for actual and efficient use are used to prevent operators from unnecessary stockpiling of numbers. One example is mobile operators locking in large amounts of numbers in Subscriber Identity Module cards for prepaid accounts distributed to retail outlets for eventual sale.

76. Licences to use numbers of substantial economic value may be granted by PTS following an open invitation to apply.[180] Such a licence is to be granted following:

(1) a comparative selection procedure;
(2) a tender procedure where the price that the applicant is willing to pay for the licence shall be decisive;
(3) a procedure with random allocation; or
(4) a combination of procedures (1)–(3).

176. Chapter 3 s.19 Electronic Communications Act.
177. PTS has issued regulations on numbering PTSFS 2003:3, 2003:4 and 2013:1.
178. Chapter 3 s. 20 Electronic Communications Act.
179. Chapter 3 s. 21 Electronic Communications Act.
180. Chapter 3 s. 22 Electronic Communications Act.

The Government and PTS are authorized to issue regulations concerning the content of an open invitation and the procedure to be used.[181]

77. Numbers that are perceived by PTS as more attractive are deemed to potentially have substantial economic value.[182] Directory service providers complained in the early 1990s that PTS had allocated the number 118118 to Telia's directory service without first offering it for sale on the market.

78. A provider of public telephony services is required to ensure that its network allows subscribers to retain their telephone numbers when changing service provider.[183] If the subscriber so requests, the telephone number used for such a service shall be transferred to another to enable it to provide the service. Where a number's digit structure has geographical significance, as is the case for most fixed-line residential subscriptions in Sweden, it only needs to be transferred for the provision of services within the same geographical area (area code district). Providers are not required to transfer numbers between fixed and mobile networks, respectively, although some choose to offer this service anyway.[184]

The Government or PTS, if authorized, may issue regulations concerning how the obligations shall be satisfied and regarding exemptions from the obligations, and may also grant exemptions in individual cases, where special reasons exist.[185]

79. Charges for number portability must be based on the operational cost for the transfer.[186] A provider that has transferred a number is only entitled to payment for the operational costs that comprise increased traffic costs for a message to the number; the charge is invoiced to the operator taking over the number; the transferring provider may not charge the subscriber for the service.[187]

80. The transferring provider is required to immediately provide such information as is necessary for routing messages to the telephone number to the Swedish Number Portability Administrative Center (SNPAC), the independent non-profit industry organization set up to administer number portability routing.[188] SNPAC operates the reference database for number portability. Other information than the telephone number and the service provider that may be directly or indirectly referable to a natural person may not be released without consent from the individual.[189]

81. The provision of domain names for Internet communication falls outside of the operational scope of PTS. Domain names under the top-level domain associated

---

181. Chapter 3 s. 22 Electronic Communications Act and ss 19 and 20 Ordinance on Electronic Communications.
182. *See* Government Bill 2002/03:110, 373.
183. Chapter 5 s. 9(1) Electronic Communications Act.
184. Chapter 5 s. 9(2) Electronic Communications Act.
185. Chapter 5 s. 9(4) Electronic Communications Act.
186. Chapter 5 s. 10(1) Electronic Communications Act.
187. Chapter 5 s. 10(2) and 10(3) Electronic Communications Act.
188. More information at, www.snpac.se.
189. Chapter 5 s. 11 Electronic Communications Act.

with Sweden (.se) are allocated by the independent private foundation *Internetstiftelsen*, the Swedish Internet Foundation.[190] PTS, however, supervises the administration of national top-level domains in accordance with the National Top-Level Domains for Sweden on the Internet Act (*lag (2006:24) om nationella toppdomäner för Sverige på Internet*).[191]

§8. Radio Spectrum

82. Radio frequencies are considered a scarce resource in the public domain. The Electronic Communications Act defines radio waves as electromagnetic waves with frequencies ranging from 9 kHz to 3,000 GHz, spread without specially arranged conductors.[192] The definition is derived from Article 2 of Decision No. 676/2002/EC of the European Parliament and of the Council of 7 March 2002 on a regulatory framework for radio spectrum policy in the European Community.

83. PTS is the designated supervisory authority for issues relating to the right to use radio spectrum and radio transmitters in Sweden.[193] PTS decides on permits and licences for such use and is authorized to issue regulations on exemptions from the licence obligation.[194]

84. Licences to use radio transmitters are awarded for a limited period of time.[195] PTS decides on conditions for the use of the licence, relating, for example, to commercial usage, geographic area, specific technology, and frequency bands.[196] The validity period for licence conditions may be shorter than the validity period of the licence itself. When determining the validity of permits and conditions, particular regard shall be given to:

(1) future changes in radio use;
(2) the period that the transmitter is intended to be used;
(3) the technical development that can be expected;
(4) the time required to achieve reasonable financial return on the equipment; and
(5) whether a licence to use radio transmitters for broadcasts in accordance with another Act constitutes a precondition for a licence to use radio transmitters.[197]

---

190. internetstiftelsen.se/en.
191. *See* Part II Ch. 6.
192. Chapter 1 s. 7 Electronic Communications Act.
193. Sections 10 and 11 Ordinance on Electronic Communication.
194. Chapter 3 s. 4 Electronic Communications Act.
195. Chapter 3 s. 12(1) Electronic Communications Act.
196. Chapter 3 s. 11 Electronic Communications Act.
197. Chapter 3 s. 12(2) Electronic Communications Act.

85. A licence is required in order to use radio transmitters in Sweden or on a Swedish vessel or aircraft abroad.[198] If the use of frequencies and the conditions and procedure for the grant of a licence to use radio transmitters have been harmonized in accordance with international agreements to which Sweden has acceded or provisions adopted in accordance with the Treaty on the Functioning of the European Union (TFEU), the party that has been granted such a licence shall be deemed to have a licence.[199] This means that when a harmonized selection procedure in accordance with Article 8 Authorization Directive has been used in granting a licence in one EU Member State, the licence will also be valid in other Member States.

86. Allocation of radio spectrum and licences for transmitters to certain public bodies relating to security and law enforcement, such as the Police (*Polisen*), the Swedish Armed Forces (*Försvarsmakten*), the National Defence Radio Establishment (*Försvarets radioanstalt*), and the Defence Materiel Administration (FMV/*Försvarets materielverk*), are decided in accordance with separate procedures.[200] PTS may also issue regulations on exemptions from the licence obligation; in such cases, conditions may be prescribed that the radio installation in which the transmitter is included should meet specific technical requirements and other usage conditions.[201]

87. In accordance with Chapter 3 section 6 Electronic Communications Act, a licence to use a radio transmitter shall be granted provided that:

(1) it can be assumed that the radio frequencies will be used in such a way that the risk of unauthorized harmful interference does not arise;
(2) the radio use constitutes an efficient use of radio frequencies;
(3) it can be assumed that the radio use will not impede radio communication that is particularly important having regard to the free formation of opinion;
(4) the radio use will not utilize radio frequencies required to maintain a reasonable preparedness for the development of existing and new radio uses or frequencies for which radio use has been harmonized in accordance with international agreements to which Sweden has acceded or provisions adopted in accordance with the TFEU;
(5) it can be assumed that the radio use will not interfere with radio frequencies required for public security and law enforcement operations; and
(6) where the applicant has previously had a licence revoked or a similar circumstance exists, there is no reasonable cause to assume that the radio use will be in violation of the licence conditions.

198. Chapter 3 s. 1 Electronic Communications Act.
199. Chapter 3 s. 2 Electronic Communications Act.
200. Chapter 3 s. 3 Electronic Communications Act. *See* www.polisen.se, www.forsvarsmakten.se, www.fra.se and www.fmv.se respectively.
201. Chapter 3 s. 4 Electronic Communications Act.

A licence to use a radio transmitter for broadcasts that require licences according to another Act or according to provisions issued under another Act may only be issued if such a licence exists.

88. The number of licences granted within one part of the radio spectrum may be restricted when this is deemed necessary by PTS to safeguard the efficient use of radio frequencies; a decision to limit the number of licences shall be reviewed as soon as there is reason to do so.[202]

89. When the number of permits has been limited in such a way, allocation shall take place following an open invitation to apply, unless particular reasons to do otherwise exist.[203] The requirement to issue an open invitation does not apply to radio use that:

(1) primarily relates to broadcasting of programmes to the public of programmes referred to in Chapter 1 section 2 Fundamental Law on Freedom of Expression (sound radio, television or other transmissions of sound, image or text by means of electromagnetic waves, along with public playback from databases);
(2) is intended for private use; or
(3) is needed for operations conducted to ensure public order, security or health.

Allocation under an open invitation is decided following a comparative selection procedure or a tender procedure, where the price that the applicant is willing to pay for the licence shall be decisive, or following a combination of these procedures. PTS may issue regulations concerning the content of an open invitation and on the comparative selection or tender procedure.

90. A licence to use a radio transmitter does not generally specify a particular radio use, such as mobile telephony and computer communications, fixed wireless access, etc.

91. A licence to use a radio transmitter may be combined with conditions concerning:[204]

(1) the frequency range;
(2) the electronic communications services or types of electronic communications networks or technologies;
(3) coverage and roll-out within Sweden;
(4) the geographical area;
(5) an obligation to share frequency space with others;
(6) such matter as in accordance with a decision on the harmonized use of radio frequencies should be imposed as conditions when the party to be allocated

202. Chapter 3 s. 7 Electronic Communications Act.
203. Chapter 3 s. 8 Electronic Communications Act.
204. Chapter 3 s. 11(1) Electronic Communications Act.

a radio frequency has been nominated in accordance with international agreements or provisions adopted in accordance with the TFEU;
(7) obligations arising from international agreements on the use of frequencies;
(8) undertakings made in conjunction with the grant of a licence in a selection procedure; and
(9) technical and other requirements to ensure actual and efficient use of the radio spectrum.

92. Conditions requiring a licence to be used for particular electronic communications services or types of electronic communications networks or technologies may only be issued if necessary,[205] to avoid harmful interference, ensure efficient use of the radio spectrum, protect people's life or health, serve the public interest that certain electronic communications services are available in certain parts of the country, or serve the public interest in promoting the provision of radio and TV services licensed in accordance with another Act.

93. A licence to use a specific radio transmitter may, in addition to the conditions set out (in paragraph 91 above), be combined with conditions relating to:[206]

(1) the nature of the antenna and the radio transmitter;
(2) the geographical area in which a mobile radio transmitter may be used;
(3) where the antenna for a fixed radio transmitter shall be located;
(4) competence requirements for those who will manage the radio equipment.

94. Recital 19 of the Framework Directive suggests that:

> Transfer of radio frequencies can be an effective means of increasing efficient use of spectrum, as long as there are sufficient safeguards in place to protect the public interest, in particular the need to ensure transparency and regulatory supervision of such transfers.

95. The Electronic Communications Act states that a licence or part of a licence to use a radio transmitter may be assigned to another party with PTS' permission.[207] Such permission shall be granted, provided:

(1) the assignee fulfils the requirements imposed on the applicant in conjunction with the grant of the licence;
(2) there is no reason to assume the transfer will have an adverse impact on competition;
(3) the transfer does not result in changed use of radio frequencies, if harmonized in accordance with provisions adopted under the TFEU; and
(4) there are no other particular reasons against doing so.

---

205. In accordance with Chapter 3 s. 11(2) Electronic Communications Act.
206. Chapter 3 s. 11a Electronic Communications Act.
207. Chapter 3 s. 23 Electronic Communications Act.

An inefficient use of radio spectrum is an example of a particular reason not to grant permission for a transfer.[208]

96. If harmful interference occurs, licence holders are required to immediately ensure that the interference ceases or is reduced as far as possible, unless the interference is permitted; this also applies to a party using a radio receiver that interferes with the use of another radio receiver.[209] Electrical or other electronic installations, excluding radio installations, that are intended to generate radio frequency energy for communications purposes in lines or for industrial, scientific, medical or any other similar purpose, may only be used in accordance with regulations issued by the Government or PTS.[210] Section 14 Ordinance on Electronic Communications prohibits possessing electrical or electronic installations whose purpose is interference with radio transmissions.

§9. Public Service Obligations and Other Public Rights and Obligations

97. Chapters 5 and 6 Electronic Communications Act set out the regulations concerning public service obligations and other public rights and obligations. The concept of public service obligations refers to universal service and services aimed at protecting the public interest. The expression 'other public rights and obligations' concerns the provision of electronic communications networks and services which, to some extent, have a public character; this includes the conveyance of emergency calls, directory services, services for the disabled, co-location, facility sharing, personal data processing, and the protection of privacy and users' rights.

I. Universal Service Obligations

98. USOs may be imposed if deemed necessary by PTS to ensure adequate public electronic communications services. They may be imposed on a party that is considered appropriate; this party is ordered to, at an affordable price, provide particular services.[211]

There is currently no operator designated to provide universal service in the form of telephony or Internet access services. Access to telephony has historically been provided by Telia (formerly operated by the Swedish State as a public service corporation, known as Televerket and later TeliaSonera), as the only operator. Before the Telecommunications Act came into force in 1993, only Televerket could offer a

208. *See* Government Bill (*Proposition*) 2002/03:110, 164.
209. Chapter 3 s.13 Electronic Communications Act.
210. Chapter 3 s. 14 Electronic Communications Act.
211. Chapter 5 s. 1 Electronic Communications Act.

telephony service; licensing conditions were imposed, requiring it to provide telephony services to anyone who requested.[212] The Telecommunications Act was replaced by the Electronic Communications Act in 2003 and the licensing conditions for TeliaSonera remained in force transitionally until April 2004. In 2005, PTS placed TeliaSonera under an obligation to meet reasonable requests for access to the public telephone network at an affordable price. TeliaSonera appealed against PTS' decision and the Stockholm Administrative Court annulled the decision on 5 February 2007.[213] No new decision requiring the provision of universal telephony service has been issued.[214]

99. In October 2008 PTS proposed the introduction of a universal service fund to finance provision of universal service of fixed telephony and other electronic communications services.[215] PTS has also studied the question of provision of a universal 'functional access' to the Internet, in the form of broadband access.[216]

100. The Electronic Communications Act authorizes PTS to order 'appropriate parties' to:[217]

(1) satisfy reasonable requirements for connection to a public communications network to a fixed network termination point at a permanent place of residence or business location;
(2) satisfy reasonable requirements for access to public telephony services to a fixed network termination point at a permanent place of residence or business location, for everyone who demands this service;
(3) make available information about all telephone subscriptions, to the extent they are not subject to secrecy or a duty of confidentiality according to law, in a subscriber directory, which shall be updated annually;
(4) provide a complete directory enquiry service regarding telephone subscriptions, to the extent that the information provided is not subject to secrecy or a duty of confidentiality according to law;
(5) provide public payphones or other places with public access to voice telephony to the extent that, as regards quality, amount and geographical distribution, satisfies the public need; or
(6) provide people with disabilities access to these services to the same extent and on equivalent terms as for other end users, and satisfy the needs of people with disabilities for such services.

---

212. The policy when the Telecommunications Act was introduced was that the state was responsible for providing access to telephony at uniform prices to everyone in Sweden.
213. Stockholm Administrative Court, Decision No. 20346-05.
214. Swedish Post and Telecom Agency (PTS), '*Telefoni, grundläggande internet och kopparnätsavvecklingen*', PTS-ER-2019:10, 28 Mar. 2019, 12.
215. Swedish Post and Telecom Agency (PTS), '*Samhällsomfattande tjänster. Rätt till telefoni*', PTS-ER 2008:20.
216. PTS report, 18 Feb. 2010, No. 10-658.
217. Chapter 5 s. 1 Electronic Communications Act.

101. Access to universal services shall be safeguarded through procurement by the state if it is necessary in view of the costs for the provision of the service or network.[218] This means that if the cost to the operator proves unreasonably burdensome, the service shall instead be procured by the state. In deciding whether costs are too high, PTS shall take regard to the costs, revenue and immaterial rights related to providing the service. Where the operator holds a dominant position for the service to be provided, additional costs are deemed to be low.

102. A party obliged to provide such a service may be required to reach specific performance targets within a given time; this given time must be at least three months.[219] An obligation to provide fixed-line access shall be designed so that it supports calls, fax and data communication with a particular specified minimum data rate that allows functional access to the Internet.[220] Section 29a Ordinance on Electronic Communications states that an access speed of 10 Mbit/s achieves functional access. A party obliged to provide subscriber directories and directory enquiry services shall treat the information in a non-discriminatory way.[221] A party obliged to provide universal service may have an obligation to:

(1) apply common tariffs throughout Sweden or apply a specified maximum price;
(2) make it possible for the consumer to pay in advance for connection to the public telephone network and for the use of public telephony services;
(3) allow the consumer to pay for a connection to the public telephone network through payments that are spread over time; and
(4) on subscriber's request give information on alternative tariffs which incur lower costs.[222]

103. PTS is empowered to designate an operator as an appropriate party to shoulder a USO.[223] The preparatory works to the Electronic Communications Act set out the requisite conditions: a decision shall be founded on objective criteria and the receiving undertaking's ability to carry out the obligation; the selection shall take in account the principle of proportionality; and no undertaking can be excluded from the possibility of receiving an obligation beforehand. Only undertakings that already offer relevant commercial services, such as operators, can in reality be deemed appropriate.[224]

104. PTS has found that several factors serve to ameliorate the burden of a service provision requirement. The operator will be able to sell other services to the subscribers gained through a USO obligation. The operator will have its coverage

218. Chapter 5 s. 1(2) Electronic Communications Act.
219. Chapter 5 s. 2(1) Electronic Communications Act.
220. Chapter 5 s. 2(2) Electronic Communications Act.
221. Chapter 5 s. 3 Electronic Communications Act.
222. Chapter 5 ss 4 and 7 a–b Electronic Communications Act.
223. Section 29 Ordinance on Electronic Communications.
224. Government Bill (*Proposition*) 2003/04:110, 217 and 383, and PTS decision of 19 Aug. 2005, No. 05-1072/23.

increased, which may increase respect for its brand. The increase of customers may lead to better economies of scale, for example, in procuring equipment. Customers gained through the service obligation may also prove more loyal to the operator than other subscribers, which would be valuable when the customer moves.[225] Even so, PTS proposed the establishment of a universal service fund to finance compensation for or procurement of service provision obligations. Funding is suggested to be collected through charges on operators who have notified service and/or network provision to PTS. Charges are to be calculated based on criteria that are transparent, objective, non-discriminatory, and proportional. No such fund has, however, been introduced.

105. A number of general public service requirements are demanded of all providers of public electronic communications services and networks. An important obligation is the requirement that operators take appropriate technical and organizational actions to ensure that operations satisfy reasonable reliability demands.[226] PTS has issued guidelines for the operator's work in this regard.[227]

106. A provider of a public communications network or a publicly available electronic communication service is required to report service disruptions or significant interruptions to PTS without undue delay. Where it is in the public interest, PTS may oblige providers to inform the general public of service disruptions or interruptions that have taken place.[228]

107. Regulations may be adopted regarding minimum service levels offered by providers of public communication networks, if necessary to prevent obstructed or slow network transmission or the degradation of the quality of publicly available electronic communication services.[229] This measure implements Article 22.3 Universal Services Directive, providing the regulator with tools in the event of an actionable breach of network neutrality.

Providers of a public telephony service are further required to:[230]

- assist in emergency calls being conveyed without interruption and free of charge;
- provide location data free of charge to those who receive emergency calls;
- satisfy reasonable requests to release subscriber information that is not subject to secrecy or a legal duty of confidentiality, to those who conduct subscriber directory services, on terms that are fair, cost-orientated and non-discriminatory;
- provide specified telephone bills for the use of a public telephone network or associated public telephony services to a subscriber free of charge;

225. Swedish Post and Telecom Agency (PTS), '*Samhällsomfattande tjänster. Rätt till telefoni*' PTS-ER-2008:20, 23 Oct. 2008.
226. Chapter 5 s. 6b Electronic Communications Act.
227. Guideline by PTS, PTSFS 2007:2.
228. Chapter 5 s. 6c Electronic Communications Act. PTS has issued Regulations and Guidelines regarding notification of service disruption or interruptions, PTSFS 2012:2.
229. Chapter 5 s. 6d Electronic Communications Act.
230. Chapter 5 s. 7(1) and 6e Electronic Communications Act.

– ensure that end users can reach all numbers in use within the EEA, provided this is technically and economically feasible and the dialled subscriber has not chosen, for commercial reasons, to restrict access for incoming calls from certain geographical areas; and
– have regard to the needs of people with disabilities.

Calls that are free of charge for the caller may not be specified on her or his telephone bill.[231] Telephony service providers are obliged, at a subscriber's request, to block numbers or certain types of calls (e.g., international calls or calls to premium numbers),[232] or to block calls when the accrued charges have reached a limit set by the subscriber.[233] Subscribers are to be informed of these rights when entering into a contract for a telephony service.

Operators providing a public communications network or publicly available electronic communication service shall have clear, comparable, adequate and up-to-date publicly available information on applicable prices, tariffs and general terms for access to and the use of the network or service.[234] Operators may be ordered to provide information to end users about the quality of their services.[235]

If a subscriber falls behind on payments, provision of the network or service may be only discontinued after the subscriber has been prompted to pay within a specified reasonable time and was informed that the service may otherwise be discontinued; if the service is paid for within the specified time, it may not be discontinued.[236] Where a subscriber has paid too late on repeated occasions, the provision of the service may be discontinued immediately; in such cases, the operator shall immediately notify the subscriber of the cessation of service and, for a period of at least ten days, allow the subscriber to make emergency calls and other free phone calls.[237] If the unpaid or repeated late payment relates to a particular service, the discontinuance may be limited to that service, provided it is technically possible and the subscriber has not previously received a demand for payment or misled the service supplier.[238]

II. Other Public Rights and Obligations

108. Operators require access for placing equipment and laying down cables across public and private property to serve end users. Rights of way are regulated in the Utility Easements Act (*ledningsrättslag (1973:1144)*) and examined by the cadastral procedure. A utility easement encompasses the power to take measures needed for the installation and use of cables or other devices on the property

231. Chapter 5 s. 7(2) Electronic Communications Act.
232. Chapter 5 s. 7a Electronic Communications Act.
233. Chapter 5 s. 7b Electronic Communications Act.
234. Chapter 5 s. 17 Electronic Communications Act.
235. Chapter 5 s. 18 Electronic Communications Act.
236. Chapter 5 s. 19(1) Electronic Communications Act.
237. Chapter 5 s. 19(2) Electronic Communications Act.
238. Chapter 5 s. 19(3) Electronic Communications Act.

unit.[239] At the request of the proprietor of the utility easement, an order can be made that the easement shall belong to that party's property unit or registered site leasehold.

The Utility Easements Act encompasses cables that are part of an electronic communications network for public use and public low-voltage cabling for signalling, remote control, data transmission or some similar purpose.[240] The easement can only be granted where the purpose could not be met in another way or where the benefits to be gained by the easement outweigh any inconvenience, from a public or individual point of view.[241] It was previously unclear if a mast carrying transmitters for a mobile network was strictly a 'utility' as in Swedish the Act speaks of 'cables'; however, the Act was clarified to include masts in 2004.

109. Recital 23 of the Framework Directive considers that facility sharing can be of benefit for town planning, public health or environmental reasons. In accordance with the Electronic Communications Act, an operator may be obliged to provide co-location or other opportunities for shared use of property or other resources in cases where it is of importance for the protection of the environment or achievement of physical planning objectives, or required to protect public health or public safety.[242] This may include strengthening or expanding an electronic communications mast or similar measures, but not an obligation to replace an existing mast with a new one.[243] The right to demand co-location is restricted to other operators; a municipality or public authority is not entitled to demand that operators co-locate, for example, for physical planning or environmental reasons. An operator may not demand co-location in order to share costs; only operators seeking access to another operator's facilities may exercise the right to request co-location. Compensation for providing co-location shall be calculated at market rates, as far as they can be established.[244]

110. Operators may also be obliged to allow reasonable requests for access to and use of networks and affiliated installations in order to provide electronic communication services. Article 12.1 and 12.3 of the Access Directive on obligations of access to, and use of, specific network facilities is implemented through detailed regulations in the Electronic Communications Act, whereby SMP operators may be required to provide a range of forms of access. PTS has issued Telia Company AB with such a requirement relating to local access to copper-based network infrastructure and co-location.[245]

239. Section 1 Utility Easements Act.
240. Section 2 Utility Easements Act.
241. Section 6 Utility Easements Act.
242. Chapter 4 s. 14(1) Electronic Communications Act.
243. Chapter 4 s. 14(2) Electronic Communications Act.
244. *See* regarding calculation of compensation Government Bill (*Proposition*) 2005/06:191, '*Ändring i lagen om elektronisk kommunikation*', 15 and 22.
245. PTS decision 19 Feb. 2015, dnr 11-9306. This requirement is still in place, amended by PTS decision 5 Jun. 2018, dnr 17-8944.

111. The Electronic Communications Act makes a distinction between subscribers, users and end users. The definitions given in Chapter 1 section 7 determine who is a beneficiary of a specific right. A subscriber is a person who has concluded a contract with a provider of public electronic communications services concerning the provision of such services; a user is a person who uses or requests the provision of a public electronic communications service; an end user is a user who does not provide public communications networks or public electronic communications services.

112. The Electronic Communications Act sets out a long list of requirements regarding contracts between network and/or service providers and subscribers.[246] A contract between a consumer and the provider of such a network or service shall contain clear, comprehensive and easily accessible information on, among other things, the provider's name and address, the services to be provided, detailed prices and tariffs, the term of the agreement, conditions for extension and termination and conditions for compensation. These requirements are also applicable to other end users following a request.[247]

If a service provider wishes to amend the contract, the subscriber must be notified of the amendment at least one month before it enters into force. A subscriber who does not accept the new conditions may terminate the contract without incurring any cost, charge or other obligation. The notification to the subscriber shall include information on the right to terminate the contract.[248]

§10. Administrative Charges

113. The Electronic Communications Act states that PTS may charge a processing fee to a party notifying operations concerning:

(1) the provision to the public of electronic communications networks;
(2) the provision to the public of electronic communications services; or applies for:
   - a licence to use a radio transmitter;
   - a licence to use numbers from the national numbering plan;
   - consent to assign a licence or part of a licence to use a radio transmitter or numbers.[249]

The fee shall correspond to the authority's costs for processing the matter. An annual fee shall also be paid by the provider of a notified network or service or a licence holder;

246. Chapter 5 s. 15(1) Electronic Communications Act.
247. Chapter 5 s. 15(2) Electronic Communications Act.
248. Chapter 5 s. 16 Electronic Communications Act.
249. Chapter 8 s. 17(1) Electronic Communications Act and s. 12 Ordinance on Financing the Operations of the Post and Telecom Agency (*förordning (2016:602) om finansiering av Post- och telestyrelsens verksamhet*).

114. PTS annually issues a regulation on the calculation of the administrative charges.[250] Operators are obliged to pay an annual percentage of their gross revenues to finance the costs incurred in the management, control and enforcement of the regulatory framework. Currently the applicable percentage is 0.147, for operators with revenue in excess of SEK 5 million; operators with less annual revenue pay a fixed sum of SEK 4,000. The fee for financing measures against serious peacetime threats and stresses that relate to electronic communications is set at 0.154, for operators with revenue in excess of SEK 30 million. The Government however sets an annual total cap of what fee may be collected for this purpose. The fees for the use of numbers and various radio transmitter usages are listed in the PTS regulation.

250. The latest regulation is PTSFS 2018:6, covering 2019.

Chapter 2. Regulation of Competition in the ICT Market

§1. General Statement

115. The present EU regulatory framework aims at reducing or even withdrawing *ex ante* sector-specific rules. The mechanism for doing so is based on an initial analysis of the relevant markets with a view to assessing whether competition is effective in a given market. If so, *ex ante* regulatory obligations should not be imposed. If there is not effective competition or if competition is not deemed durable, *ex ante* obligations may be imposed on undertakings having an SMP.[251]

§2. Market Definition Procedure

116. PTS is in charge of defining the relevant markets concerning the provision of electronic communications networks and services. In doing so, it must take into account the EU Commission guidelines for market analysis and the assessment of SMP, as well as the Recommendation on relevant product and service markets.[252] PTS is tasked to continuously determine which product and service markets have such characteristic features that it may be justified to impose obligations under the Electronic Communications Act.[253]

§3. Market Analysis Procedure

117. For each market, PTS shall determine whether effective competition prevails. Where it is concluded that effective competition does not prevail in a given market, undertakings with significant power are identified and notified of decisions concerning obligations.[254] Where it is concluded that effective competition prevails, any existing obligations will be revoked; the timing of revocation shall be determined taking into account the interests of the parties concerned.[255] As regards cross-border markets, as determined by the European Commission, measures shall be decided following consultation with the competent authorities of the States affected.[256]

§4. Operators with SMP

118. An undertaking shall be deemed to have significant power if it, either individually or together with others, has a position of such financial strength that it can

251. *See* Art. 16 Framework Directive.
252. *See* Art. 15 Framework Directive.
253. Chapter 8 ss 5 and 6 Electronic Communications Act.
254. Chapter 8 s. 6(2) Electronic Communications Act.
255. Chapter 8 s. 6(3) Electronic Communications Act.
256. Chapter 8 s. 6(4) Electronic Communications Act.

to a significant extent act independently of its competitors, its customers and ultimately of consumers.[257] PTS is tasked with issuing regulations on guidelines and supporting documentation for making an assessment.[258] The Electronic Communications Act uses a concept of SMP equivalent to the one established in the EU Framework Directive and to the concept of dominance as defined by case law of the Court of Justice of the European Union (CJEU).[259]

119. If an operator has been found to have SMP, PTS shall decide on appropriate obligations to be imposed. A catalogue of available obligations is listed in Chapter 4 of the Electronic Communications Act; the aim of any chosen obligation(s) is to achieve effective competition.[260] An operator may, for example, be obliged to:

- publish specified information on accounting, technical specifications, network characteristics, conditions on access and usage, pricing, or other matters necessary for transparency regarding interconnection or other forms of access;[261]
- apply non-discriminatory conditions, ensuring equivalent conditions towards others who offer equivalent services;[262]
- maintain separate accounts and report specified activities relating to interconnection and other forms of access;[263]
- accommodate reasonable requests for access to and use of networks and related installations in order to supply electronic communication services. This may entail granting access to specified network components, including such access necessary to enable carrier selection and pre-selection as well as offers for retail subscriptions; extending previously granted access; offering other operators specified retail services; granting access to technical interfaces, protocols or other key technologies necessary for service interoperability; offering co-location or other opportunities for shared use of related installations; offering specified services necessary to ensure interoperability of services to end users; offering access to operational support systems or similar systems necessary to ensure fair competition in the provision of services; offering access to services that enable, support or may support the provision of services over an electronic communications network or electronic communications services; interconnecting or otherwise acting to enable the connection of networks or related installations. Such obligations may be combined with conditions necessary to ensure normal network operations; conditions for complying with particular technical standards or specifications must correspond to standards designated as obligatory by the European Commission and published in the *Official Journal* of the EU;[264]
- apply cost-covering or cost-oriented pricing or other set pricing for specific types of interconnection or access; this can include applying a specified method of

257. Chapter 8 s. 7(1) Electronic Communications Act.
258. Chapter 8 s. 7(2) Electronic Communications Act.
259. *See* Case 27/76 *United Brands v. Commission* [1978] ECR 207.
260. Chapter 4 s. 4 Electronic Communications Act.
261. Chapter 4 s. 5 Electronic Communications Act.
262. Chapter 4 s. 6 Electronic Communications Act.
263. Chapter 4 s. 7 Electronic Communications Act.
264. Chapter 4 s. 8 Electronic Communications Act.

accounting for costs and making a description of the method available to the public. The operator is to show its prices are fair and reasonable with regard to costs and may be ordered to adjust its pricing. In imposing this obligation, the investment made by the operator is taken into account, allowing the operator a reasonable return on capital investment.[265]

120. Under exceptional circumstances, a vertically integrated operator that has been obliged to provide access may be required to detach activities related to the access obligation at an organizational level in what is known as 'functional separation'. The detached business unit shall operate independently, ensuring non-discrimination and transparency.[266] Where functional separation is imposed, it may be combined with conditions aimed at ensuring operational independence, such as being placed in a separate legal entity or under an independent management.[267]

121. Where an operator, who could be subject to functional separation, undertakes to separate such activities in order to ensure non-discrimination and transparency, this commitment may be accepted where exceptional reasons exist. Such acceptance obliges the operator to comply with the commitment, and as long as the decision is in force functional separation may not be imposed.[268] The acceptance decision may be revoked, should the circumstances fundamentally change, the operator fails to honour the commitment or where the decision was based on incomplete, false or misleading information provided by the operator.[269]

122. An operator that has SMP in an end user market may be ordered to take appropriate action, where obligations that can be imposed in accordance with Chapter 4 are insufficient.[270] Such action may be:

(1) the application of a particular maximum or minimum price;
(2) not implementing measures that impede competition; or
(3) not providing a service that can be provided independently as a result of another service also being provided.

265. Chapter 4 ss 11 and 12 Electronic Communications Act.
266. Chapter 4 s. 12 a Electronic Communications Act.
267. Chapter 4 s. 12 b Electronic Communications Act.
268. Chapter 4 s. 12 c(1) Electronic Communications Act.
269. Chapter 4 s. 12 c(2) Electronic Communications Act.
270. Chapter 5 s. 13 Electronic Communications Act.

Chapter 3. Regulation of Cryptography and Other Dual-Use Products

§1. THE REGULATION OF CRYPTOGRAPHY

123. In Sweden, the import, use and production of cryptographic products is not restricted. It is also possible to import and produce cryptography products.

The Swedish Commission for ICT (*IT-Kommissionen*, hereinafter 'ICT Commission')[271] was an advisory board that was set up by the Swedish Government and advised the Government on issues relating to information technology. It has in various reports provided guidance to the Swedish Government on the issue of cryptography. One of the conclusions it came to was that it was impossible to separate cryptography from normal computer technology. In a report entitled 'The Importance of the Use of Encryption', the ICT Commission indicated that the discussion on cryptography involves three areas: (1) the availability of strong encryption techniques and products; (2) the use of encryption together with attempts to limit its use; and (3) the export control of encryption techniques and products. The ICT Commission furthermore made the following proposals:

- All forms of mandatory system for depositing keys should be opposed.
- Swedish users need to be able to use encryption products to the same extent as companies.
- Encryption is important for international communication.
- Government policy should encourage the use of strong encryption.
- Government should send a clear message that it is acceptable to use strong encryption.

Finally, the ICT Commission recommended that exports of cryptography should be stimulated and encouraged as well as the import and use of strong cryptography products.

124. The Swedish policy on cryptography was proposed in Government Communication 1998/1999:116 on cryptography.[272] The origin of this Government Communication is the establishment in 1996 of a Swedish Government Office Reference Group in order to formulate a national policy with regard to encryption. The Swedish Government presented this Communication to the Swedish Parliament on 6 May 1999. It outlined the Swedish Government's attitude towards cryptography and a main area of focus was the use of cryptography, both in regard to its import as well as export.

271. The ICT Commission ceased to exist on 30 May 2003, www.itkommissionen.se. *See* Introduction Ch. 5 *supra* (para. 34).

272. Skrivelse 1998/99:116 Om kryptografi. The basis of this Communication was a report from the ICT Commission entitled 'Inför en svensk policy för säker elektronisk kommunikation', IT-kommissio nens rapport 6/97, SOU 1997:73.

According to the Government Communication, the following points should be considered when deciding on a policy with regard to cryptography products:[273]

- The importance of trustworthy electronic documents.
- The trustworthiness of electronic signatures as well as attaining confidentiality for electronic communication and other information.
- The fight against crime.
- Export controls to prevent cryptography ending up in the wrong hands.

In Communication 1998/1999:116, the Swedish Government also stated that there was no reason to limit the use of cryptography in Sweden. Rather, emphasis was on the fact that all should be free to choose technology themselves. Therefore, there were to be no limitations on the import of encryption products. Here the emphasis was on the advantages that could be gained from these products. For example, encryption is a means of ensuring security within e-commerce, it enhances ways of attaining privacy and it secures communications not only between individuals, but also between individuals and public authorities.

125. It can also be mentioned that authorities investigating a crime are able to use various means in order to get access to cryptographic keys; however, a person who is suspected of committing a crime cannot be forced to actively assist or participate in the investigation of the crime.

Therefore, in summarizing the status of cryptography within Sweden, there are no restrictions regarding the import, use and production of cryptographic products. However, considering that cryptography is also considered a dual-use product, its export is regulated together with other dual-use products.

§2. The Regulation of Dual-Use Goods

126. The term 'dual-use' has its origin in the fact that certain products, due to their nature, can be used for both civilian purposes and military ones. Therefore, dual-use products can have consequences which jeopardize the security interests of nations. However, dual-use products can also have far-reaching benefits. For example, cryptography is important in the creation of a secure information technology environment and the technology is used in e-commerce and digital signature technologies. However, in the wrong hands, it could also be used to conceal crime or acts of terrorism. Cryptography is considered a dual-use product and most of the legislation in respect of other dual-use products also applies to cryptography.

In the opinion of the ICT Commission, referred to above, it was unfortunate that cryptography fell under the same regulations as other dual-use products, due to the fact that it has many commercial advantages, and it is important that trade in cryptography products be allowed to occur, with Swedish companies being allowed to trade on equal footing with other international companies.[274]

---

273. *Ibid.*, 4.
274. IT Commission, 'The Importance of the Use of Encryption', Dnr ITK99/19, 9.

I. Legislative Framework

127. The legal framework with regard to dual-use products is comprised of international regime controls, EU legislation and national legislation. Most of the legislation on dual-use products originates from EU Regulations, supplemented by national legislation regarding export control.

International policy in regard to the export of dual-use products is determined by five multilateral regimes of which Sweden is a member. They are the following:

- The Zangger Committee.[275]
- The Nuclear Supplies Group.[276]
- The Australia Group.[277]
- The Missile Technology Control Regime.[278]
- The Wassenaar Arrangement.[279]

The main aim of these regimes is to restrict export and in so doing prevent the spread of weapons of mass destruction and dual-use products. The regime specifically dealing with cryptography products is the Wassenaar Arrangement.[280] It was established in 1995 and Sweden became a signatory that same year. The arrangement has as its aim the prevention of the dissemination of ammunitions and dual-use products in order to create international security. Each signatory to the Wassenaar Arrangement is required to implement the arrangement by enacting national legislation.

128. Council Regulation No. 428/2009[281] regulates the export of dual-use products both within the EU and to countries outside of the region. Article 3(1) of the Regulation states that authorization is required for the export of dual-use products listed in Annex I. In addition, an authorization may also be required if the dual-use product is not specified in Annex 1, according to Article 3(2). Annex I stipulates which types of products may be exported as well as what type of licence is required. This annex is updated on a regular basis. The overriding factors to be considered in determining whether a specific product is to be considered a dual-use product are the type of dual-use product as well as its proposed destination. According to the Regulation, dual-use products should be subject to effective control when they are exported from the EU. Adherence to this principle in turn allows for the free movement of dual-use products within the EU.

National legislation in Sweden is comprised of the Act on Control Over Dual-use Products and Over Technical Assistance (*lag (2000:1064) om kontroll av produkter*

275. www.zanggercommittee.org.
276. www.nuclearsuppliersgroup.org.
277. www.australiagroup.net.
278. www.mtcr.info.
279. www.wassenaar.org.
280. Wassenaar Arrangement on Export Controls for Conventional Arms and Dual-Use Goods and Technologies.
281. Council Regulation (EC) No. 428/2009 of 5 May 2009 setting up a Community regime for the control of exports, transfers, brokering and transit of dual-use items.

med dubbla användningsområden och av tekniskt bistånd), and the corresponding Ordinance (*förordning (2000:1217) om kontroll av produkter med dubbla användningsområden och av tekniskt bistånd*). The Department for Disarmament and Non-Proliferation at the Swedish Ministry for Foreign Affairs determines policy, initiates legislation and regulates international negotiations in this area.[282] The public authority responsible for export controls of dual-use products is the Inspectorate of Strategic Products (ISP, *Inspektion för strategiska produkter*).[283] The Inspectorate has enacted a Regulation relating to the export of strategic products (TFS 2000:25), setting out the application document to be used and information to be given when applying for an export licence.[284]

129. The term 'export' is defined in Article 2(2) of the Regulation. It refers to goods leaving the Community, the re-export of non-Community goods and the transmission of software or technology by electronic media, including by fax, telephone, email or any other electronic means to a destination outside of the European Community. The export of cryptography products without the required licence can lead to someone being convicted of the crime of smuggling, in accordance with the Act on Control Over Dual-use Products and Over Technical Assistance.

II. Supervision of Cryptography and Dual-Use Exports

130. The main function of the National Inspectorate of Strategic Products (ISP, subsequently referred to as the Inspectorate) is to control not only the export of military equipment, but also the export of equipment that could have both civilian and military uses, in other words, dual-use products. The role of the Inspectorate is to see to it that dual-use products are not exported to certain governments and other actors, thereby contributing to the production of weapons of mass destruction. It therefore can be said to play a role in Swedish foreign and security policy. It is also responsible for ensuring compliance with the regulations that must be observed in connection with dual-use products as well as the handling of targeted sanctions aimed at specific countries.

The Export Control Council (ECC) is an advisory body of the Inspectorate, consisting of twelve members. All export matters are referred to the ECC, along with cases where the Inspectorate needs advice where developments have occurred or when assessing new recipient countries.[285] The members are appointed by the Government, and represent the various Swedish political parties.

131. In determining matters of export control, there is a general presumption in favour of allowing the export of dual-use products. In other words, the export of dual-use products is allowed unless there are specific reasons for not allowing this.

282. www.government.se/government-of-sweden/ministry-for-foreign-affairs/organisation/, 18 Sep. 2019.
283. isp.se/eng/about-the-isp/, accessed 18 Sep. 2019.
284. *Inspektionens för strategiska produkter föreskrifter (TFS 2000:25) om ansökan om exporttillstånd.*
285. isp.se/eng/about-the-isp/our-councils/, accessed 18 Sep. 2019.

According to the Inspectorate, matters concerning the export of dual-use products are dealt with either by focusing on the dual-use product itself or by focusing on the end use of the dual-use product.

As mentioned above, cryptography products are treated as dual-use products and are subject to export control if they meet the conditions set down in Council Regulation No. 428/2009, namely that they have a key length that exceeds 56 bits for symmetric keys and 512 bits alternatively 112 bits for asymmetric keys (dependent upon the mathematical function used).[286] Authorization is not required for the transfer of cryptography that is intended for personal use, for example, for individuals to secure personal files.

132. When focusing on the dual-use product itself, the general rule is that a licence is required for the export of dual-use products if they appear in Annex I of the Regulation. However, exports within the EU do not require a licence, except in those circumstances involving dual-use products that are very specialized and appear in Annex IV of the Regulation.

If a company is unsure of whether a dual-use product can be exported, it is able to ask the Inspectorate for advice on the matter. The Inspectorate will then respond in writing after carrying out an assessment of the product's classification, and thus whether an export licence is required.[287]

133. The end use approach to dual-use products is relevant in circumstances where a product is not found on the product list, but which may still be subject to export controls. For example, the Inspectorate may suspect that a dual-use product is to be exported to a country which intends to use it for undesirable ends. In such cases, the Inspectorate has the authority to classify dual-use products with reference to a specific end user as controlled even if it does not appear on the abovementioned Annex I. This is known as a catch-all clause, and is referred to in Article 4 of the Regulation. Any denial by the Inspectorate for an export licence is reported to the EU or to the relevant regime, for example, the Wassenaar Arrangement, if it concerns cryptography products.

In circumstances where a licence is required, the Inspectorate can also require an end user certificate, which verifies what the dual-use product is, the purposes that the dual-use product will be used for, contract numbers and finally also what it can be used for.

Also, Article 7 states that the Regulation does not apply to the supply of services or the transmission of technology if it involves the cross-border movement of persons. Therefore, a person travelling with, for example, a laptop which contains a cryptography product is not subject to the Regulation.

134. There are various types of export licences applicable to the export of dual-use products. Article 9(1) of the Regulation refers to a Community General Export

286. As set out in Annex I Category 5 Part 2 of Commission Delegated Regulation (EU) 2018/1922 of 10 October 2018 amending Council Regulation (EC) No. 428/2009 setting up a Community regime for the control of exports, transfer, brokering and transit of dual-use items.

287. isp.se/pda/klassificering-av-produkt-och-teknik/ (in Swedish), accessed 18 Sep. 2019.

Authorization (CGEA) for exports. It specifies certain non-EU countries to which the export of dual-use products is treated the same as exports to countries within the EU.[288] The original Regulation provided for one CGEA, EU001, and allowed for export to specified countries, namely Australia, Canada, Japan, New Zealand, Norway, Switzerland and the US. This list has, following Council Regulation (EU) No. 1232/2011, been updated to include Lichtenstein and there are now six general licences, EU001–EU006, including licences for export of a temporary nature and export after repair or replacement.

Article 9(2) of the Regulation states that authorizations required for any other exports shall be granted by the relevant authority in Member States. All such authorizations are valid throughout the EU. The Swedish authority, the Inspectorate, can in accordance with the Regulation issue three other types of export licences, namely an individual licence, a global licence, and a general licence. They become relevant in cases where the export of a dual-use product is not covered by the CGEA. An individual licence is applicable to a certain dual-use product from a specified exporter and to a specific destination. A global licence can be granted to a specified exporter. This allows for unlimited export to multiple countries while the licence is valid. The general licence is an open authorization and does not require an application, only notification of use.

288. As provided for in Annex II of the Regulation.

Chapter 4. Legal Status of Standardization

135. In Sweden, developments with respect to standardization in the area of ICT are reflected in both the private sector as well as within the public administration. Sweden is a country with a long tradition of developing a sound and well-functioning public administration and standardization has been identified as necessary in order to stimulate progress within this sector.

Since 1 January 2012, the main organization involved in standardization in Sweden is the Swedish Standardisation Federation.[289] The Federation is a collaborative organization for the three Swedish National Standardization Bodies (NSBs): the NSB for telecommunication, *Informations- och Telekommunikationstekniska Standardiseringen*,[290] the NSB for electricity, SEK (*Svensk Elstandard*),[291] and the Swedish Institute for Standards (SIS).[292] These bodies in turn are members of international standardization organizations. For example, SIS is a member of the International Organization for Standardization (ISO)[293] and the European Committee for Standardization (CEN).[294]

The purpose of the Standardization Federation is to promote standardization in Sweden, promote the use of standards, streamline standardization through collaboration and apply for state funding.[295] The organization does not maintain an official register of adopted standards, but rather refers to the respective standardization organization's website, where a full catalogue is kept.[296]

A national IT Standards Council was established in 2014 under the authority of the E-Government Delegation, managed by SIS, with the role of being the Government's platform for addressing standardization issues specifically within the area of ICT. After the delegation was discontinued in 2015, the council ceased to exist.

The initiative for the inception of a standard can come from individuals, private organizations or public government authorities. When a standard is proposed, the matter is investigated by experts who then form committees and working groups. This process ends with an open consultation before the standard is approved. In addition, all standards that are adopted on the European level are almost always accepted on the national level.[297]

---

289. *Sveriges Standardiseringsförbund*, www.standardiseringsforbundet.se. The Swedish Standards Association replaced Swedish Standards Council (*Sveriges Standardiseringsråd, SSR*), the public authority previously responsible for the oversight and control of standards in Sweden.
290. www.its.se.
291. www.elstandard.se.
292. www.sis.se.
293. www.iso.org.
294. www.cen.eu.
295. www.standardiseringsforbundet.se/about-us/, accessed 19 Sep. 2019.
296. SSR previously maintained an official register of adopted standards in Sweden. However, this is no longer available since October 2012, *see* www.standardiseringsforbundet.se/register-over-svensk-standard.
297. www.its.se/om-standardisering/hur-standard-blir-till/, accessed 19 Sep. 2019.

§1. PRIVATE SECTOR

136. The legal framework in Sweden within the area of standardization in the private sector is regulated by a number of acts and ordinances that implement EU legislation.

The rationale behind the EU legislation is that the EU merely specifies the technical demands that need to be met by products, and then it is for manufacturers to determine how these demands can technically be achieved. For example, it is the responsibility of the manufacturers of radio and telecommunications terminal equipment to see to it that products adhere to the standards set on the European level.[298] The CE certification[299] in turn functions as a guarantee that products put on the market adhere to the Directives' specifications.[300] An effect of this is that States may not prohibit or hinder the placing of products on the market that bear the CE mark.[301] It is then the function of the responsible authority to determine whether these standards have been adhered to.

137. The Act on Radio Equipment (*radioutrustningslag (2016:392)*) as well as a corresponding Ordinance (*radioutrustningsförordning (2016:394)*) is one such example of the above-mentioned legislative technique. The above legislation puts into effect Directive 2014/53/EU of the European Parliament and of the Council of 16 April 2014 on the harmonization of the laws of the Member States relating to the making available on the market of radio equipment and repealing Directive 1999/5/EC.[302] According to the Ordinance on Radio Equipment, PTS[303] is the authority specializing and having jurisdiction within the operation area of the corresponding Act. Sections 4–8 give it the authority to introduce Regulations within the above-mentioned area.[304]

138. The aim of Directive 2014/53/EU is to allow for the free movement of radio equipment as long as it fulfils the Directive's essential requirements, such as health and safety. Another aim is to set out additional means for market surveillance to track and monitor products which fail to comply with the Directive's essential requirements. Directive 2014/53/EU specifies 'essential requirements' that need to be met in order to provide a high level of protection to users of this equipment. Article 3(1) specifies two general essential requirements. They are to ensure: (a) the protection of the health and safety of persons and domestic animals and the protection of property and (b) an adequate level electromagnetic compatibility found in

---

298. Previously, manufacturers of radio and telecommunications terminal equipment were required to obtain clearance prior to putting a product on the market. Manufacturers now do not need to wait for a decision by local authorities before putting products on the market, often causing delay.
299. CE stands for Conformité Européenne (European Conformity).
300. For general principles surrounding use of the CE certification, *see* Regulation (EC) No. 765/2008 of the European Parliament and of the Council of 9 Jul. 2008 setting out the requirements for accreditation and market surveillance relating to the marketing of products and repealing Regulation (EEC) No. 339/93.
301. ec.europa.eu/growth/single-market/ce-marking/, accessed 19 Sep. 2019.
302. This Directive is also referred to as the RE-Directive or RED.
303. www.pts.se.
304. PTS has issued a regulation with detailed requirements for radio equipment, PTSFS 2016:5.

Directive 2014/30/EU.[305] The article also contains other essential requirements regarding, for example, use of the radio spectrum and accessibility of radio equipment. However, it does not specify how these essential requirements are to be fulfilled and it is up to each manufacturer to devise the best methods of achieving this end. Compliance is mandatory and products are not allowed to be placed on the market until they have satisfied the necessary requirements.[306]

139. Another Directive having a bearing on the private sector is Directive 2001/95/EC of the European Parliament and of the Council of 3 December 2001 on General Product Safety. The aim of this Directive is to decrease trade barriers within the EU by standardizing all products as far as health, the environment and safety issues are concerned. Directive 2001/95/EC has been incorporated into national legislation in the form of the Product Safety Act (*produktsäkerhetslag (2004:451)*) with a corresponding Ordinance (*produktsäkerhetsförordning (2004:469)*). The aim of the Product Safety Act is to ensure that goods and services do not cause any personal injury. Section 8 of the Act defines a good or product 'safe' where it, under normal or foreseeable use will not entail any risks to personal health or safety, or only a low risk. The risk must be acceptable considering how the goods or services are used. Section 9 sets out the factors that must be taken into account when determining whether or not the risk is acceptable. These factors include the characteristics of the good, information that is provided, the good's effect on other goods where it can be assumed it will be used in conjunction with other goods, and the risk that the good may have for certain categories of people, for example, children. Section 11 contains a presumption in favour of goods being safe if they adhere to a Swedish standard that transforms a European standard. Finally, according to section 3 Product Safety Ordinance, it is the Swedish Consumer Agency (*Konsumentverket*)[307] that is the supervisory authority for matters relating to the Product Safety Act.

§2. Public Authorities

140. Sweden has a large public administration and the issue of standardization in this sector has been examined in the form of a Government consultation. In 2006, the Swedish Government ordered an enquiry, one of the aims of which was to examine the status of standardization as well as the coordination of standardization within this public administration. The results of the enquiry were published in 2007 in the form of a SOU.[308] One aspect that was highlighted was the role of open software. The conclusions of the Report must be seen in the light of Directive 98/34/EC, which had the aim of preventing national IT standards from creating trade barriers

305. Directive 2014/30/EU of the European Parliament and of the Council of 26 February 2014 on the harmonization of the laws of the Member States relating to electromagnetic compatibility.
306. *See* further Guide to the Radio Equipment Directive 2014/53/EU, Version of 19 December 2018, 20, ec.europa.eu/docsroom/documents/29782/attachments/1/translations/en/renditions/pdf, accessed 20 Sep. 2019.
307. www.konsumentverket.se.
308. Government Official Report SOU 2007:47, 'Den osynliga infrastrukturen – om förbättrad samordning av offentlig IT-standardisering'.

within the EU.[309] The point of departure was the definition of the term 'standard', which was seen both as a commonly accepted example against which something is measured as well as the outcome of a standardization process.[310] The Report stated that the issue of IT standards must be seen in relation to the following factors:

- Swedish coordination in response to EU decisions.
- E-government.
- Industrial policy.
- Gaining an overall view of IT standardization as an organizational system.

In addition, the Report referred to a Government Bill concerning general IT policy.[311] One of the points advocated in the Bill was that the use of open standards should be promoted where possible. These are standards that have been established by recognized European institutions and include the CEN,[312] the European Telecommunications Standards Institute (ETSI)[313] and the European Committee for Electrotechnical Standardization (CENELEC).[314] The Report alluded to the fact that there were other standards with a large degree of openness. In addition, it was proposed that Sweden should promote direct reference to informal standards, for example, those developed by bodies such as the Internet Engineering Task Force,[315] the Organization for the Advancement of Structured Information Standards,[316] the World Wide Web Consortium,[317] and the United Nations (UN) Centre for Trade Facilitation and Electronic Business.[318]

The Report stated that Swedish public authorities should be able to receive all types of documents that are widely used in the market by the general public and based on formal standards. However, it also stated that it is for each public authority to decide if it wants to use open document formats in other contexts, for example, when communicating with the general public.

Highlighted in the Report is that no single body assumes control or takes a leading role in IT standardization. It therefore suggested the creation of a body to oversee the entire organizational system in relation to IT standardization. It proposed that the SIS[319] was the organization best placed to take on this function.

---

309. Directive 98/34/EC of the European Parliament and of the Council of 22 Jun. 1998 laying down a procedure for the provision of information in the field of technical standards and regulation. This Directive has now been repealed and replaced with Directive (EU) 2015/1535 of the European Parliament and of the Council of 9 September 2015 laying down a procedure for the provision of information in the field of technical regulations and of rules on Information Society services.
310. Government Official Report SOU 2007:47, 30.
311. Government Bill (Proposition) 2004/5:175, 'Från IT-politik för samhället till IT-politik för IT-samhället'.
312. www.cen.eu.
313. www.etsi.org.
314. www.cenelec.eu.
315. www.ietf.org.
316. www.oasis-open.org.
317. www.w3.org.
318. www.unece.org/cefact/, accessed 20 Sep. 2019.
319. www.sis.se.

141. A consequence of the move towards an increased reliance on and use of e-government in Sweden has also resulted in the fact that there is an increased exchange of information between the various Swedish public administrations. In addition, there is an increased number of ways in which the general public is able to communicate with these public administrations. The result is that information security has an increased significance. In the Report, reference is made to information security accreditations under ISO/IEC Standard 27001, as well as the Swedish version. Reference in the Report is also made to BITS[320] which is a document with recommendations issued by the Swedish Civil Contingencies Agency that can be used in order to increase the levels of security within an organization.

142. Reference must also be made to another SOU, 'Strategy for the Government Agencies' Work on e-government', published in 2009.[321] The e-Government Delegation was given the task of providing proposals as to how public authorities and government agencies could become more productive and efficient.

One recommendation was in respect to the National Guidelines for public sector websites. The original guidelines were developed by the Swedish Administrative Development Agency (VERVA) and published in 2006.[322] The Report proposed that the above Guidelines be developed so that they meet the WCAG 2.0 standards, which are a set of non-technology specific guidelines for making web content more accessible, not only to the general public but also to people with disabilities.[323] The e-Government Delegation published a new version of the Guidelines in 2012, incorporating the recommended WCAG 2.0 standards proposed, with updated versions being published on a monthly basis on a dedicated website.[324] This website is now administered by the DIGG, established in September 2018.[325] DIGG is responsible for ensuring compliance with the law implementing Directive (EU) 2016/2102 of the European Parliament and of the Council of 26 October 2016 on the accessibility of the websites and mobile applications of public sector bodies.

§3. Conclusion

143. Standards themselves have no inherent legal status in Sweden. However, they are incorporated into various forms of legislation and thereby have an influence from within legislation. As for the Swedish Government's view on standardization, an increased interest in investment has been shown[326] and the need for

320. BITS stands for Basic Level for Information Security (*Basnivå för informationssäkerhet*), *see* Swedish Civil Contingencies Agency (MSB) www.msb.se/en/.
321. Government Official Report SOU 2009:86, 'Strategi för myndigheternas arbete med e-förvaltning'.
322. VERVA was closed at the end of 2008.
323. Web Content Accessibility Guidelines, www.w3.org/TR/WCAG20, accessed 20 Sep. 2019.
324. www.webbriktlinjer.se/riktlinjer/alla-riktlinjer-som-pdf/, accessed 20 Sep. 2019.
325. www.digg.se/about-us.
326. In 2016 the Government awarded 3 million SEK to the Swedish Standardisation Federation in order to facilitate the process of assuming secretariat responsibility for international standardisation in

increased standardization has recently been identified in order to maintain competitiveness.[327] The Government has developed a strategy for standardization and intends to strengthen Sweden's participation in the international and European standardization organizations. The strategy emphasizes stronger collaboration between Swedish actors, a focus on spreading European standardization internationally and working to increase the participation of Swedish experts in the development of standards.[328]

---

areas such as digitalization, environment and climate and life science. *See* Press Release '*Regeringen satsar på internationell standardisering*', 23 May 2016, www.regeringen.se/pressmeddelanden/2016/05/regeringen-satsar-pa-internationell-standardisering/.

327. Debate article from the Ministry for Foreign Affairs, '*Ökat välstånd kräver mer standardisering*', 26 Jul. 2018, www.regeringen.se/debattartiklar/2018/07/okat-valstand-kraver-mer-standardisering/.

328. The strategy is available (in Swedish) on the Government's website www.regeringen.se/49ced1/contentassets/6cd7c3221c3448a683ddec2e2b3390e3/regeringens-strategi-for-standardisering.pdf, accessed 20 Sep. 2019.

Chapter 5. Legal Status of Out-of-Court Dispute Settlement in the ICT Sector

§1. General Statement

144. Disputes between contracting parties in the ICT sector are, as a starting point, regarded as civil matters in the sense that they are amenable to out-of-court settlement. They normally concern disagreements/interpretations regarding once voluntary agreed contractual relationships and the parties may therefore also amicably resolve their disagreements/interpretations within these relationships. A settlement may be reached either before a dispute is brought before the court or during the courts' handling of it. In the latter situation, the settlement will result in the plaintiffs' withdrawal of its action and the court writing it off, or a joint request from the parties that the court enters into a judgment confirming the settlement.[329] Also non-contractual liability claims for damages brought within the ICT sector, for example, by an operator or an end user under Chapter 7 section 13a Electronic Communications Act (*lag (2003:389) om elektronisk kommunikation*); claims under the Copyright Act (*lag (1960:729) om upphovsrätt till litterära och konstnärliga verk*); claims under section 1 Product Liability Act (*produktansvarslag (1992:18)*); as well as claims under the general Tort Liability Act (*skadeståndslag (1972:207)*) because of alleged violation of the Electronic Commerce Act (*Lag (2002:562) om elektronisk handel och andra informationssamhällets tjänster*) and/or the Electronic Bulletin Boards Act (*lag (1998:112) om ansvar för elektroniska anslagstavlor*), are considered as disputes which in principle are amenable to out-of-court settlement.[330] This also includes that disputes within the ICT sector involving mandatory rules which parties to a contract may not set aside in advance,[331] in principle, are amenable to out-of-court settlement.

145. A court handling a civil dispute amenable to out-of-court settlement shall to the extent appropriate, and considering the nature of the case and other circumstances, work for the parties to reach a settlement. If the court considers that the case is suitable for mediation, it may suggest the parties to appear at a mediation session before a mediator appointed by the court.[332] In practice, parties seldom choose to enter into mediation when their dispute is already ongoing in court. One reason for this is that mediation as opposed to the court action is more costly since the parties will not only have to assume their respective counsel's fees but also a fee to the mediator.

329. Chapter 17 s. 6 Code of Judicial Procedure (*rättegångsbalk (1942:740)*).
330. *See*, e.g., Government Official Report SOU 2006:88, 'Effektivare LEK. Slutbetänkande av Utredningen om översyn av lagen om elektronisk kommunikation', 239; and Government Bill (*Proposition*) 2006/07:119, 'En effektivare lag om elektronisk kommunikation', 37.
331. *See*, e.g., s. 5 Product Liability Act.
332. Chapter 42 s. 17 Code of Judicial Procedure.

§2. Out-of-Court Dispute Settlement with Regard to Access and/or Interconnection

146. The Swedish Electronic Communications Act (*lag (2003:389) om elektronisk kommunikation*) confers upon the national regulatory authority, PTS, to adjudicate conflicts arising between those who provide electronic communication networks or electronic communication services; or associated services as regards obligations ensuing from the Electronic Communications Act; or from regulations, licence conditions or decisions concerning obligations that have been issued under the Electronic Communications Act.[333] In 2016 the Swedish parliament passed the Expansion Act (*lag (2016:534) om åtgärder för utbyggnad av bredbandsnät*) which implements Directive 2014/61/EU of the European Parliament and of the Council of 15 May 2014 on measures to reduce the cost of deploying high-speed electronic communications networks and also confers upon PTS to adjudicate conflicts regarding obligations ensuing from the Act. PTS' mandate under the Electronic Communications Act and the Expansion Act includes ruling upon conflicts regarding *inter alia* rights/duties to interconnect and/or rights to access another operator's or network operator's[334] facilities, as well as to decide terms in the operator's relationships, for example termination and/or access charges and/or any other term which derives from obligations that may have been imposed *ex ante* on one or both operators. A prerequisite for PTS' jurisdiction is that the invoked obligations and requested remedies ensue from the Electronic Communications Act (or the Expansion Act), its regulations, licensed conditions or decisions which follow from the Act or formally have been issued by PTS, or otherwise are *related* to obligations which stem from the Electronic Communications Act.[335] It is notable that PTS' mandate to adjudicate conflicts between operators according to Chapter 7 section 10 Electronic Communications Act and Chapter 2 section 4 Expansion Act only comes into play if one, or both, operator(s) so request. The decision issued by PTS in a dispute between operators is binding and regarding decisions rendered under Chapter 7 section 10 Electronic Communications Act replaces any former agreement made between them on the substantive matter.[336] This means that even if the parties already have an earlier agreement covering the disputed issues, for example a certain level of termination charge, a party may initiate a dispute resolution procedure against the other, and request PTS to decide a new term (charge) to apply and replace the term on which the parties earlier have agreed. PTS' decision may be

333. Chapter 7 s. 10 Electronic Communications Act.

334. *See* definition in Art. 2 in Directive 2014/61/EU which comprises also undertakings other than authorized telecom operators under the Electronic Communications Act, e.g., network operators of gas, electricity and heating.

335. *See* Government Bill (*Proposition*) 2008/09:159, 'Vissa ändringar i lagen om elektronisk kommunikation'; and C-426/05 *Tele2 Telecommunication GmbH v. Telekom-Control-Kommission*, s. 39, REG 2008 I-685.

336. Article 20 Framework Directive; and Government Bill (Proposition) 2002/03:110, 'Lag om elektronisk kommunikation, m.m.', 303–304. *See*, e.g., Decision of the Stockholm Administrative Court of Appeal of 22 Jun. 2017 in Case 8481-15.

appealed to administrative courts – the County Administrative Courts (*Förvaltningsrätten*) in first instance and, provided that leave to appeal is granted to a second instance, i.e., the Administrative Courts of Appeal (*Kammarrätten*).

147. When an operator requests PTS to resolve a dispute under Chapter 7 section 10 Electronic Communications Act PTS may, instead of adjudicating upon it, refer the dispute for *mediation*. The parties shall in such a case be afforded an opportunity to submit proposals to the authority concerning an appropriate party to act as mediator.[337]

If mediation has proceeded for four months or has been discontinued before that without the parties reaching agreement, the authority shall, upon a new application by any of the parties, consider the dispute in accordance with Chapter 7 section 10 Electronic Communications Act. The parties shall be jointly liable to pay reasonable compensation to a mediator for work and disbursements.[338] If a dispute referred to PTS has also been referred to an authority in another state within the EEA, PTS shall, when processing the matter, consult the foreign authority.[339]

PTS has so far referred very few disputes for mediation and the reason for this is probably (at least) two-fold. One is the cost aspect. The other and more significant reason is that PTS often chooses a third alternative when an operator requests dispute resolution. Instead of resolving the dispute in accordance with Chapter 7 section 10 or refer it to mediation according to section 11, it can resort to act in its capacity of supervisory body under the Electronic Communications Act. In this capacity PTS may, for example, compel an involved operator to adhere to *ex ante* obligations imposed on it by virtue of earlier rendered decisions on SMP. PTS also has a mandate to decide interim measures during the supervisory process.[340] Supervision instead of dispute resolution and/or mediation sometimes also serves as an attractive and cost saving alternative for a party who wishes to interconnect with a reluctant operator demanding unreasonable conditions[341] for it or simply refuses to interconnect. If a dispute concerns past time termination charges, supervision procedures will however not be an alternative since supervision is solely a *forward-looking procedure* and cannot be used to remedy historical overcharges. For this latter purpose, dispute resolution[342] is the sole alternative. It is then important to note that in such pecuniary disputes, for example when an operator wishes to recover historical overcharges from another operator, there are certain time-limits which must be observed, and that PTS may only issue binding decisions which *establishes* the correct charge level. If an operator, despite PTS' decision refuses to pay, the entitled operator must turn to an ordinary civil court in order to obtain an enforceable award.

---

337. Chapter 7 s. 11 Electronic Communications Act.
338. Chapter 7 s. 12 Electronic Communications Act.
339. Chapter 7 s. 13 Electronic Communications Act.
340. Chapter 7 ss 1–9 Electronic Communications Act.
341. Compare Decision by PTS from 2 Oct. 2007, No. 07-10669/23.
342. Chapter 7 s. 10 Electronic Communications Act and Decision of Supreme Court 1 Jul. 2012, NJA 2012 p. 498.

148. The above-described means for resolving disputes regarding issues falling within the scope of the Electronic Communications Act or the Expansion Act do not prevent parties to voluntarily solicit Alternative Dispute Resolution (ADR), for example, mediation, on their own initiative instead of employing the rules in Chapter 7 Electronic Communications Act or the Expansion Act. It should however be observed that certain issues are not susceptible to other courts or adjudicating bodies except PTS. Thus PTS has an exclusive competence to rule and issue decisions which replace former agreements made between the parties on issues which could be characterized as 'core' issues of the Electronic Communications Act, for example, assessments of access charges and the right to interconnection and/or access. Such matters are considered to fall exclusively within PTS' competence.[343]

In 2012 The Supreme Court rendered an important decision and opened up for ordinary civil courts to rule upon disputes regarding interpretation of interconnection agreements. In addition, the Supreme Court stressed that civil courts have competence, *inter alia*, to comply a party to pay debts under the interconnection agreement in order to enable the party to bring its claim to the enforcement authority, which, PTS does not have the competence to do.[344] Civil courts also have jurisdiction in disputes between operators regarding issues in interconnection/access agreement which are only remotely connected to the Electronic Communications Act, for example, offset clauses, confidentiality undertakings, trademark issues, etc.

149. When operators solicit ADR (e.g., mediation) to reconcile their disagreements, it often results in a revised or a new agreement. If the new terms involve SMP obligations or other mandatory rules which stem from the Electronic Communications Act, a party who is discontent with the result of the reconciliation could still submit the disputed issues to PTS in accordance with Chapter 7 sections 10–13 Electronic Communications Act. This is possible because of the public interest and objectives vested in the EU Directives[345] which in turn are implemented into Swedish law through the Electronic Communications Act. The Directives and the Act aim at ensuring that private individuals, legal entities, and public authorities shall have access to secure and efficient electronic communications and the greatest possible benefit regarding the range of electronic communications services and the price and quality. Further, when applying the Act, particular regard shall be given to the importance of electronic communications for the freedom of expression and freedom of information.[346]

343. *See* Stockholm City Court Decision of 26 Apr. 2005 in Case T 4715-02 *TeliaSonera Mobile Networks AB v. Telenor AB*. *See also* Government Bill (*Proposition*) 2002/03:110, 117 and 303; and Government Bill (*Proposition*) 2004/05:175, 'Från IT-politik för samhället till politik för IT-samhället', 282 and 304.
344. Decision by Supreme Court from 11 Jul. 2012, NJA 2012 p. 498.
345. Directive 2002/21/EC (Framework Directive), Directive 2002/20/EC (Authorization Directive), Directive 2002/19/EC (Access Directive), Directive 2002/22/EC (Universal Service Directive) and Directive 2002/58/EC (Directive on Privacy and Electronic Communications), Directive 2009/136/EC and Directive 2009/140/EC.
346. Chapter 1 s. 1 Electronic Communications Act.

§3. Out-of-Court Dispute Settlement Involving Consumers and Other End Users

150. Disputes between operators and consumers and other end users are solved through the dispute resolution clauses in the subscriber (service-) agreements. An example of a dispute resolution clause in a consumer agreement is the following:

> Disputes
>
> Any disputes concerning the interpretation or application of the Agreement must be decided by a Swedish court, in accordance with Swedish law. The dispute may also be considered by the Swedish National Board for Consumer Disputes [Swe: *Allmänna reklamationsnämnden]* (P O Box 174, 101 23 Stockholm, www.arn.se), whose decision is a recommendation to the Parties for how the dispute should be resolved. The National Board for Consumer Disputes does not consider disputes that solely concern the basis for invoicing Services.[347]

The National Board for Consumer Complaints (ARN)[348] is a public body authorized to impartially try disputes between consumers and business operators in a variety of consumer's product and service fields. Petitions are filed by the consumer and ARN recommends how the dispute should be resolved. ARN's recommendations are not binding, but a majority of business operators follow them.

151. More importantly, as it especially focuses on providing free information, guidance and assistance for telecom, TV and Internet consumers, is the Swedish Telecom Advisors.[349] The Swedish Telecom Advisors is an organization that provides free information, guidance, and assistance for telecom, TV and Internet consumers. It was set up in 2006 by the Swedish IT and Telecom Industry Association after an initiative from PTS and is financed by telecom, TV and Internet operators. All telecom, TV and Internet operators who enter into an agreement with consumers are invited and offered the opportunity to co-finance the bureau. The Swedish Telecom Advisors can act as a mediator in disputes between individual consumers and telecom, TV and Internet operators. The creation of The Swedish Telecom Advisors in 2006 was an important step for the Swedish telecom, TV, and Internet industry efforts to promote a generally accepted industry practice towards consumers and other end users. The organization's board comprises representatives of telecom, TV, and Internet operators and the government. The government is represented by PTS and the Swedish Consumer Agency (*Konsumentverket*), a public body. The authorities and industry representatives have an equal number of votes on the board, and one of the state authorities has the casting vote if this is necessary to facilitate a decision on the bureau's operations.

---

347. *TeliaSoneras* General Terms and Conditions for Services to Consumers, applicable from and including 25 May 2018.
348. Allmänna reklamationsnämnden, www.arn.se.
349. Telekområdgivarna, www.telekomradgivarna.se.

152. Swedish consumer protection legislation, such as the Consumers Sales Act (*konsumentköplag (1990:932)*) and the Consumer Services Act (*konsumenttjänstlag (1985:716)*), is not directly applicable on telecom, TV, and Internet services but many of its principles (mandatory in favour of the consumer) are often said expected to apply analogous if and when such disputes appear before civil courts. Chapter 5 section 15 Electronic Communications Act enumerates certain information about, for example, quality of services, price conditions, duration, etc. which must be contained in contracts between end users and operators providing electronic communications services or a connection to a public telephone network. The information is mandatory and PTS may employ its supervisory powers and compel operators who fail to live up to these minimum standards to adhere to them.

Part II. Protection of Intellectual Property in the ICT Sector

Chapter 1. Application of Copyright in the Area of ICT

§1. General Statement

153. Sweden has been a member of the Paris Convention for the Protection of Industrial Property (Paris Convention) since 1885, and joined the Berne Convention for the Protection of Literary and Artistic Works (Berne Convention) in 1904, as well as ratified the latest amendments. Both Conventions are administered by the World Intellectual Property Organization (WIPO), a specialized agency of the United Nations. The Berne Convention was complemented in 1996 by the WIPO Copyright Treaty (WCT), which entered into force in 2002.

Regarding neighbouring rights, Sweden entered the Rome Convention for the Protection of Performers, Producers of Phonograms, and Broadcasting Organizations (Rome Convention) in 1962, and signed and ratified its successor, the WIPO Performances and Phonograms Treaty, in 1996.

As a contracting party of the World Trade Organization, Sweden signed and ratified the Agreement on Trade-Related Aspects of Intellectual Property Rights (TRIPS).

154. On a European level, though neither the Treaty on European Union nor the TFEU explicitly states any legal competence within the field of intellectual property rights, Article 36 TFEU[350] stipulates that prohibitions or restrictions on imports and exports are allowed if they are justified on grounds of the protection of industrial and commercial property to the extent they do not 'constitute a means of arbitrary discrimination or a disguised restriction on trade between Member States'. According to Article 345 TFEU,[351] the Treaty 'shall in no way prejudice the rules in Member States governing the system of property ownership'. Despite these rules, intellectual property rights have been an important issue for the internal market which has led to a number of Directives within this area.[352]

350. Ex Art. 30 Treaty establishing the European Community.
351. Ex Art. 295 Treaty establishing the European Community.
352. *See*, e.g., Recital 4 Computer Program Directive: 'Certain differences in the legal protection of computer programs offered by the laws of the Member States have direct and negative effects on the functioning of the internal market as regards computer programs.'

Examples include:

- Council Directive 87/54/EEC of 16 December 1986 on the legal protection of topographies of semiconductor products.
- Council Directive 93/83/EEC of 27 September 1993 on the coordination of certain rules concerning copyright and rights related to copyright applicable to satellite broadcasting and cable retransmission.
- Directive 96/9/EC of the European Parliament and of the Council of 11 March 1996 on the legal protection of databases (hereinafter 'Database Directive').
- Directive 2001/29/EC of the European Parliament and of the Council of 22 May 2001 on the harmonization of certain aspects of copyright and related rights in the information society (hereinafter 'InfoSoc Directive').
- Directive 2004/48/EC of the European Parliament and of the Council of 29 April 2004 on the enforcement of intellectual property rights (hereinafter 'Enforcement Directive').
- Directive 2006/116/EC of the European Parliament and of the Council of 12 December 2006 on the term of protection of copyright and certain related rights.
- Directive 2009/24/EC of the European Parliament and of the Council of 23 April 2009 on the legal protection of computer programs. (hereinafter 'Computer Program Directive').

Some of them will be discussed more in detail below.

§2. Legislative Framework in Sweden

155. Sweden protects intellectual property, especially copyright, in its Constitution. Chapter 2 of the Instrument of Government (*regeringsform (1974:152)*) states fundamental rights and freedoms, and Article 16 stipulates: 'Authors, artists and photographers shall own the rights to their works in accordance with rules laid down in law.'

The first Swedish legislation on intellectual property rights was the King's Decree (*reglemente*) for book publishers in the year 1752. Today's statute was enacted in 1960: Act on Copyright in Literary and Artistic Work (*lag (1960:729) om upphovsrätt till litterära och konstnärliga verk*; hereinafter 'Copyright Act'). Its wording was written and designed to allow its application and validity over a long period of time.[353]

156. The Copyright Act grants the authors of literary and artistic works economic[354] and moral rights.[355] With a few exceptions, most of the rules are not mandatory, which allows for the economic rights to be transferred by contractual agreements.

353. Governmental Bill to the original Copyright Act, Proposition 1960:17, 'Upphovsrätt till litterära och konstnärliga verk. Rätt till fotografisk bild', published in NJA II 1961 s. 1, 48.
354. Chapter 1 Art. 2 Copyright Act.
355. Chapter 1 Art. 3 Copyright Act.

The copyright protection starts at the moment of creation, in accordance with Article 5(2) Berne Convention stipulating that '[t]he enjoyment and the exercise of these rights shall not be subject to any formality'. The copyright sign © has therefore no legal validity in Sweden.

In accordance with Council Directive 93/98/EEC of 29 October 1993, harmonizing the term of protection of copyright and certain related rights, the time of protection is seventy years after the year of death of the author (*post mortem auctoris*).[356] Neighbouring rights are protected for fifty years in accordance with EC Directive 93/98, and databases enjoy fifteen years of protection.[357]

§3. Object of Protection

157. According to Chapter 1 Article 1 Swedish Copyright Act, literary and artistic works include:

(1) fictional or descriptive representations in writing or speech;
(2) computer programs;
(3) musical or dramatic works;
(4) cinematographic works;
(5) photographic works or other works of fine arts;
(6) works of architecture or applied art;
(7) works expressed in some other manner.

Maps and other works of a descriptive nature executed as drawings, engravings or in a three-dimensional form shall be considered literary works.

The expression 'literary or artistic work' (*litterärt eller konstnärligt verk*) in other words includes all types of cultural products and media content. For example, the term 'literary works' includes not only books but also scientific writings, presentations, seminar papers, meeting notes, encyclopaedias, newspaper articles, technical descriptions, texts in instruction manuals and forms, advertising texts, computer programs, and database collections. Artistic works mainly include musical compositions, film art (including video art), theatrical performances and art works (paintings, drawings, graphics, photography, sculpture, collage, textile art, and art as computer-created pictures), as well as architectural designs.[358]

The Copyright Act does not make any distinction between literary, musical, and artistic works. Some exemptions, however, are reserved for a specific type, such as literary works.

158. Swedish copyright law explicitly exempts certain works from protection. According to Article 9, copyright does not subsist in laws and other regulations;

356. Chapter 4 Art. 43 Copyright Act. Compare Art. 7 Berne Convention that requires a minimum of fifty years.
357. *See also* Art. 10 Database Directive.
358. Mogens Koktvedgaards & Marianne Levin, *Lärobok i immaterialrätt* (Stockholm: Norstedts Juridik, 2007), 69 et seq.

decisions by public authorities; reports by Swedish public authorities; or official translations of these texts. In other words, there is no Crown Copyright in Sweden.

Important to mention here is also the Swedish constitutional right of access to information and public records, which supersedes copyright to some extent. For example, patent applications are considered public records unless otherwise stated in the Swedish Public Access to Information and Secrecy Act (*offentlighets- och sekretesslag (2009:400)*).[359]

159. In order for a work to be protected, it has to be created by a human being and be the result of a personal creative effort. There is no qualitative or quantitative requirement in order for the work to be worthy of protection.

160. Pictures can be protected as photographic works[360] or as photographic pictures.[361] The former requires a higher level of originality; the latter protects all types of photographs, also the ones taken by amateurs, or within medicine or science. The protection requires some sort of photographic technique being used, which includes digital cameras as well as holograms created by laser technique.[362] The difference between the two types of work is the term of protection, which amounts to seventy years after the death of the author of a photographic work as opposed to fifty years from the year in which the photographic picture was taken.

161. Photographs always consist of still images, not sequences of pictures that amount to moving pictures which would be covered as cinematographic works[363] if they are original. A film that does not amount to a cinematographic work is protected for fifty years, pursuant to Article 46.

The Swedish Supreme Court (*Högsta Domstolen*) decided in the Nintendo case[364] that videogames are not regarded as cinematographic works as they include an interactive moment. Instead, they are protected as computer programs. Video art, however, is regarded as a cinematographic work.

§4. Subject of Protection

162. As mentioned above, a work has to be created by a human being and be the result of a personal creative effort.

It can be discussed in this context to what extent works completely created by computer programs can be protected under the Copyright Act. Literary or artistic works, created with the help of a software program or a machine, are protected by

359. *See* s. 22 Swedish Patents Act (*patentlag (1967:837)*) and Ch. 31 s. 20 Public Access to Information and Secrecy Act.
360. Article 1 point 5 Copyright Act.
361. Chapter 5 Art. 49a Copyright Act.
362. Koktvedgaards & Levin, 101 et seq.
363. Article 1 point 4 Copyright Act.
364. Decision by Supreme Court from 22 Nov. 2000, NJA 2000 s. 580.

copyright law, as the user of the computer would be the author of the work.[365] This also applies to music created on a computer.

163. The Swedish Copyright Act does not contain any general provisions with regard to works created in an employment relationship.[366] Therefore, an employee creating literary or artistic works as part of the employment is also considered to be the author of the created works. Sweden does not, in other words, follow the works made for hire principle as the UK or US.

The employer can, however, obtain exclusive rights through contractual agreements with the employee. These licensing agreements can also be included in the employment contract. In accordance with Chapter 3 Article 27 Copyright Act, the economic rights may be transferred to the employer in whole or in part, with no additional form requirements. The moral rights, however, stay with the author, that is, the employee. Sweden has recognized a general principle that an employer commonly has the right, unless otherwise agreed, to exploit the copyright of an employee's work, which is created within the work tasks or due to direct instructions.[367]

§5. Exclusive Rights

164. The Swedish Copyright Act grants two types of exclusive rights for works in Chapter 1 Article 2: the right to make copies and the right of making them available to the public. Making of copies (*framställning*) is defined as 'any direct or indirect, temporary or permanent preparation of copies of the work, regardless of the form or through which method this is carried out and regardless of whether it concerns the work in whole or in part'. This also includes temporary copies on the computer or any other system, such as caches, etc.

165. The term 'making available to the public' (*tillgängliggörande för allmänheten*) includes communication to the public (*överföring till allmänheten*), public performance (*offentligt framförande*), public exhibition (*offentligt visning*), and distribution (*spridning*) such as sale, lease or rent.

The term 'communication to the public' was introduced when transposing the InfoSoc Directive into Swedish law in 2005. Before that, on-demand services were interpreted as either public performance or, in a few cases, public exhibition. Today's term includes 'any making available of the work to the public by wire or by wireless means that occurs from a place other than that where the public may enjoy the work. Communication to the public includes also acts of communication that occur in such a way that members of the public may access the work from a

365. Henry Olsson, *Upphovsrättslagstiftningen – En kommentar*, 2nd edn (Stockholm: Norstedts, 2009), s. 1.
366. With the exception of computer programs created as part of an employment.
367. Sanna Wolk (ed.), *Ownership of the Copyright in Works and the Patent Right in Inventions Created by Employees in Finland, Sweden, Germany, Austria, the United Kingdom, Estonia and Argentina*, Gröna Serien, No. 120 (Stockholm: Institute of Intellectual Property Law and Marketing Law – Institutet för Immaterialrätt och Marknadsrätt (IFIM), 2002), 8–11.

place and at a time individually chosen by them'. This includes traditional radio and TV broadcasts, webcasting, publication on a website, as well as any peer-to-peer file sharing.[368]

A decision by the Swedish Supreme Court in 2000 discussed if deep linking was to be considered a public performance.[369] The Court held that deep linking from a website to infringing music files on the Internet constitutes either public performance itself or abetting public performance and thereby infringes copyright. Deep linking was to be understood as linking from one web page to the other without the visitor being aware of the change of address. The Supreme Court did not deal with the question of reference links, where the visitor clearly is made aware of the change of website. The Governmental Bill transposing the InfoSoc Directive stated that this decision could still be relevant in relation to the limits of exclusive rights, even though the linking would now fall under the rights of communication to the public and not public performance.[370]

166. Another term that has been discussed is 'to the public'. The governmental bill transposing the InfoSoc Directive defines public in the context of public performance as the possibility for anyone to join the communication. Even a requirement of membership can be considered public if anybody can become a member. In order for a communication to be private, it has to be aimed at one or a few people or in case it is aimed at a more general public, the requirements must be too strict for everybody to fulfil them. Even password protection or other protection measures do not exclude a communication from being public.[371]

When transposing the InfoSoc Directive, the meaning of 'public performance' was somewhat changed in Swedish law. Before the Directive, public performance included radio, TV, and other distance broadcasting. Now the term comprises 'only such cases where the work is being made available to the public, with or without the use of a technical device, at the same place as the one where the public may enjoy the work'. This definition covers the live performance of a musician or a theatrical play, the showing of video or playing of music on a CD player publicly, or last but not least, the showing of a radio programme or a TV broadcast publicly in a restaurant. The last situation involves both public performance and communication to the public. The term 'public' has the same meaning as regarding communication to the public.

The InfoSoc Directive also led to a change in the meaning of the term 'public exhibition'. Today it includes 'such cases where a copy of a work is being made available to the public, without the use of a technical device, at the same place as the one where the public can enjoy the copy'. If a technical device is being used, the Copyright Act considers it as a public performance. Before the amendment it was unclear if the display of a work on a TV or computer screen was to be considered as a performance or an exhibition; now the legal situation is clear as this

368. Henry Olsson, *Upphovsrättslagstiftningen,* s. 2; and Government Bill (*Proposition*) 2004/05:110, 'Upphovsrätten i informationssamhället – genomförande av direktiv 2001/29/EG, m.m.'.
369. Decision by Supreme Court of 15 Jun. 2000, NJA 2000 s. 292.
370. Government Bill (*Proposition*) 2004/05:110, 70.
371. Olsson, *Upphovsrättslagstiftningen,* s. 2; and Government Bill (*Proposition*) 2004/05:110, 57.

situation is covered by performance and not exhibition, as it is not the work itself that is being displayed but the content of a file.

167. According to Chapter 5 Article 48 Copyright Act, sound radio or television organizations have exclusive rights to exploit a sound radio or television broadcast, which include recording the broadcast in material format so it can be reproduced, making copies and distributing these copies, and permitting a recording to be communicated to the public.

§6. EXEMPTIONS TO THE EXCLUSIVE RIGHTS

168. Chapter 2 Swedish Copyright Act contains provisions on the limitations of copyright. Some of these exceptions are voluntary and can be changed in a contract, whereas some are mandatory and surpass even contrary contractual obligations, for example Article 26g and 26h Swedish Copyright Act.

In general, the limitations can be divided into three categories:

(1) provisions that allow free use;
(2) provisions that allow limited use for remuneration (*tvångslicenser*);
(3) provisions that allow collective licences, that is, agreements between right holders' organizations and users, which are also applicable for authors not represented in these organizations (*avtalslicenser*).[372]

169. Chapter 2 Swedish Copyright Act was drafted in accordance with the Berne Convention, especially the three-step-test of Article 9.2,[373] as well as Article 13 TRIPS[374] and Article 5(5) InfoSoc Directive.[375]

The limitations mainly concern published works, that is, works that have been lawfully made available to the public.[376] The idea behind this is that only the author should be able to decide on the publication of a work.

In the following sections, two exemptions are explained in detail, as they are particularly relevant in an Information and Communications Technology (ICT) context: temporary and private copies.

372. Recital 18 InfoSoc Directive explicitly allows for collective licenses: 'This Directive is without prejudice to the arrangements in the Member States concerning the management of rights such as extended collective licences.'
373. 'It shall be a matter for legislation in the countries of the Union to permit the reproduction of such works in certain special cases, provided that such reproduction does not conflict with a normal exploitation of the work and does not unreasonably prejudice the legitimate interests of the author.'
374. 'Members shall confine limitations or exceptions to exclusive rights to certain special cases which do not conflict with a normal exploitation of the work and do not unreasonably prejudice the legitimate interests of the right holder.'
375. 'The exceptions and limitations provided for in paras 1, 2, 3 and 4 shall only be applied in certain special cases which do not conflict with a normal exploitation of the work or other subject-matter and do not unreasonably prejudice the legitimate interests of the right holder.'
376. Chapter 1 Art. 8 Copyright Act.

I. Temporary Copies

170. As mentioned above, temporary copies are covered by the exclusive right of reproduction. In accordance with Article 5(1) InfoSoc Directive, Chapter 2 Article 11a Swedish Copyright Act states:

> Temporary forms of copies of works may be made, if the making of the copies is an integral and essential part of a technological process and if the copies are transient or have only a secondary importance in that process. The copies must not have any independent economic importance.
>
> The making of copies under the first Paragraph is permissible only if the sole purpose of that making is to enable:
>
> 1. a transmission in a network between third parties by an intermediary, or
> 2. a lawful use, that is, a use that occurs with the consent of the author or her or his successor in title or another use that is, not un-permissible under this Act.
>
> The provisions under the first and second Paragraphs do not confer a right to make copies of literary works in the form of computer programs or compilations.

Article 11a has to be seen in relation to the Swedish Electronic Commerce Act (*lag (2002:562) om elektronisk handel och andra informationssamhällets tjänster*), as well as the Directive on Electronic Commerce,[377] which exempt service providers from liability for mere conduit, caching and hosting.[378] The legislation on electronic commerce does, however, only cover service providers and not the temporary copying for individuals, making Article 11a Copyright Act necessary to cover this exemption.

171. The main purpose of Article 11a is to allow users to browse and surf the web without meeting the risk of infringing copyright. As the exclusive right of reproduction includes direct or indirect, temporary or permanent copies of a work,[379] temporary copies in caches, both on different routers, host and access providers, as well as on individuals' computers, fall within this exclusive right. With caching being an integral part of web browsing, the exemption of Article 11a is therefore necessary.

Besides the requirement that temporary copies are only permitted if the copying is an integral and essential part of the process and the copies are not the most important part of the process, paragraph 2 in Article 11a Copyright Act states that the making must try to enable either a transmission in a network or a lawful use. The typical example for the first case would be Internet Service Providers (ISPs) storing

377. Directive 2000/31/EC of the European Parliament and of the Council of 8 Jun. 2000 on certain legal aspects of information society services, in particular e-commerce, in the Internal Market (hereinafter 'Directive on Electronic Commerce').

378. *See* Part V Ch. 3 *infra* (paras 355 et seq.).

379. Chapter 1 Art. 2 Copyright Act.

copies of websites and emails in the cache of their servers. Important to remember here is Recital 33 InfoSoc Directive, which although not explicitly transposed into Swedish law, states:

> To the extent that they meet these conditions, this exception should include acts which enable browsing as well as acts of caching to take place, including those which enable transmission systems to function efficiently, provided that the intermediary does not modify the information and does not interfere with the lawful use of technology, widely recognized and used by industry, to obtain data on the use of the information.

In other words, an intermediary should not tamper with the information, otherwise the right does not apply and it could be liable for copyright infringement. An example of the second possibility for making temporary copies, that is, the lawful use, would be private copying according to Chapter 2 Article 12 Copyright Act. This also corresponds to Recital 33 InfoSoc Directive: 'A use should be considered lawful where it is authorized by the right holder or not restricted by law.'

Article 11a paragraph 3 Copyright Act further states that this right does not include making copies of computer programs or compilations.

II. Private Copying

172. Chapter 2 Article 12 Swedish Copyright Act deals with private copies and in which situations they constitute legal exceptions to the exclusive rights granted by copyright law. The provision in the Swedish Act was amended due to the implementation of the InfoSoc Directive. It now contains four paragraphs that stipulate the following:

> *On the Making of Copies for Private Purposes*
>
> Article 12. Anybody is entitled to make, for private purposes, one or a few copies of works that have been made public. As regards literary works in written form the making of copies may, however, concern only limited parts of works, or such works of limited scope. The copies must not be used for purposes other than private use.
>
> The provisions in the first Paragraph do not confer a right to 1. construct works of architecture 2. make copies of computer programs, or 3. make copies in digital form of compilations in digital form.
>
> Furthermore, the provisions in the first Paragraph do not confer a right to engage, for private purposes, another person to 1. make copies of musical works or cinematographic works 2. make utilitarian articles or sculptures, or 3. copy another person's work of fine art by means of artistic reproduction.
>
> This Article does not confer a right to make copies of a work when the copy that constitutes the real master copy has been prepared or has been made available to the public in violation of Article 2.

Paragraph 1 of Article 12 stipulates the general rule for private copies being exempted from the exclusive right of reproduction. According to the provision, anybody can reproduce a literary or artistic work for private purposes. The number of copies have to be kept to a minimum, and with regard to literary works, reproducing more than half a book, either in digital or in analogue format, is not covered by Article 12.[380]

173. In general, all types of works can be copied for private purposes – regular literary works, music, film (e.g., movies on DVD or on TV), and other artistic works. Paragraph 2, however, exempts, among others, computer programs from the right to private copying. Acts of reproduction can include photocopying, recording of musical and film works, as well as downloading creative works on a personal computer.

Furthermore, Article 12 only allows reproduction of works that have been made public. In other words, the author or right holder must have agreed to the publication of the work.[381]

Private purposes cover copying for one's own use or for use within family or close circle of friends.[382] Not only the reproduction as such but also the following use has to be for private purposes. Recordings of music for private purposes can therefore not be sold to the public afterwards.

174. In transposing the InfoSoc Directive, a new paragraph 4 was introduced in Article 12 limiting the right to private copying to real master copies. In other words, private copying is only allowed for works that either have been reproduced with the consent of the author or in exercising one of the exemptions in Chapter 2 of the Copyright Act. With regard to the Internet, this means that the original copy that was made available online has to be authorized or otherwise be legal according to Chapter 2.

This new provision also led to an amendment regarding liability for infringement. According to Chapter 7 Article 54 paragraph 4 Swedish Copyright Act infringement of Article 12 paragraph 4 can only lead to civil liability in case of intent or gross negligence. In addition, an infringement can only lead to criminal liability if the individual carried out the violation intentionally or with gross negligence.[383]

175. As Article 12 is voluntary, the right holders can limit its application in a contract with the user. Standard terms and conditions for video rental, for example, often include such provisions. Not abiding by these contractual rules then constitutes breach of contract, and not copyright infringement.

---

380. Government Bill (*Proposition*) 2004/05:110, 383.
381. *See* Chapter 1 Art. 8 Copyright Act: 'A work is deemed to have been made public when it has lawfully been made available to the public.'
382. Before transposition of the InfoSoc Directive, the scope of private purposes even included copies for colleagues at one's workplace. *See* Olsson, *Upphovsrättslagstiftningen,* s. 12.
383. Chapter 7 Art. 53. *See* more relating to sanctions in paras 178 et seq.

§7. Transfer of Rights

176. An author can transfer the exclusive economic rights entirely or partially to somebody else.[384] The Swedish terms are *överlåtelse* for a complete transfer and *upplåtelse* for a partial transfer or rights. The moral rights, however, can never be transferred:

> Article 27: Subject to the limitation that follows from Article 3, copyright may be transferred entirely or partially.
>
> The transfer of a copy does not include a transfer of the copyright.

177. The licensing agreements have to be specified with regard to which rights are being transferred wholly or in part. Otherwise, in line with general copyright law principles, the contract terms will be interpreted restrictively and might not cover specific rights originally thought of.[385]

The transfer of rights can also concern future works, even including all future works of the author. Under specific circumstances, contracts concerning future creative results can, however, be invalid according to Swedish contract law. In a decision from 24 April 1989, the Svea Court of Appeal (*Svea hovrätt*) came to the conclusion that a contract transferring the rights of all future works of an artist combined with the right for the other party to solely decide which of the works are published infringes Article 36 Swedish Contracts Act and therefore was considered invalid.[386]

§8. Enforcement/Sanctions

178. Infringement of copyright provisions can lead to both civil and criminal liability, as prescribed by Chapter 7 Copyright Act. According to Chapter 7 Article 53 Copyright Act, infringing acts that are committed wilfully or with gross negligence are punishable by a fine or imprisonment for a maximum of two years. Chapter 7 Article 54 further stipulates that anyone who exploits a work in violation of copyright rules shall pay 'a reasonable compensation for the exploitation' to the author. In case of intent or negligence, the liability also covers 'the further damage that the infringement' has caused.

According to Article 54 the compensation should consider lost profit, any profit that has been made by the infringer, damage caused to the reputation of the work, moral damage, as well as the interest of the author or the right holder in that infringements are not committed.

The one who claims a copyright infringement has to prove it in court. The Swedish Supreme Court stated in a case in 1994 that a striking resemblance with a work

384. Chapter 3 Art. 27 Swedish Copyright Act.
385. *See* more in Part III Ch. 2 *infra* (paras 229 et seq.).
386. The decision is published in Nordiskt Immateriellt Rättsskydd (Nordic Intellectual Property Law Review) NIR 1989 s. 394.

can represent a strong argument for reproduction of that work. In this case, the suspected infringer would have to show it was more likely that the second work was created independently in order to avoid conviction for infringement.[387]

179. In 2004, the EU enacted Directive 2004/48/EC of the European Parliament and of the Council of 29 April 2004 on the enforcement of intellectual property rights (hereinafter 'Enforcement Directive') in order to 'approximate legislative systems so as to ensure a high, equivalent and homogeneous level of protection in the internal market'.[388] Though it did not aim to harmonize rules for judicial cooperation, jurisdiction, or the recognition and enforcement of decisions in civil and commercial matters, it established several 'procedures and remedies necessary to ensure the enforcement of intellectual property rights'.[389] The Directive was transposed into Swedish national law by introducing some amendments in the Copyright Act, including the right of information.

A new Article 53c that implements Article 8 Enforcement Directive ('right of information'), introduces into Chapter 7 Copyright Act the possibility for right holders to apply for an 'order to provide information' (*informationsföreläggande*) before the Court, which obliges a party 'to provide information to the applicant concerning the origin and distribution networks for the goods or services in respect of which the infringement or the violation has been committed'. Such orders can only be issued 'if it can be assumed that the information would facilitate an inquiry into the infringement' and can only relate to parties that have committed or contributed to such an infringement.

The order to provide information covers Internet access providers submitting information about the subscribers to certain IP numbers that have been used in the course of copyright infringement.[390] Some cases were initiated before the District Court of Stockholm, mainly requiring host providers and access providers to release information about their customers. The Swedish Supreme Court issued a judgment on the matter[391] after a preliminary ruling from the CJEU.[392] The Supreme Court, taking into account privacy and data retention issues, confirmed that such orders to provide information may be issued, provided that rights holders have demonstrated probable cause of copyright infringement, as required under Article 53c Copyright Act. The interests of rights holders to investigate and potentially prosecute alleged copyright infringement was therefore deemed to outweigh interests of individual privacy.[393] In a more recent court case, the Svea Court of Appeal (*Svea hovrätt*) found that a reasonable time to carry out disclosure of information following the obligation in Article 53c was, in cases involving a large number of IP addresses (in this case, over 8,000) four months.[394]

387. Decision by Supreme Court from 23 Feb. 1994, NJA 1994 s. 74.
388. Recital 10 Enforcement Directive.
389. Article 1 Enforcement Directive.
390. Government Bill (*Proposition*) 2008/09:67, 'Civilrättsliga sanktioner på immaterialrättens område – genomförande av direktiv 2004/48/EG', 263.
391. Decision by Supreme Court from 21 Dec. 2012, NJA 2012 s. 975.
392. Case C-461/10 *Bonnier Audio AB and Others v. Perfect Communication Sweden AB*.
393. *See* Part VI Ch. 2 §3 III B *infra* (para. 441).
394. Decision by Svea Court of Appeal from 25 Jan. 2017, RH 2017:25.

180. In the context of enforcement, the Swedish Copyright Act also contains a chapter on the protection of technological measures, which was introduced in the transposition of the InfoSoc Directive. The chapter covers provisions on the protection of technological measures as well as electronic information on the management of rights. In accordance with the Act,[395] 'technological measure' means 'any effective technology, device or component designed to prevent or restrict, in the normal course of its operation, the reproduction or the making available to the public of a copyright-protected work without the consent of the author'.

'Information on the management of rights' is defined as:

> any information, also in the form of numbers or codes, that is linked to a copy of a copyright-protected work or appears in connection with the communication to the public of such a work and which aims at identifying the work or the author or her or his successor in title or at informing about the conditions of use of the work. The information must have been provided by the author or her or his successor in title.[396]

Chapter 6a Article 52d prohibits any circumvention of technological protection measures. It is furthermore prohibited, according to Chapter 6 a Article 52e, to manufacture, import, transfer, distribute or possess for commercial purposes any devices, products or components, or to make available services, which:

(1) are promoted, advertised or marketed for the purpose of circumvention of a technological measure;
(2) other than to circumvent a technological measure, have only a limited interest from a commercial point of view, or a limited scope of commercial use; or
(3) are primarily designed, constructed, adapted or produced for the purpose of enabling or facilitating a circumvention of a technological measure.

In addition, it is prohibited to remove or alter any electronic rights-management information relating to a work protected by copyright.[397]

395. Chapter 6 a Art. 52b para. 2 Copyright Act, as well as Art. 6(3) and Art. 7(2) InfoSoc Directive.
396. Chapter 6 a Art. 52b para. 3 Copyright Act.
397. Chapter 6 a Art. 52g Copyright Act.

Chapter 2. Legal Protection of Software

§1. General Statement

181. Chapter 1 Article 1 point 2 Swedish Copyright Act explicitly grants copyright protection to computer programs. Sweden introduced this protection in 1989 before the Computer Program Directive entered into force. The Directive led, however, to smaller amendments in the Act, among others the introduction of Chapter 2 Article 26g and 26h Copyright Act.

§2. Object of Protection

182. In accordance with Article 10 TRIPS[398] and Article 4 WCT,[399] as well as Article 1(1) Computer Program Directive,[400] computer programs are protected as literary works, as stipulated in Chapter 1 Article 1 point 2 Swedish Copyright Act.

Neither the Act nor the Directive defines the term 'computer program'. A Swedish governmental report,[401] however, suggested a similar definition as the WIPO Model provisions on the protection of computer software from 1978:[402] 'A computer program is [a] set of instructions capable, when incorporated in a machine-readable medium, of causing a machine having information processing capabilities to indicate, perform or achieve a particular function, task or result.'

183. The copyright in software covers all expressions of a program, including any immediately readable form or any machine-readable format, such as source or object code, whether it is stored on a disk, CD, in the computer's read-only memory or on paper.[403] In accordance with the Computer Program Directive, the protection also covers the preparatory design material,[404] such as design drafts, and all other preparatory material.

Documentation for a program, however, is not protected as a computer program but as literary work in general.

398. 'Computer programs, whether in source or object code, shall be protected as literary works under the Berne Convention (1971).'
399. 'Computer programs are protected as literary works within the meaning of Art. 2 of the Berne Convention. Such protection applies to computer programs, whatever may be the mode or form of their expression.'
400. 'Member States shall protect computer programs, by copyright, as literary works within the meaning of the Berne Convention for the Protection of Literary and Artistic Works.'
401. Government Official Report SOU 1985:51, 'Upphovsrätt och datorteknik. Delbetänkande 3 av upphovsrättsutredningen', 87.
402. International Bureau of the World Intellectual Property Organization, 'Model provisions on the protection of computer software' (Geneva: WIPO, 1978).
403. Koktvedgaards & Levin, 96.
404. Chapter 1 Art. 1 Copyright Act.

The protection extends to neither the underlying ideas and principles, such as algorithms and the like, nor the interface of the program.[405] Programming languages are also not protectable by copyright.[406] This is one of the weaknesses and strengths related to software, as the algorithm can be the most valuable part of the whole software, while preventing distribution and use of good programming ideas is not in the best interest of the society as a whole. This is also an important principle in relation to interoperability and interaction between software.[407]

The program as such has to be 'the author's own intellectual creation', no additional qualitative criteria is required for it to be eligible for protection.[408]

§3. Subject of Protection

184. The general principle that the author receives all the exclusive rights to the work at the moment of creation also applies here.

185. With regard to computer programs created in employment relations, the Swedish Copyright Act, in accordance with Article 2 Computer Program Directive, regulates in Chapter 3 Article 40a:

> The copyright in a computer program created by an employee as a part of her or his tasks or following instructions by the employer is transferred to the employer unless otherwise agreed in contract.

The automatic transfer of rights according to Article 40a not only includes the economic rights but, contrary to the Computer Program Directive,[409] also the moral rights.[410]

As clear from its wording ('unless otherwise agreed in contract'), Article 40a Swedish Copyright Act is non-mandatory and can be changed in the contract of employment.

§4. Exclusive Rights

186. The Swedish Copyright Act does not stipulate any specific exclusive rights for computer programs, but the general rule of Chapter 1 Article 2 applies, which states that copyright includes making copies of a work or making it available to the

405. *See* Recital 11 and Art. 1(2) Computer Program Directive.
406. Recital 11 Computer Program Directive.
407. Koktvedgaards & Levin, 98.
408. Article 1(3) Computer Program Directive.
409. Article 2(1) Computer Program Directive: 'The author of a computer program shall be the natural person or group of natural persons who has created the program.'
410. Wolk, *Ownership of the Copyright in Works*, 11; and Government Bill (*Proposition*) 1992/93:48, 'Regeringens proposition om ändringar i de immaterialrättsliga lagarna med anledning av EES-avtalet m.m.', 117.

public. The term 'making available to the public' in turn covers communication to the public, public performance, public exhibition, and distribution such as sale, lease or rent.

As mentioned above[411] the definition of reproduction[412] is rather broad and includes, for example, temporary copies in the internal memory of a personal computer as well as cache copies on servers, which might not have a value in themselves.

This choice of legislative technique was already taken in the Computer Program Directive. In order to balance the interests of society as a whole, an exemption was introduced covering temporary copies.[413]

§5. Exemptions

187. Some of the general exemptions for literary and artistic works mentioned above[414] do not apply for computer programs.

The right of the user to make temporary copies, for example, only exists 'if the making of the copies is an integral and essential part of a technological process and if the copies are transient or have only a secondary importance in that process'. This provision does, however, 'not confer a right to make copies of literary works in the form of computer programs or compilations'.[415]

In addition, the right to make private copies is limited when it comes to computer programs. According to Chapter 2 Article 12 paragraph 2 Swedish Copyright Act, the private copying exemption does not apply to computer programs.

188. Users with a right to use a computer program are, however, allowed to:

- 'make such copies of the program and to make such changes to the program which are necessary' in order to enable use of the program for its intended purpose. This also applies to the correction of errors;[416]
- 'to make back-up copies of the program, if this is necessary for the intended use of the program'.[417] Contracts in contrast to this provision are void;[418]
- 'observe, study or test the function of the program in order to ascertain the ideas and principles which lie behind the various details of the program'. The right to reverse engineer applies 'provided that the act is performed in connection with

411. *See* Ch. 1 §5 *supra* (para. 164).
412. Chapter 1 Art. 2 Copyright Act: 'any direct or indirect, temporary or permanent preparation of copies of the work, regardless of the form or through which method this is carried out and regardless of whether it concerns the work in whole or in part'.
413. *See* Ch. 1 §6 I *supra* (paras 170 et seq.).
414. *See* Ch. 1 §6 *supra* (paras 168 et seq.).
415. Chapter 2 Art. 11a Copyright Act.
416. Chapter 2 Art. 26g para. 1 Copyright Act.
417. Chapter 2 Art. 26g para. 2 Copyright Act.
418. Chapter 2 Art. 26g para. 6 Copyright Act.

such loading, display on a screen, processing, transmission or storing of the program that the user is entitled to make'.[419] Contractual stipulations which limit these rights are void.[420]

Interesting to note here is that the rights to make backup copies (point b) and to reverse engineer (point c) are mandatory, and cannot be limited through contractual agreements. In a recent Supreme Court judgment, the mere passive storage of software following the end of a licence period was not considered to be copyright infringement.[421]

189. Another provision based on the Computer Program Directive is Chapter 2 Article 26h Swedish Copyright Act concerning decompilation to ensure interoperability. According to the provision, codes of computer programs can be copied or translated if this is necessary to obtain interoperability between the program and another program. In order to fall under Article 26h reverse engineering has to meet the following requirements:

- the acts are performed by a person who has the right to use the program or by a person who is authorized to perform those acts;
- the information necessary to achieve interoperability has not previously been readily available to the persons referred to in the point above;
- the acts are confined to those parts of the original program which are necessary to achieve interoperability.

The information obtained through reverse engineering may not be used for the development, preparation or marketing of a computer program substantially similar in its expression to the protected program.[422] As above, contractual stipulations limiting these rights are void.[423]

§6. Enforcement/Sanctions

190. As for all other copyright infringements, not adhering to any of the exclusive rights concerning computer programs can lead to both criminal and civil liability.[424]

Under certain conditions, however, copying of a computer program that was lawfully published is exempted from criminal liability if the master copy is not used in commercial or public activities, and the individual only uses the copies for private purposes.[425]

419. Chapter 2 Art. 26g para. 4 Copyright Act.
420. Chapter 2 Art. 26g para. 6 Copyright Act.
421. Decision by Supreme Court from 25 Sep. 2018, NJA 2018 s. 725.
422. Chapter 2 Art. 26h para. 2 Copyright Act.
423. Chapter 2 Art. 26h para. 3 Copyright Act.
424. *See* in general Ch. 1 §8 *supra* (paras 178 et seq.).
425. Chapter 7 Art. 53 para. 2 Copyright Act.

Chapter 3. Legal Protection of Databases

§1. General Statement

191. Sweden introduced protection for databases in 1960 by enacting Article 49 Copyright Act protecting catalogues, tables and other similar works where a large amount of data was collected and gathered. In 1997, the rule was somewhat amended due to the implementation of the Database Directive which stipulates a sui generis right for the content of databases in addition to protection for the structure.[426]

§2. Object of Protection

192. Chapter 5 Article 49 Swedish Copyright Act protects catalogues, tables or similar products:

- in which a large number of information items have been compiled (catalogue protection); or
- which are the result of a significant investment (sui generis right).

As a kind of neighbouring right, the compilation does not have to reach a certain quality or originality, and it is rather the efforts of creating the database that are being protected. If a compilation reaches a certain level of originality it can, however, be protected as a literary work according to Chapter 1 Article 2 Swedish Copyright Act.

The first possibility for a database to receive protection is if a large amount of information has been collected. This is the case for sales and exhibition catalogues, timetables, compilations of currency and stock exchange prices.[427] It does not matter in which format the information is compiled; both analogue and digital versions fall within the scope of Article 49.

The second possibility for protection is databases that are the result of a significant investment. This provision transposes Article 7 Database Directive into Swedish law, which can serve as a guideline for interpreting the meaning of significant investment. Article 7 of the Directive speaks about 'qualitatively and/or quantitatively of the substantial investment in either the obtaining, verification or presentation of the contents'. In other words, the investment can be quantitatively substantial considering the time or money invested in the collecting or organizing of the material. A qualitative aspect can be, on the other hand, if the choice of material or its collection were challenging.[428]

---

426. Koktvedgaards & Levin, 109.
427. Governmental Bill (*Proposition*) 1960:17, 322.
428. Henry Olsson, *Upphovsrättslagstiftningen*, s. 49.

The Swedish Supreme Court decided in a case in 2005,[429] following the preliminary ruling of the CJEU,[430] that investment refers 'to the resources used to seek out existing independent materials and collect them in the database, and not to the resources used for the creation as such of independent materials'. The Court of Justice further stated that: 'the purpose of the protection by the sui generis right provided for by the Directive is to promote the establishment of storage and processing systems for existing information and not the creation of materials capable of being collected subsequently in a database'.[431]

193. Important to notice is that the protection covers the compilation and database as such and not the information stored in it. Chapter 5 Article 49 does, however, not exclude any potential rights for the works collected in the catalogue or compilation. In other words, the compiled data may – with a sufficient level or originality – be protected as literary or artistic works.[432] The database as a whole, however, will be protected according to Article 49.

194. The time of protection for databases is fifteen years 'from the year in which the product was completed',[433] which reflects Article 10 Database Directive.

To summarize, Swedish law provides three possibilities to protect databases:

(1) protection as a work pursuant to Chapter 1 Article 2 (and according to time for protection);
(2) catalogue protection pursuant to Chapter 5 Article 49 (compilation of a large number of data);
(3) sui generis right pursuant to Chapter 5 Article 49 (database as the result of a significant investment).

§3. SUBJECT OF PROTECTION

195. As Chapter 5 Article 49 Copyright Act states, anyone who produced a catalogue enjoys the copyright protection. In other words, it is the producer of the database who is granted exclusive rights. Contrary to general copyright law rules, the producer can be a legal person, not only a natural person.

This does not, however, affect any potential rights of individuals in works collected in the database.

429. Decision by Supreme Court from 28 Dec. 2005, NJA 2005 s. 924.
430. Case C-338/02 *Fixtures Marketing Ltd. v. Svenska Spel AB* [2004] ECR I-10497.
431. Point 24 in the Judgment.
432. Chapter 1 Art. 2 Copyright Act.
433. Chapter 5 Art. 49 para. 2 Copyright Act.

§4. Exclusive Rights

196. Chapter 5 Article 49 Swedish Copyright Act grants 'the exclusive right to make copies of the product and to make it available to the public'. Article 7(1) of the Database Directive, which stipulates the right to prevent 'extraction and/or re-utilization of the whole or of a substantial part, evaluated qualitatively and/or quantitatively, of the contents of that database', was, in other words, not transposed literally into Swedish law. Chapter 5 Article 49 protects the structure of a database, not the information compiled in it.[434]

197. The third paragraph of Chapter 5 Article 49 was added when implementing the InfoSoc Directive and refers to the general exclusive rights granted by the Copyright Act.

The right to make copies covers all types of reproduction, including temporary copies. With regards to Article 7(1) of the Database Directive, a copy emerges if it concerns the whole or substantial parts of the database. Copying single bits of information or a smaller amount of data contained in the compilation does not constitute copyright infringement, unless these parts are considered literary or artistic works according to Chapter 1 Article 2 Copyright Act, in which case the individual copying the works infringes Chapter 1 Article 2, but not Chapter 5 Article 49.[435]

In addition, the producer of the database has the exclusive right of making it available to the public, which includes communication to the public, public performance, public exhibition, and distribution.[436] Publishing a database online would therefore fall under 'communication to the public'.[437]

198. According to paragraph 4 of Chapter 5 Article 49 Copyright Act, contractual agreements that extend the exclusive rights are not valid.[438] However, within the framework of the exclusive rights, the producer can agree on specific terms and conditions regarding the licences.[439]

§5. Exemptions

199. As for computer programs, users are not allowed to 'make copies in digital form of compilations in digital form'.[440] Digital copying of digital databases is therefore an infringement of copyright, even for private purposes.[441] However, analogue paper copies of digital material as well as digital copies of analogue material for private purposes are allowed.[442]

434. Government Bill (*Proposition*) 1996/97:111, 'Rättsligt skydd för databaser, m.m.', 59.
435. Government Bill (*Proposition*) 1996/97:111, 59.
436. Chapter 1 Art. 2 paras 3 and 4 Copyright Act.
437. Government Bill (*Proposition*) 1996/97:111, 59.
438. In this sense the provision protects the users of a database.
439. Koktvedgaards & Levin, 170–171.
440. Chapter 2 Art. 12 para. 2 point 3 Copyright Act.
441. Digital in this context means electronic information in binary code, i.e., zeros and ones.
442. Government Bill (*Proposition*) 1996/97:111, 53–54.

An authorized user has the right to make use of a database in any way that is necessary to fulfil 'its intended purpose'.[443] Typical use of a database is, therefore, allowed. This provision reflects Article 6(1) Database Directive.[444]

200. As mentioned above, only the structure of the database is protected by Chapter 5 Article 49 Copyright Act, not the content. Therefore, copying a part of the compilation is allowed as long as it does not constitute a substantial part of the whole database. Other people can use the data for a new compilation, provided it is built upon another structure.[445]

§6. Enforcement/Sanctions

201. The general sanctions for copyright infringement, including criminal and civil liability, also apply to violations of Chapter 5 Article 49 Copyright Act.

The second paragraph of Chapter 7 Article 53 Copyright Act states an exemption from criminal liability, if a digital copy of a publicly available digital database is made for private purposes, the master copy is not used in commercial or public activities and the individual only uses the copy for private purposes.

443. Chapter 2 Art. 26g para. 5 Copyright Act.
444. Article 6(1) Database Directive: 'The performance by the lawful user of a database or of a copy thereof of any of the acts listed in Art. 5 which is necessary for the purposes of access to the contents of the databases and normal use of the contents by the lawful user shall not require the authorization of the author of the database.'
445. Government Bill (*Proposition*) 1996/97:111, 59; Koktvedgaards & Levin, 199.

Chapter 4. Legal Protection of Computer Chips

§1. General Statement

202. In 1986, Sweden introduced a law on the protection of topographies for semiconductor products which led to a specific protection for computer chips. This new legislation had been influenced by American legislation on 'mask works' in 1984. The American Act required reciprocity for the protection of foreign semiconductor products; as Sweden had its own production of computer chips it was important for Swedish companies to have legal protection in America as well.[446]

203. In transposing the Council Directive 87/54/EEC of 16 December 1986 on the legal protection of topographies of semiconductor products, Sweden passed the Act on the Protection of Topographies for Semiconductor Products (*lag (1992:1685) om skydd för kretsmönster för halvledarprodukter*), which is the applicable legislation today.

Accordingly, Chapter 1 Article 10 Swedish Copyright Act now explicitly exempts semiconductor products from copyright protection: 'Copyright does not subsist in layout designs in semiconductor products. Special provisions apply to the rights in such designs.'

§2. Object of Protection

204. The Swedish Act on the Protection of Topographies for Semiconductor Products does not define semiconductor products. However, guidance can be found in the Directive, which states in Article 1(1):

(1) a 'semiconductor product' shall mean the final or an intermediate form of any product:
   - consisting of a body of material which includes a layer of semiconducting material;
   - having one or more other layers composed of conducting, insulating or semiconducting material, the layers being arranged in accordance with a predetermined three-dimensional pattern;
   - intended to perform, exclusively or together with other functions, an electronic function.

(2) the 'topography' of a semiconductor product shall mean a series of related images, however fixed or encoded:
   - representing the three-dimensional pattern of the layers of which a semiconductor product is composed; and
   - in which series, each image has the pattern or part of the pattern of a surface of the semiconductor product at any stage of its manufacture.

446. Government Bill (*Proposition*) 1992/93:48, 'Regeringens proposition om ändringar i de immaterialrättsliga lagarna med anledning av EES-avtalet m.m.', 44.

In accordance with the Directive, the Swedish Act requires the topography to be the 'creator's own intellectual effort' and 'not commonplace in the semiconductor industry'.[447] No further requirements are necessary. The protection for computer chips concerns their design.

205. Article 4 of the Directive allows for the requirement of registration with a public authority. Contrary to many other EU Member States, Sweden does, however, not require any registration of the topography. The protection starts at the moment of creation and lasts ten years after the topography was used commercially for the first time in some part of the world.[448]

'Commercial exploitation' is defined in Article 1(1)(c) Directive as 'the sale, rental, leasing or any other method of commercial distribution, or an offer for these purposes'.

§3. Subject of Protection

206. Section 3 Swedish Act on the Protection of Topographies for Semiconductor Products stipulates that the exclusive right applies to the physical person who is the creator of the topographies of semiconductor products. The creator has to be a citizen of or have their habitual residence in a Member State of the EEA.[449]

207. If the topography was created as part of the creator's employment, the right to protection shall apply in favour of the creator's employer unless terms of employment are to the contrary. The employer has to be a natural person who is a citizen or has habitual residence in a Member State of the EEA, or a legal person with the place of commercial establishment in the territory of a Member State.[450]

§4. Exclusive Rights

208. According to section 2 Swedish Act on the Protection of Topographies for Semiconductor Products, the protection includes the exclusive rights to authorize or prohibit any of the following acts:

(1) reproduction of the topography;
(2) importation of the topography for commercial exploitation/purposes; and
(3) making the topography available to the public through sale, rental or other ways of distribution to the public.

447. Section 1 Act on the Protection of Topographies for Semiconductor Products.
448. Section 4 Act on the Protection of Topographies for Semiconductor Products.
449. *See also* Art. 3(1) Directive on the Legal Protection of Topographies of Semiconductor Products.
450. Section 3 para. 2 Act on the Protection of Topographies for Semiconductor Products. *See also* Art. 3(2) Directive on the Legal Protection of Topographies of Semiconductor Products.

These exclusive rights also include computer chips that have been produced by using the topography.[451]

The right holder can, in other words, control the reproduction, distribution as well as the import of topographies and any computer chips that are built on the same design.

§5. Exemptions

209. Sections 5–7 Swedish Act on the Protection of Topographies for Semiconductor Products list the exceptions to the exclusive rights. According to section 5, topographies may be copied for teaching purposes or in order to analyse the pattern (reverse engineering). Single copies may also be made for private purposes. These copies may, however, not be used for other purposes in these cases.

According to section 6, exclusive rights do not apply to topographies that have been distributed to the public within the EEA with the consent of the right holder. This principle of exhaustion reflects Article 5(5) of the Directive.

§6. Enforcement/Sanctions

210. Infringing the rights stipulated in the Swedish Act on the Protection of Topographies for Semiconductor Products can lead to civil and criminal liability. Section 9 stipulates a fine or imprisonment for up to two years in cases of intent or gross negligence and also criminalizes the attempt or preparation of such infringements. Section 11 allows for compensation for damages. Compensation is given for any infringing use; in cases of intent or gross negligence the damages can also include lost profit, any profit the infringer gained, as well as damages to the reputation of the topography.

If somebody acquires a copy of a protected topography and is neither aware of nor has a reason to believe that the topography is protected, she or he has the right to continue using the computer chip even after being made aware of the protection. However, compensation for the use shall be paid by her or him.[452]

211. In accordance with the Enforcement Directive and similar to the Swedish Copyright Act, section 9c Act on the Protection of Topographies for Semiconductor Products grants right holders the possibility to apply for an 'order to provide information' (*informationsföreläggande*) which can be issued by a court.

451. Section 2 para. 2 Act on the Protection of Topographies for Semiconductor Products.
452. Section 10 Act on the Protection of Topographies for Semiconductor Products.

Chapter 5. Other Intellectual Property Rights in the ICT Sector

§1. Patents

212. Chapter 1 section 1 Swedish Patent Act (*patentlag (1967:837)*) explicitly exempts computer programs or business plans from the definition of invention.[453] According to paragraph 1 of the same section, only inventions can be eligible for patent protection, which therefore excludes computer programs. Section 1 paragraph 2 states the following.

The following shall never be regarded as an invention: that which is merely:

(1) a discovery, scientific theory or mathematical method;
(2) an aesthetic creation;
(3) a scheme, rule or method for performing mental acts, for playing games or for doing business, or a program for computers;
(4) a presentation of information.

213. Following a decision by the Supreme Administrative Court (*Regeringsrätten*) in 1974, computer programs were not protectable by patent in Sweden.[454] This situation changed, however, with a court decision from 1990.[455] In its decision,[456] the Supreme Administrative Court dealt with the patentability of an invention concerning a method of determining the pitch in human speech, for which the Swedish Patent and Registration Office (*Patent- och registreringsverket*)[457] originally denied a patent registration. The Court held that the Swedish patent legislation aims to comply with the European Patent Convention (EPC), which is why the term 'which is merely' corresponds to 'such subject-matter' in Article 52 EPC. Though Swedish law is applicable on patent registrations in Sweden, case law by the European Patent Office (EPO)[458] has been of importance.

The EPO did not have a clear standpoint on patentability of inventions using computer programs. In 1985, the Guidelines for Examination in the EPO were amended and stated then that an invention that contributes with a technical step shall not be denied patentability solely on the grounds that a computer program is involved in the inventive step.

The presently valid Guidelines stipulate that a computer program that is capable of causing, when running on a computer, a further technical effect going beyond the normal physical effects is eligible for patentability.

A further technical effect which lends technical character to a computer program may be found, for example, in the control of an industrial process or in processing data which represent physical entities or in the internal functioning of the computer itself or its interfaces under the influence of the program and could, for example,

453. Section 1 para. 2 Patent Act.
454. Decision by Supreme Administrative Court from 22 Jan. 1974, RÅ 1974 ref 11.
455. Koktvedgaards & Levin, 251–253.
456. Decision by Supreme Administrative Court from 13 Jun. 1990, RÅ 1990 ref 84.
457. www.prv.se.
458. www.epo.org.

affect the efficiency or security of a process, the management of computer resources required or the rate of data transfer in a communication link.[459]

In order to comply with the common framework of the EPC, the Swedish Supreme Administrative Court (*Regeringsrätten*) held in the case from 1990[460] that the speech signal invention was not excluded from patentability simply because of the fact that a computer program was involved to a certain extent.

At present, case law is, in general, sparse within the area of patent protection for computer programs; a more open-minded granting of patents for computer programs can, however, be noted[461] in line with the development on a European level.

§2. Trade Secrets

214. Unauthorized use of know-how is protected according to the Swedish Act on Trade Secrets (*lag (2018:558) om företagshemligheter*). This law updated existing national legislation on trade secrets, and was a result of Directive 2016/943 on the protection of undisclosed know-how and business information (trade secrets) against their unlawful acquisition, use and disclosure, coming into force on 1 July 2018 and replacing the Act on the Protection of Trade Secrets (*lag (1990:409) om skydd för företagshemligheter*). Protection is given where information is kept secret and the use of it could lead to damage for a company.[462] The knowledge does not have to be documented; even information in somebody's mind can be protected. The new Act widens the scope of prohibited acts, increases the circumstances under which damages are to be paid and introduces more severe criminal sanctions.

According to section 26 Act on Trade Secrets, any unauthorized intentional access to trade secrets can lead to criminal liability with imprisonment for a maximum of two years (for aggravated offences this increases to a maximum of six years). Following the implementation of Directive 2016/943, unlawful possession of trade secrets can also lead to criminal liability, with imprisonment for a maximum of two years (for aggravated offences the maximum is four years) in accordance with section 27. Any intentional or negligent use of trade secrets leads to civil liability for damages caused by the use.[463]

In a Supreme Court case from 2001, an employee's copying of electronic data from a customer database only resulted in civil liability for damages, as the employee had lawful access to the data and did therefore not fulfil the requirements for criminal liability under the 1990 Act.[464] This type of action would now fall under the definition of 'acquisition', as found in section 3(1) of the 2018 Act.

A decision by the Labour Court (*Arbetsdomstol*) dealt with the case of three former employees who had created a computer program at their new workplace, which was very similar to software the former employer was using. The Court held

459. European Patent Office, 'Guidelines for Examination in the European Patent Office', November 2018, Part G Ch. II 3.6.
460. Decision by Supreme Administrative Court from 13 Jun. 1990, RÅ 1990 ref 84.
461. Koktvedgaards & Levin, 251–253.
462. Section 2 para. 1 Act on Trade Secrets.
463. Sections 6-10 Act on Trade Secrets.
464. Decision by Supreme Court from 1 Jun. 2001, NJA 2001 s. 362.

that the employees had had access to a computer program during their work, and that this constituted a trade secret. The next question concerned the requirement of using the trade secret in an unauthorized way. The Swedish Labour Court held that only similarities in the two computer programs were not evidence enough to prove unauthorized use, as there were other plausible reasons for the similarities. Neither did the mere fact of a short development period for the new software provide sufficient grounds for an unauthorized use of a trade secret. The employees were therefore acquitted.[465]

As is apparent by the Labour Court's decision, a conviction not only requires the proof of a trade secret but also demonstration of the fact that the trade secret was actually acquired or used in an unauthorized way.

465. Decision by Labour Court from 2 Sep. 2009, AD 2009 No. 63.

Chapter 6. Internet Domain Name Registration

§1. General Statement

215. In 2006, Sweden introduced the National Top-Level Domains for Sweden on the Internet Act (*lag (2006:24) om nationella toppdomäner för Sverige på Internet*) (hereinafter 'Top-Level Domains Act') as part of its strategy to achieve a more secure Internet.[466] The Act aims at enabling a secure and effective administration of the Swedish top-level country domain names and to allow state control over the administration.[467]

Though the registration as such is mainly done by outsourced organizations (registrars), the general terms and conditions of the main Swedish registry, the Swedish Internet Foundation (*Internetstiftelsen*),[468] apply and take precedence over conflicting terms and conditions in individual contracts between registrars and domain holders.[469]

§2. Administration

216. The Swedish Top-Level Domains Act applies to the technical administration and registration of domain names for Sweden.[470] Technical administration with regard to domain names traditionally includes maintaining databases such as who is, approve registrars, support name servers as well as maintain the DNS-service which translates domain names to IP addresses.[471]

Section 5 Top-Level Domains Act sets up several requirements that registries have to meet. The provision mainly concerns security aspects but also stipulates obligations such as providing correct and easily accessible information to the name servers for the top-domain, ensuring traffic between the name servers and the Internet (i.e., safeguarding the accessibility of the DNS-service), securing the information on top domains and following routines that meet certain accepted standards. Registries also have to maintain a register of issued domain names and make backup copies of the data on a regular basis.[472]

Registries have to notify the Swedish supervisory authority of their services. According to the National Top-Level Domains for Sweden on the Internet

---

466. Prior to the enactment in 2006 the Swedish State was not involved in the administration of domain names.
467. Government Bill (*Proposition*) 2004/05:175, 'Från IT-politik för samhället till politik för IT-samhället', 1.
468. Previously called Internet Infrastructure Foundation.SE (*Stiftelsen för Internetinfrastruktur*).
469. Section 1.3 Terms and conditions of registration applicable for the top-level domain.SE from 6 Feb. 2019.
470. Section 1 Top-Level Domains Act.
471. Government Bill (*Proposition*) 2004/05:175, 245.
472. Section 6 Top-Level Domains Act.

Ordinance (*förordning (2006:25) om nationella toppdomäner för Sverige på Internet*) (hereinafter 'Top-Level Domains Ordinance'), PTS is the responsible supervisory authority.[473]

217. At the moment, the Swedish Internet Foundation (*Internetstiftelsen*) is the only registry for the Swedish top-level and country-level domain.se. Since September 2013, the foundation also administers the top-level domain.nu.[474] Established in 1997, it is an independent public interest foundation and not only administers Swedish domain names, but also aims at promoting a positive development of the Internet in general in Sweden.

§3. Registration

218. The rules for registration are not stipulated in any statutory provisions but are provided in the terms and conditions of registration applicable for the top-level domain.se, issued by the Swedish Internet Foundation (*Internetstiftelsen*).

As in most other countries, the principle 'first come, first served' applies.[475] This means that in principle any domain name will be registered as long as it is available,[476] and no general consideration is given to possible intellectual property rights to the name.

Both natural and legal persons can apply for registration of domain names.[477] The general terms and conditions issued by the Swedish Internet Foundation set up some technical requirements for domain names as well as some exemptions as to which domain names can be registered.[478]

219. According to section 3.2.1 of the terms and conditions of registration applicable for the top-level domain.se, a domain name may only comprise ASCII characters, which include the letters a–z, numbers 0–9 and hyphens (though the domain name cannot consist only of hyphens). Domain names have to include at least two and maximum of sixty-three characters.[479]

Certain domain names are reserved and can only be registered after a special assessment (reserved) or not at all (blocked). Examples include:[480]

- example and test domains (blocked), such as example.se, localhost.se;
- misleading domains (blocked), such as whois.se;

473. Section 2 Top-Level Domains Ordinance.
474. This domain is seen as popular due to its meaning 'now' in Swedish, Danish and Dutch.
475. Section 3.1.2 Terms and conditions of registration applicable for the top-level domain. SE from 6 Feb. 2019.
476. *Ibid.*, s. 3.2.6.
477. *Ibid.*, s. 3.1.1.
478. For statistics on Swedish domain names *see* internetstiftelsen.se/en/domain-statistics/, accessed 15 Jan. 2020.
479. Section 3.2.5 Terms and conditions of registration applicable for the top-level domain.SE from 6 Feb. 2019.
480. *See* for a complete list data.internetstiftelsen.se/barred_domains_list.txt, accessed 15 Jan. 2020.

– specific second-level domains (blocked), such as org.se, parti.se and press.se;
– domain names related to Swedish law (blocked), such as cern.se, epo.se, euratom.se and interpol.se.

§4. Intellectual Property Rights

220. As mentioned above the registration process for domain names does not take into account potential intellectual property rights in the names. This is very common in other European countries and internationally.

There can, however, be rights in a word or a name, both according to the Swedish Trademarks Act (*varumärkeslag (2010:1877)*) as well as the Swedish Trade Names Act (*firmalag (1974:156)*). Individuals may also have a right to their personal name.

Trademarks have to be registered with the Swedish Patent and Registration Office (*Patent- och registreringsverket*),[481] according to Chapter 1 section 6 and Chapter 2 section 1 Trademarks Act, or can be protected due to usage pursuant to Chapter 1 section 7 Trademarks Act. In addition, trade names can be protected upon registration with the Swedish Companies Registration Office (*Bolagsverket*)[482] or through usage, according to section 2 Trade Names Act.

Though rights on trademark or trade names are not considered during the registration of domain names, the Swedish Internet Foundation takes account of intellectual property rights, especially trademarks, in allowing right holders to apply for a transfer or deregistration of a domain name through ADR.

In exceptional circumstances domains can be forfeited to the state. In a recent judgment the Supreme Court ruled that domain names are considered property that can be forfeited.[483] The case involved the well-known Pirate Bay domain names 'piratebay.se' and 'thepiratebay.se'. Due to copyright infringement carried out by the registered holder of the domain names, the domains could be forfeited according to the Copyright Act's rules on forfeiture.

§5. Disputes

221. Just as WIPO's Domain Name Dispute Resolution (Uniform Domain-Name Dispute-Resolution Policy, UDRP), the Swedish organization requests individuals and companies registering a domain name under.se to agree to their General terms and conditions and thereby agree to the use of dispute resolution when settling a conflict. Since June 2017 dispute resolution for the top domain.se has been administered by WIPO.[484]

481. www.prv.se.
482. www.bolagsverket.se.
483. Decision by Supreme Court from 21 Dec. 2017, NJA 2017 s.1070.
484. *See* www.wipo.int/amc/en/domains/cctld/se/, accessed 15 Jan. 2020.

222. Under certain conditions, a registered domain name can be deregistered or transferred after an ADR proceeding.[485] Point 7.2 of the General terms and conditions stipulates the following requirements which all have to be fulfilled:

(1) the domain name is identical or similar to:
   - a trade symbol (trademark or service mark);
   - a trade name or secondary name;
   - a family name;
   - an artist's name (if the name is not associated with someone who deceased a long time ago);
   - a title of another party's copyrighted literary or artistic work;
   - a name that is protected by the Regulation concerning Certain Official Designations (*förordning (1976:100) om vissa officiella beteckningar*);[486] or
   - the name of a government authority that is listed in the registry that Statistics Sweden must maintain under the Swedish Code of Statutes SFS 2007:755 (Government Agencies Register Ordinance), or its generally accepted abbreviation.

(2) the domain name has been registered or used in bad faith; and
(3) the domain holder has no rights or justified interest in the domain name.

All relevant circumstances are assessed when determining whether a domain name has been registered or used in bad faith.[487] Examples of circumstances supporting bad faith claims (a lack of which potentially implying that bad faith does not exist) are:

- the domain holder is utilizing or plans to utilize the good reputation, market position or characteristic feature of the petitioner[488] to attract traffic to the own website or to increase revenue in this matter;
- the domain holder's registration of the domain name prevents or makes it difficult for the petitioner to register the brand as domain name;
- the domain name is being used or planned to be used to disrupt the petitioner's operations;
- the domain name has been registered with a view to a sale to the petitioner.

As above, all relevant circumstances are assessed when determining whether a domain holder has no right or justified interest in the domain name.[489] Examples of

485. Section 6.3 Terms and conditions of registration applicable for the top-level domain.SE from 6 Feb. 2019.
486. For example the Council of Europe (*Europarådet*) or the International Monetary Fund (*Internationella valutafonden*).
487. Instructions pertaining to ADR (para. 7), Instructions concerning the bad faith condition (condition 2), internetstiftelsen.se/docs/Instructions-pertaining-to-ADR-paragraph-7.pdf.
488. That is, the party requesting dispute resolution proceedings.
489. Instructions pertaining to ADR (para. 7), Instructions concerning the right or justified interest condition (condition 3), internetstiftelsen.se/docs/Instructions-pertaining-to-ADR-paragraph-7.pdf, accessed 15 Jan. 2020.

circumstances supporting such claims (a lack of which potentially implying that the domain holder does not have any right or justified interest) are:

- the domain holder owns a registered brand (or other right) that is identical or similar to the domain name;
- the domain name is being used or has been registered to be used in its linguistic meaning; or
- the domain name is being used or has been registered to be used in commercial or private operations that do not infringe on the petitioner's rights;
- the domain name is older than the brand (or other right) on which the petitioner bases the application.

223. As of April 2014, 566 decisions have been taken through ADR; out of these, 384 were in favour of the plaintiff.[490] Since the transfer of dispute resolution to WIPO in 2017, over 100 decisions have been issued.[491] Normally, if the trademark is not registered, the plaintiff has to prove usage with evidence such as number of sales, costs for and extent of marketing, or use market research to show the trademark's reputation on the market.[492]

The requirement 'similar to'[493] has been confirmed for the domain name locket.se with the trademark blocket.se, the domain name vovlo.se with the trademark Volvo, iloveikea.se with the trademark IKEA, and igoogle.se as well as googlephone.se with Google. In many ADR cases, the domain name and trademark were identical and therefore did not require any further investigation in this respect, for example, vuitton.se, kawasaki.se, esso.se, dole.se as well as google.se.

If a domain name is not used for commercial purposes, the domain owner is able to keep it, even though it might infringe someone else's trademark. A non-commercial purpose of a domain name cannot, however, be claimed if the website has not been launched.[494] In accordance with trademark legislation, the term 'commercial purposes' is rather broad and can include not only websites with a purpose of profit-making, but also non-profit or educational, scientific and cultural activities if they involve an economic interest and can therefore be considered businesses.[495]

Regarding the requirement of bad faith, case law by arbitration proceedings has shown that the fact that the domain holder should have known about the trademark because of its reputation and does not reply in the proceedings, lead to the presumption of bad faith at the time of registration of the domain name. Registration of several domain names in a systematic way may also be an indication of bad faith.[496]

---

490. For ongoing disputes and previous decisions *see* www.iis.se/domaner/tvistlosning/for-se-domaner/atf-arenden/, accessed 15 Jan. 2020.
491. *See* Decisions at www.wipo.int/amc/en/domains/cctld/se/, accessed 15 Jan. 2020.
492. Henrik Bengtsson, 'Svenska domännamnstvister: Praxis enligt den s.k. II-stiftelsens systems för alternativ tvistelösning', *Nordiskt Immateriellt Rättskydd* 3(2005): 257 and 263.
493. Previously referred to as 'likely to be confused'.
494. *See*, e.g., Decision No. 9, from 27 Aug. 2003, Peugeot.se.
495. Bengtsson, 266–267.
496. Bengtsson, 270 and 272.

224. According to Point 6.4 General Terms and Conditions, a domain name shall be deregistered or transferred if the applicant presents a judgment by a court stipulating that the domain name shall be deregistered or transferred. There are no statistics to what extent this is being used, but the ADR system seems to work very well regarding cybersquatters, and as it works faster than trials before the district courts, most trademark owners will prefer to use it.

Part III. ICT Contracts

Chapter 1. Hardware Contracts

225. Swedish law does not specifically govern ICT hardware contracts. In essence, such contracts stipulate the buyer's and the seller's rights and obligations in relation to the transfer (or leasing, where applicable) of movable property. This means that all hardware transfer contracts between commercial parties are subject to the Sale of Goods Act (*köplag (1990:931)*). Consumer sales and certain international sales are subject to specific legislation in the form of the Consumer Sales Act (*konsumentköplag (1990:932)*) and the Convention on Contracts for the International Sale of Goods respectively. The Sale of Goods Act is non-mandatory legislation, which means that it is normally possible and also customary in ICT contracts, to overrule this legislation through the actual agreement entered into by the parties, that is, the agreed provisions in the hardware contract will take precedence in the case of any conflict with the Sale of Goods Act.

In addition, according to section 3 Sale of Goods Act, 'commercial custom or other customs which must be regarded as binding on the parties' will take precedence over the Sale of Goods Act. Within the Swedish ICT sector, standard contracts issued by trade associations play a fairly important role, and it is not unusual for small or even medium-sized IT businesses and transactions to be conducted on the basis of, or with reference to, such standard contracts. In relation to hardware contracts, Agreement 90[497] is the most common standard contract, despite the fact that it mainly focuses on turnkey contracts and system deliveries. Since Agreement 90 is often used when interpreting ICT contracts, it has been argued that Agreement 90 should be considered as customary practice within the market.[498] In such cases, the provisions in Agreement 90 could – in connection with section 3 Sale of Goods Act – be used as a reference to define the commercial custom for ICT hardware and turnkey contracts that would prevail over the Sale of Goods Act. Regardless, the explicit terms and the content of the parties' agreement will of course have precedence over both the Sale of Goods Act and Agreement 90.

226. Within the Swedish ICT sector, it has been an ongoing trend over the past decades to shift the focus from hardware specifications and descriptions to more

497. Agreement 90 was issued by IT & Telekomföretagen and SILF in Swedish and English. The latest version was issued in 2014.

498. Agne Lindberg & Daniel Westman, *Praktisk IT-rätt*, 3rd edn (Stockholm: Norstedts Juridik AB, 2002), 390.

functional aspects of the delivery, that is, hardware has become more of a commodity closely connected to different services and also more of an instrument to run software applications and hosting data. This would be particularly clear in the light of the cloud computing trend. In addition, many customers today tend to prefer to lease or rent hardware rather than purchase it, especially in commercial ICT deals. Such financial arrangements allow the customer to maintain agility and flexibility as well as avoid making large investments and having to deal with old or obsolete equipment. The changed focus towards functionality, services, cloud and financing models has caused many suppliers to bundle hardware with software and different types of services, such as software-as-a-service, maintenance services, mobile solutions, financing, and consumable supplies. Such structures are often referred to as 'functional' or 'as-a-service' deliveries, where the customer pays a fee per week/month/usage which includes the costs for hardware as well as the included software and services. Where the hardware contract includes maintenance services, it is crucial for the customer to ensure that the hardware contract includes necessary service-related provisions (e.g., maintenance frequency, availability requirements, response and resolution requirements, etc.), as well as the right to receive financial compensation in case of the supplier's non-performance or non-compliance. Contracts for such bundled service offerings, which include hardware, software and services, are typically tied to a separate service level agreement, where the parties agree on suitable key performance indicators and service levels to ensure a high and consistent delivery from the supplier.

Another trend relevant for IT hardware is the ongoing digitalization of Swedish industries and corporations, often tied to initiatives related to the so-called Internet-of-Things. Such digitalization initiatives will include hardware deliveries (e.g., sensors) as a key component.

227. For hardware contracts, a critical issue to negotiate are the warranties provided by the supplier with regard to defects in the hardware. The customer will generally strive to include more functionality-based warranties, where the supplier warrants that the hardware is fit for a specific purpose or use in a specific environment, whereas the supplier will strive to limit any warranty or representation to standard documentation and descriptions of the hardware. According to section 32 Sale of Goods Act, the supplier is, as a general rule, liable for defects occurring during a period of two years after the delivery. However, this rule is usually set aside and/or modified in the hardware contract.

Further, in any hardware contract it is essential to ensure suitable contractual protection (as well as insurance coverage) in regards to product liability, e.g., in the form of warranties and/or indemnities in relation to potential liability for damage to persons or other tangible objects. Swedish law contains mandatory legislation and strict product liability for safety deficiencies in hardware, the Product Liability Act (*produktansvarslagen (1992:18)*).

228. In conclusion, traditional hardware contracts are becoming increasingly unusual in Sweden due to the bundling of hardware with services, cloud computing, software and financing. From a legal perspective, commercial parties to a hardware contract have a general freedom of contract and may freely dispose of the agreement. Standard contracts such as Agreement 90 could, to some extent, serve as a benchmark. It is important to note, however, that these standard contracts are generally considered to be more favourable to the supplier than the customer.

Chapter 2. Software Contracts

229. A software contract can refer to different types of ICT contracts, such as licence agreements, development or distribution contracts. Since distribution agreements are covered in Chapter 4 below, this chapter will focus on software licence and development agreements.

Software licensing contracts are, as far as copyright issues are concerned, subject to the Swedish Copyright Act *(lag (1960:729) om upphovsrätt till litterära och konstnärliga verk)*, which sets out specific provisions with regard to both the transfer of copyright to software as well as licensing. Although not directly applicable, it is also widely accepted that the Sale of Goods Act, in regard to the principles of commercial transactions as such (e.g., regarding issues such as when a delivery is considered to be delayed, or within which time a complaint must be raised by the customer from the time when the customer discovered a defect), will apply analogously on software contracts to the extent that the software contract does not specifically stipulate otherwise.[499]

230. A software contract is generally different from other commercial contracts since the software licence concerns the provision of a licence (a right to use) rather than the *transfer* of property.[500] A software licence can be either exclusive or non-exclusive, although it is obviously unusual for any commercial software to be licensed on an exclusive basis.

231. The object for a software licence is typically the software code along with the accompanying documentation and manuals for the software. Except for specific source code escrow arrangements (*see* below), the customer will not be provided with, or have the general right to modify the source code of the software. However, it should be noted that Article 26g Swedish Copyright Act stipulates that a licensee has a mandatory right to correct errors in computer software as well as make amendments for the purpose of compatibility. Furthermore, the licensee is free to make copies of the software for backup purposes to the extent necessary for the intended use of the software. Finally, the licensee may observe, examine and test the software as long as such activities are performed within the scope of the licensed rights.

According to Article 26h Swedish Copyright Act, the licensee also has a mandatory but limited right to decompile the software. Decompilation may, however, only be performed for the purpose of achieving intended interoperability between the licensed software and the other software. The result from the decompilation must not be disclosed to third parties unless such disclosure is necessary in order to achieve the intended interoperability. It is explicitly stated in the Swedish Copyright Act that any information gained by decompilation shall not be used for the development of software that has a similar expression as the decompiled software.

---

499. *See* Lindberg & Westman, 374 et seq.

500. Note that intellectual property rights to software can theoretically be transferred as well as licensed. The question whether to transfer or license software is a commonly negotiated part of many development agreements (*see infra*).

232. The so-called specification principle (*specifikationsprincipen*) is a fundamental aspect of Swedish copyright law. This principle states that only such rights explicitly granted in the software contract will be transferred or licensed to the licensee. This principle is partly incorporated in Article 28 Copyright Act, which states that a transfer of copyrighted material will not – unless explicitly agreed to – include a right for the buyer to modify or reassign the material. To the extent that such rights are intended to pass to the buyer, the transfer agreement should include explicit provisions regarding the right to change and reassign the copyrighted material.

233. Important provisions in a software contract based on traditional licensing include liability for defects (typically limited to a standard warranty valid for a short period from delivery, e.g., thirty or ninety days), source code escrow, support and maintenance services,[501] and infringement. The latter has gained in importance in the light of open source challenges. Warranty undertakings will generally be connected to the support and maintenance agreement between the parties, if applicable.

234. Source code escrow arrangements are rather common in Sweden for software that has been developed specifically for one customer or project but where the copyright has not been transferred to the customer. Perhaps the most important clause to negotiate in an escrow agreement is to agree on which events that should trigger release of the materials placed in escrow. Examples of commonly used release events include the supplier's insolvency, the winding-up of its business, change of ownership, and/or substantial breach of (or non-performance) the maintenance agreement. In escrow agreements between Swedish parties, the Stockholm Chamber of Commerce is widely selected as the escrow agent, often by virtue of their model contract.[502]

235. In recent years, many software suppliers have started to distribute their software through a Software-as-a Service (SaaS) model rather than by use of a traditional licensing model. SaaS is a broad market, and services can include anything from rather simple web-based email solutions to complex Customer Relationship Management Systems. However, any SaaS would typically be highly standardized. The SaaS trend has been driven not only by suppliers, who can decrease costs for distribution and maintenance, but also by customers, who prefer not to handle issues regarding licensing, maintenance, and hosting of the software. A SaaS-contract will, compared to a traditional software licence agreement, focus less on the right to use the software, and more on functional service descriptions, service levels (e.g., availability and maintenance requirements), service level remedies (e.g., liquidated damages), data security, and exit management provisions to ensure cooperation and transfer of data upon the termination or expiration of the SaaS-contract. The extent of copyright use (and hence the need for an explicit licence provision) in a SaaS-contract is dependent on the technical solution and whether the end user is duplicating the software when using it or making it available to a third party.

---

501. *See* Ch. 5 *infra* (paras 246 et seq.).

502. *See* in English, english.chamber.se/escrow-services.htm, accessed 6 Mar. 2020; for more information in Swedish *see* www.chamber.se/kallkod/hur-gor-man.htm, accessed 6 Mar. 2020.

The trade organization Swedish IT and Telecom Industries, who has published i.a. Agreement 90, has also published a standard contract on SaaS. However, most often the SaaS vendors would require the transaction to be governed by the vendor's standard terms. This is particularly the case for large global SaaS vendors. Nevertheless, our experience is that these vendor standard contracts are negotiable to some extent provided that the customer is considered important and/or that the deal is large enough.

The SaaS vendors' standard contract terms are generally unbalanced in favour of the vendor. This would typically deviate from the Swedish view and customs as regards commercial agreements. General contract law principles in Sweden (as set out in, e.g., the Sale of Goods Act), which would apply in the absence of a written contract, are significantly more favourable to the customer than any standard SaaS vendor terms and conditions. However, in recent years we have noted that the willingness among large SaaS vendors to negotiate standard terms has increased.

SaaS vendors sometimes argue that standardized services require standardized contract terms. This is obviously not a relevant argument, since standardized services would require nothing more than standardized service descriptions. Terms and conditions for the legal and commercial relationship between a SaaS vendor and the customer are, and should be, a result of the commercial forces at hand.

A SaaS customer should be extra cautious with information security issues and data protection regulations in vendor standard contracts. In some cases, SaaS and other public cloud services will not be a viable option due to the lack of 'legal information security', for example in relation to jurisdictional risk and loss of control over confidential information. Further, regulatory requirements, if applicable, as well as data protection rules need to be taken into consideration when sourcing SaaS.

236. Software development contracts deal with a number of important issues. First of all, and provided that the project is based on a so-called 'waterfall' methodology, the development project and the management and governance thereof need to be described in detail in order to ensure a successful project. Another important aspect of a software development contract is the clauses regarding intellectual property rights and, specifically, whether the customer will only have a right to use the result, hence a licence, or if the intellectual property rights to the result shall be transferred to and vested in the customer. In most cases, this issue can be resolved by either a grant-back licence to the supplier (if rights to results are transferred to the customer) or a wide licence grant for the customer (if rights to results are retained by the supplier). It should be noted that, as a main rule and in accordance with the specification principle, the intellectual property rights to results will remain with the supplier unless otherwise explicitly agreed. Furthermore, delay incentives in the form of payment plans tied to milestones and/or delay penalties are customary in a software development contract based on a 'waterfall' methodology.

An increasingly common type of development methodology is so-called agile development. In particular, such agile development projects are often based on the

SCRUM[503] or KANBAN[504] methodology frameworks. Somewhat simplified, agile development methodology means that the parties work under an iterative process where the project is intended to deliver smaller parts (so-called 'minimum viable products') successively throughout the project, rather than one major final delivery on a specific date. The results in an agile development project are provided to the customer in numerous smaller parts where the customer will react on each part during the course of the project. Hence, the outcome of a project based on agile development is not as clearly defined as in traditional development contracts. An agile development methodology requires a contract that can accommodate the close interaction between the parties during the development project. The statement of work, which is basically a list of the activities of each party, as well as liability issues, confidentiality undertakings and provisions on delay and incentives for the supplier need to be made as clear as possible. On a general level, a development project implementing an agile methodology will typically mean that the customer needs to be more closely involved in the actual development process and that the customer, in most cases, should be prepared to assume a higher level of project and financial risk compared to a traditional delivery model.

There are several standard contracts for software development projects. For development projects using a traditional development model, the most commonly used standard contract is IT Projects version 2008. For agile development projects, the standard contract typically used is called Agile Projects version 2012.[505] These standard contracts are, however, supplier-friendly and will often require significant negotiation in order to reach a balanced agreement.

237. To summarize, the provisions in the Swedish Copyright Act need to be considered when drafting a software contract regardless of whether it is a licence or development contract. The general rules set out in the Sale of Goods Act would also need to be taken into consideration. The software contract has traditionally been based on a grant of licence, development and maintenance services. Due to the rise of cloud computing, SaaS-contracts have given rise to new issues to be dealt with by the parties.

503. For more information on SCRUM in relation to software development, *see* www.scrum.org.

504. For more information on KANBAN in relation to software development, *see* Anderson, David, 'Agile Management for Software Engineering: Applying the Theory of Constraints for Business Results', New Jersey: Prentice Hall, September 2003.

505. Both IT Projects version 2008 and Agile Projects 2012 are issued by IT & Telekomföretagen in Swedish and English.

Chapter 3. Turnkey Contracts

238. The primary purpose of a turnkey contract is to provide the customer with a complete solution or system which is (more or less) customized to meet the customer's specific requirements. This means that the turnkey contract will per se be rather extensive and include several different types of deliverables, often including a combination of hardware, software and services (e.g., adaptations of standard software or other implementation services). Maintenance services are generally not considered to be a part of the turnkey contract and will typically be subject to a separate agreement. The maintenance agreement will however often be linked to the turnkey contract, so that the maintenance undertakings will enter into effect upon the completion of the acceptance test in the turnkey contract.

The key element of a turnkey contract is that the supplier will assume responsibility for the entire system that is delivered to the customer. Hence, the different parts of the supplier's performance (hardware, software, and services) need to fulfil the agreed specification separately as well as jointly. Since the supplier assumes responsibility for the complete system delivered under a turnkey contract, it is essential for the parties to allow due consideration and time when preparing the specifications and project plans of a turnkey contract. In many cases, a large step towards ensuring the successful purchase of an entire IT system can be taken through careful preparation measures along with effective contract mechanisms.

239. The Sale of Goods Act is directly applicable to the hardware delivery component of a turnkey contract, but not to the licensing of standard software.[506] This means that, unless otherwise explicitly agreed to by the parties, the hardware part of a turnkey contract is governed by the Sale of Goods Act while the licensing part is subject to mandatory requirements set out in the Copyright Act.[507]

As already mentioned above in Chapter 1, the use of standard contracts is common within the Swedish ICT market. With regard to turnkey contracts, Agreement 90 is a well-established standard contract and the principles set out therein could to some extent be considered as commercial customs when applying the Sales of Goods Act on ICT contracts. However, it is important to point out that Agreement 90 is not mandatory in any respect, and that the parties have the freedom of contract in relation to all aspects of the turnkey contract, except for the mandatory copyright legal principles regarding, for example, compatibility changes and decompilation.[508] Agreement 90 includes all the essential aspects of a turnkey contract, such as provisions regarding installation, delivery dates, inspection/acceptance tests, delay, payment, software licence, liability for defects, confidentiality obligations, infringement indemnity, limitations of liability, and dispute resolution.

240. Most turnkey contracts include delivery of third party products, and the parties will need to stipulate the level of liability that the supplier should assume for such third party products. In general, the supplier will strive to make the third party

506. Lindberg & Westman, 372 et seq.
507. *See* Ch. 2 *supra* (paras 229 et seq.).
508. As described in Ch. 2 *supra* (paras 229 et seq.).

supplier's terms and conditions applicable, especially in situations where the customer has made an active selection to use a specific third party product for the delivery. This is also the general rule according to Agreement 90.

Another important component of the turnkey contract is the implementation and customization of the supplier's products and solutions to the customer's IT environment and specific requirements. Such implementation is usually set up as a joint project, where the supplier assumes the role of project manager and the customer's responsibilities are limited to allowing access for the supplier's personnel to the customer's facilities and IT environment. Due to the close cooperation between the parties in the implementation project, it is essential for the turnkey contract to include adequate undertakings with regard to non-disclosure obligations and compliance with applicable security policies.

Further, the turnkey contract will typically include an acceptance test procedure. It is essential for the customer to ensure that the acceptance criteria are properly defined and customized to suit the needs and demands of the customer. The acceptance test will also constitute the difference between 'delay' and 'error', since an error cannot occur before the system is actually delivered and accepted in accordance with the acceptance test criteria.

241. A common cause for problems and disputes during the implementation of customized solutions is the supplier's delay of the implementation project. In order to provide incentives for the supplier to provide the system on time, a turnkey contract generally includes a right for the customer to receive financial compensation (e.g., liquidated damages) in the case of delay. In addition to financial remedies, the customer should also strive for the contract to minimize and clarify all actions that the customer needs to perform in order for the supplier to successfully implement the solution. Such undertakings are often listed in a separate document. In the case of a substantial delay for which the supplier is responsible, the turnkey contract should include a right for the customer to terminate the contract prematurely.

Since it is customary in Sweden to settle disputes in commercial relationships by arbitration, case law on IT-contract disputes is scarce. However, recently a dispute that is highly relevant for the interpretation and design of turnkey contracts was tried by a Swedish court.[509] A customer terminated a turnkey agreement with immediate effect, due to delays in the supplier's performance and due to defects and errors in the supplied services that were not delayed. The customer furthermore claimed a refund of paid amounts, liquidated damages and reimbursement of costs. The court ruled that the customer did not have the right to terminate the agreements since the delays in delivery were actually caused by the customer and the customer had not otherwise proven a ground to cancel the agreements. The Stockholm District Court therefore ruled that the supplier had the right to full compensation for the damages suffered due to the termination of the agreements. The ruling shows the need for customers to be very specific on the statements of work as well as mechanisms for acceptance of the supplier's performance.

509. Decision by Stockholm District Court from 2 Feb. 2017, T 14204-14. The ruling has been appealed to Svea Court of Appeal.

Chapter 4. Distribution Agreements

242. With regard to distribution of hardware, software and services in Sweden, the most important forms of distribution are through the appointment of distributors and agents. Under a distribution agreement, the supplier will appoint a distributor to market, resell or sub-license the supplier's products and/or services on a designated market or worldwide. A distributor will purchase and resell products and/or services in its own name and its own account/risk. A commercial or commission agent will not purchase products or services from the supplier, but rather act as an intermediary between the supplier and the customer.

To distinguish between distributors and agents is essential from a legal perspective, since agents are subject to the Commercial Agents Act (*lag (1991:351) om handelsagentur*)[510] and the Commission Agents Act (*kommissionslag (2009:865)*) respectively. These statutes contain several mandatory protective provisions for the agent, such as the right to minimum termination notice periods and the right to receive severance pay in case of termination. A distributor, however, is not covered by any specific protective legislation under Swedish law (although distributors will need to comply with applicable competition and antitrust laws, *see* below). It is important to note that the Commercial Agents Act is only directly applicable in relation to supply of 'goods', that is, tangible items, and not to services and/or intangible items.

243. Specifically with regard to the distribution of software, the Swedish Supreme Court made an important ruling in 2008.[511] In this case, a German commercial agent claimed severance payment according to the Commercial Agents Act from a Swedish software supplier due to the supplier's termination of an agency agreement. The Court ruled that the provisions in the Commercial Agents Act regarding severance pay can be applicable for distribution of software. However, since software is not 'goods' according to Swedish law, the otherwise mandatory provisions in the Commercial Agents Act can be set aside by the provisions in the software agency agreement. The Court also indicated that the most important aspect of a software agency agreement which also includes ancillary services (such as after sales services) is in fact the licensing of software and not providing the services.[512]

244. In addition, there is also an important difference between distributors and agents in relation to mandatory antitrust and competition law. Whereas a distribution agreement will often conflict with such laws (*see* below), a commercial/commission agency agreement is normally not subject to antitrust/competition legislation, provided that the agent does not take any financial risks.

510. The Act is based on Council Directive 86/653/EEC of 18 December 1986 on the coordination of the laws of the Member States relating to self-employed commercial agents.

511. Decision by Supreme Court from 4 Jan. 2008, NJA 2008 s. 24.

512. *See* Johan Hübner, 'Analog tillämpning av lagen om handelsagentur på återförsäljare av datorprogram', *Lov & Data* 93 (2008): 14–15.

For a distribution agreement, non-competition clauses and territorial/customer restrictions are especially sensitive from an antitrust point of view. Further, the distributor must always be free to set its own prices in relation to its customers. Recommended prices or fixed maximum retail prices are however generally accepted under the block exemptions for vertical agreements,[513] provided that the supplier has a market share below 30%. With regard to non-competition clauses, the block exemptions for vertical agreements allow for such clauses to last no more than five years except in cases where the distributor's premises are owned or leased by the supplier or it is question of a franchise agreement. If the supplier's market share is below 15%, a non-compete obligation is however permissible under the European Commission's *de minimis* notice, regardless of its duration.[514] Competition restrictions after the termination of the agreement are permitted for a period of one year, provided that the restrictions are limited to the premises of the distributor and are indispensable to protect the supplier's know-how.[515] Further, under sections 36 and 38 Swedish Contracts Act (*lag (1915:218) om avtal och andra rättshandlingar på förmögenhetsrättens område*), a non-competition clause (and/or a penalty clause tied to the non-competition clause) can be deemed invalid and, hence, unenforceable to the extent that such a clause is considered unreasonable 'having regard to the contents of the agreement, the circumstances prevailing at the time the agreement was entered into, subsequent circumstances and circumstances in general'.[516]

245. Other important provisions in a distribution agreement include minimum purchase obligations, forecasting and reporting requirements. Such provisions often entitle the supplier to terminate the agreement (or, in case of an exclusive agreement, change the agreement into a non-exclusive agreement) if the distributor/agent fails to reach the applicable minimum purchase obligations or forecasted sales targets. Finally, many distribution agreements include a responsibility for the distributor/agent to handle customer complaints, warranty claims and all other after sales matters. The distributor/agent will generally be reimbursed by the supplier for such after sales work during the warranty period. Unless otherwise agreed by the parties, a two year warranty period for defects applies according to section 32 Sale of Goods Act.

---

513. Act on group exceptions for vertical agreements and restrictive practices (*Lag (2008:581) om gruppundantag för vertikala konkurrensbegränsande avtal*). The Act is based on Commission Regulation (EU) No. 330/2010 of 20 Apr. 2010 on the application of Art. 101.3 of the Treaty on the Functioning of the European Union to categories of vertical agreements and concerted practices.
514. Commission Notice on agreements of minor importance which do not appreciably restrict competition under Art. 81(1) of the Treaty establishing the European Community.
515. Article 5 Commission Regulation (EC) No. 2790/1999 of 22 Dec. 1999 on the application of Art. 81(3) of the Treaty to categories of vertical agreements and concerted practices.
516. Article 36 Contracts Act.

Chapter 5. Maintenance Contracts

246. The objective of maintenance services is basically to keep the maintenance object 'alive', up-to-date and well-functioning. A maintenance contract may complement or substitute a software warranty in a licence or intellectual property rights transfer contract by including an error resolution undertaking governed by a detailed service level agreement. It is common for different types of maintenance contracts that the supplier's obligation will be limited to deliver specified services to the customer in relation to one or more maintenance objects. This means that neither the Sale of Goods Act nor any other Swedish statute will be directly applicable, except for serving as supplementary legal principles for the interpretation of the maintenance contract. Further, since a large part of the supplier's undertakings in a software maintenance contract consist of providing computer code to the customer, copyright issues will need to be addressed in such maintenance contracts.

As for many other ICT contracts, there is a Swedish standard contract with regard to maintenance services. This standard contract is called 'IT-Maintenance Version 2008',[517] and includes many of the provisions necessary in a maintenance contract, such as general obligations for both parties, exceptions to the supplier's maintenance obligations, liability (and limitations), security, confidentiality and termination rights. Needless to say, each maintenance contract based on the IT-Maintenance standard contract will require careful considerations and adaptations to the actual deal. Specifically, IT-Maintenance must be supplemented with a service description, specific service levels and remedies, fees and payment terms.[518]

247. A maintenance contract will normally include both pro-active and reactive error rectification, as well as support services. Even though software maintenance is a complex and common type of maintenance contract, such services could also include an undertaking for the supplier to perform error rectification of both hardware and software. The general purpose of the rectification undertaking is to eliminate interruptions in the operations of the maintained systems, which in relation to hardware often include performance of technical repair services and replacement of parts. In relation to software, the supplier is normally obligated to: (i) reactively provide rectification and corrective measures (e.g., bug fixes, patches, etc.); (ii) advise and inform on how to work around the defect; or (iii) pro-actively provide a new version of the software where known errors are rectified. If the maintenance services are provided by the software licensor, the maintenance contract may also include an undertaking to provide the customer with new versions of the software, which may include not only error rectification but also new functionality. An essential aspect for the supplier is to have the option to carry out rectification work remotely (i.e., via virtual private network or similar network connection). Such a right to perform error correction remotely should be explicitly set out in the contract. In relation to such remote access to the customer's systems on distance, security arrangements may call for specific regulations in the maintenance contract.

---

517. IT-Maintenance is issued by IT & Telekomföretagen in Swedish and English. The latest version was issued in 2014.

518. *See* Lindberg & Westman, 478.

Pro-active maintenance services for hardware will normally include functional control and adjustments, replacement of worn-out parts, cleaning and similar activities. In relation to software, pro-active maintenance work can include development of the software (updates, upgrades, etc.) as well as updates and maintenance of information within databases. In addition, so-called soft maintenance services are often used for software, and will generally include an undertaking to provide the customer with new versions and updates.[519]

Furthermore, it is not uncommon to include elements of support services in maintenance contracts, which means that the contract will in fact constitute a support and maintenance agreement. In this respect, 'support' refers to the supplier's provision of a helpdesk that end users of the supported object may contact in case of errors or where there is a need of assistance in relation to the supported equipment or software. In order to avoid minor issues being reported to helpdesk, many agreements will include an undertaking for the supplier to provide education and training to a limited number of 'super-users' who will deal with Frequently Asked Questions and the resolution of minor issues. Such 'super-users' will then provide first line support and they will be the only users authorized to contact the supplier's helpdesk (which in such circumstances will be the second line support).

248. When negotiating a maintenance contract, much effort will normally be spent on identifying and regulating suitable service levels. The most commonly used service level is 'response time', meaning the time within which the supplier shall respond to customer inquiries and handle such in accordance with a specified escalation routine. A more demanding service level from a supplier perspective is 'resolution time'. Resolution time means the time from when an incident or problem in relation to the maintenance object is reported to the supplier until the incident or problem is solved. It is essential for the supplier to exclude factors outside the supplier's control affecting the service level results. Common exceptions include errors caused by the customer and errors caused by third party factors.

249. In cases of a service level breach/default, the maintenance contract should also contain adequate remedies. Such remedies can include both financial sanctions and other incentives for the supplier to adhere to the stipulated service levels. Such incentives and sanctions can be parallel and include a right for the customer to: (i) receive liquidated damages (penalties); (ii) price reductions and/or damages; (iii) terminate the contract; and/or (iv) intervene in the service delivery itself or through a third party (step-in). In recent years, however, many outsourcing and sophisticated maintenance contracts have also tried to incorporate pro-active remedy models such as 'balanced scorecards' that connect the service performance with the parties' governance structure by measuring certain key performance indicators. The objective for such models is to identify problems before they have caused a damage or default, rather than only providing compensation in arrears.[520] Another approach

519. *Ibid.*, 481.

520. *See* Agne Lindberg, Johan Kahn & Björn Krouthén, *IT-avtal – särskilt om outsourcing* (Stockholm: Norstedts Juridik AB, 2009), 119.

is to combine penalties for poor performance with incentives (bonus) in case the quality of the services exceeds the agreed or expected service levels.

250. In conclusion, there are many different types of maintenance contracts and the level of detail and sophistication varies. There is no Swedish legislation which specifically governs maintenance (or any other services in a commercial context), which means that business standards and standard agreements play an important role. For the customer, it is crucial to ensure that the maintenance contract contains adequate service levels and remedies.

Chapter 6. Facilities Management

251. There is no commonly accepted definition of a facilities management contract in Sweden. With regard to ICT contracts, a 'facility' will generally refer to premises, such as a data centre or part thereof (so-called co-location).

252. Transfer and leasing of premises, or space within premises, may be subject to the Swedish Land Code (*jordabalken (1970:994)*).[521] Transfer of immovable property (real estate) is further subject to certain legal formalities under Swedish law. The purchase contract for such transfer must be in writing and contain the following information:[522]

– the names of the seller and the buyer;
– the name of the real estate as registered with the Swedish Land Registry (*Lantmäteriet*);[523]
– an explicit transfer of the real estate;
– the purchase price.

The transfer will also require registration with the Swedish Land Registry within three months of the execution of the sale.[524]

253. With regard to facilities management services, such services will generally be provided by the proprietor of such facility, who in turn may outsource such services to one or several subcontractors. In terms of co-location or storage facilities, perhaps the most important aspects of a facilities management agreement will be network access and capacity of the facilities in terms of cooling and power along with the level of security within the facilities. It is rather common for such agreements to contain strict provisions on the security of the facilities and, for example, explicit wordings to ensure that a supplier of storage facilities is responsible for maintaining a certain level of security within the premises. In some cases, the supplier will be liable for incidents which would normally be considered as force majeure events (such as fire, floods, etc.) to the extent that such incidents could have been avoided by implementing adequate pre-emptive security measures.

521. Chapters 7–12 specifically governs leasing of premises (or parts thereof).
522. Chapter 4 Art. 1 Land Code. *See also* Folke Grauers, *Fastighetsköp* (Lund: Juristförlaget i Lund, 2006), 45.
523. www.lantmateriet.se/.
524. Chapter 20 Arts 1 and 2 Land Code.

Chapter 7. Network Services

254. Network services are the foundation of a networked computing environment. Generally, network services are installed on one or more servers to provide shared resources to client computers (LAN,[525] WAN,[526] etc.). Except for the Electronic Communications Act (*lag (2003:389) om elektronisk kommunikation*), which is the regulatory framework for electronic communications in Sweden, there is no specific legislation regarding the commercial service aspect of Network Services Contracts.

255. The main aspects for the customer in a network services agreement is to ensure a high quality of availability and service, which of course is closely linked to the network capacity of the service provider. Hence, service availability as well as specific service quality criteria will regularly be included in a Service Level Agreement which forms a part of the network services agreement. Fees are usually connected to usage of the network services, and could be based on an hourly, weekly, or monthly basis. Fixed subscription fees, which may include a certain level of usage, are also common. As in the case for other long-term service contracts, incentives in relation to the service levels are a central issue in network services contracts. Such incentives would generally consist of monetary penalties in relation to service level defaults. The main service level is of course availability (uptime) of the service. It should also be noted that network services by their nature are more likely to be affected by force majeure events and that the force majeure clause will need to be carefully designed.

256. Finally, it should be noted that the providers of Network Services mainly rely on their own standard contracts and service levels. In that respect, it can be argued that communication services are more standardized than other deliverables within the ICT industry. Many service providers are very reluctant to negotiate their standard terms.

525. Local area network.
526. Wide area network.

Chapter 8. Government Contracts

257. Depending on the nature of a government contract and its value, such a contract may be subject to EU public procurement directives[527] and one of the Swedish public procurement Acts.[528] If this is the case, the awarding authority may be required to:

- Advertise the contract in the *Official Journal* of the EU and follow special procedures.
- Ensure that all bidders are treated equally and in accordance with the fundamental principles of transparency, mutual recognition and proportionality.

258. The public procurement Acts are applicable to the awarding of all contracts that are not expressively excluded from their scope. This means that this legislation will also apply to the awarding of contracts where the contract value does not reach the thresholds for application of the EU public procurement directives. In such cases, however, the rules are less strict than those applicable to contracts which exceed the thresholds. For example, no advertisement in the *Official Journal* is required and advertisement in a publicly accessible database is sufficient.

259. To the extent that they are applicable, the EU public procurement rules are likely to have a significant impact on the:

- Timing of the pre-contract procedure.
- Award criteria adopted.
- Duration of the government contract.

260. A specific element of government contracts is the fact that the awarding authority will unilaterally, as a part of the tender request information, dictate a large number of the terms and conditions in the contract. The opportunity for suppliers to negotiate such terms in the government contract is often very limited, which means that the supplier must consider whether any legally or commercially unsatisfactory terms should have an impact on the pricing offered in the tender.

---

527. Directive 2014/24/EU of the European Parliament and of the Council of 26 February 2014 on public procurement and repealing Directive 2004/18/EC, Directive 2014/25/EU of the European Parliament and of the Council of 26 February 2014 on procurement by entities operating in the water, energy, transport and postal services sectors and repealing Directive 2004/17/EC and Directive 2014/23/EU of the European Parliament and of the Council of 26 February 2014 on the award of concession contracts.

528. *Lag (2016:1145) om offentlig upphandling, lag (2016:1146) om upphandling inom försörjningssektorerna* or *lag (2015:1147) om upphandling av koncessioner.*

Part IV. Electronic Transactions

Chapter 1. Legal Status of Electronic Transactions

§1. Contracts

261. Swedish contract law builds upon the principles of autonomy of will and freedom of contract. Once a contract is concluded, the principle of *pacta sunt servanda* applies. As common in other jurisdictions, a contract is legally established when a consensus is reached between two parties regarding the essential elements of the contract.[529]

262. Unlike other European civil law countries, such as Germany with its Bürgerliches Gesetzbuch (BGB), Sweden has not codified its civil law, and the statutory provisions dealing with sales of goods and services are spread over several different Acts.

The main statute for Swedish contract law is the Contracts Act (*lag (1915:218) om avtal och andra rättshandlingar på förmögenhetsrättens område*). It comprises forty-one sections and mainly deals with the formation of a contract, rules on representation, and the grounds for invalidity of certain legal acts. It does not stipulate any rules regarding performance under a contract or remedies for breach of contract. These are to be found in other legislation, such as the Sales of Goods Act (*köplag (1990:931)*), that deals with delivery of goods, balance of risk, quality of the goods, remedies in the event of delay in delivery or for defective goods (including damages) and remedies for breach of contract by either party.

In addition, the Consumer Sales Act (*konsumentköplag (1990:932)*), the Consumer Services Act (*konsumenttjänstlag (1985:716)*) and the Consumer Credit Act (*konsumentkreditlag (2010:1846)*),[530] as well as the Act on Terms of Contract between Undertakings (*lag (1984:292) om avtalsvillkor mellan näringsidkare*) and the Act on Terms of Contract in Consumer Relations (*lag (1994:1512) om särskilda avtalsvillkor i konsumentförhållanden*), cover provisions regarding enforcement of a contract, potentially invalid contract terms and conditions, and other requirements

529. Jan Ramberg & Christina Ramberg, *Allmän avtalsrätt*, 6th edn (Stockholm: Nordstedts Juridik AB, 2002), 101 et seq.

530. The Act transposes Directive 2008/48/EC of the European Parliament and of the Council of 23 April 2008 on credit agreements for consumers and repealing Council Directive 87/102/EEC; and replaced the earlier in force Consumer Credit Act (*konsumentkreditlag (1992:830)*).

for specific contracts. Although these Acts mainly apply in consumer-business relationships, they often serve as guidelines for interpreting agreements between two businesses as well.

I. Formation of a Contract

263. In general, a contract is legally established when an offer to enter into a contract is accepted by the recipient. In other words, a consensus concerning the essential elements of a contract has to be reached by the contracting parties.

Though section 1 Swedish Contracts Act refers to other ways of concluding a contract ('from any other custom'),[531] the offer-acceptance model is still the prevailing thought on the Swedish market.[532]

264. According to the Contracts Act (section 1), the offer (as well as the acceptance) is binding for the offeror unless otherwise stated, that is the offer cannot be revoked after it has reached the offeree. This general principle (*löftesprincipen*) differs from the principle of contracts only being binding once both parties agree (*kontraktsprincipen*), as applied in the UK or the US.[533]

Offers also have to be distinguished from invitations to tender if they are addressed to a larger group of people. There are no formal requirements on what can constitute an offer; but traditionally, it must contain the object of the contract, as well as quantity and quality of the goods.[534]

The time spans stipulated by law (i.e., if nothing is specified in the offer) can differ depending on the form of the offer. If the offer is made in a letter the offer is binding for a reasonable time, which is 'such period of time as, at the time of the offer, the offeror could reasonably have estimated to be required'. When calculating this time, account should be paid to the message reaching the recipient in due time, leaving reasonable time for consideration for the offeree, and the reply not being delayed.[535] Oral offers must be accepted immediately, unless otherwise specified.[536]

The acceptance must reflect the offer. If it adds, restricts or includes reservations to the original offer, it will be considered a new offer.[537] Traditionally, the acceptance does not have to be explicit or in writing; acceptance by action (*konkludent handlande*) or by performance are considered valid expressions of intent to conclude a contract.

---

531. Section 1 Contracts Act: 'The provisions of the aforementioned sections shall apply unless the contrary may be inferred from the offer or the reply, from commercial practice, or from any other custom.'
532. Ramberg & Ramberg, 78.
533. In some cases, the principle of contract also applies in Swedish law, for example, for real estate purchases. *See* Ramberg & Ramberg, 84.
534. Carlson, 224.
535. Section 3 Contracts Act.
536. Section 3 para. 2 Contracts Act.
537. Section 6 Contracts Act.

265. Due to the freedom of contract and the absence of general form requirements (with a few exceptions mentioned below), both emails and any other forms of electronic messages, including SMS and chat messages, have been considered valid offers and acceptances.

II. Grounds for Invalidity

266. Besides typical grounds for invalidity and lack of consent, such as duress,[538] fraud[539] and usury,[540] the Swedish Contracts Act also contains provisions for mistake in section 32. The law distinguishes between mistakes concerning the content of an offer or an acceptance (paragraph 1, *förklaringsmisstag*) and mistakes in the transmission of the offer or acceptance (paragraph 2, *befordringsfel*). In both cases, the mistakes only result in invalidity if the other party realized or should have realized the mistake. In other words, even if a mistake occurred the sender is still bound by it if the receiver acted in good faith.

Both types of mistake have been discussed with regards to electronic messages. In relation to mistakes in transmissions, the law refers to the situation that, where a statement of intent which has been forwarded by telegram or transmitted orally through a messenger, has been distorted due to a telegraphic error or an inaccurate rendition by the messenger. It is questionable if electronic messages can be distorted during the transmission without the receiver noticing; for example, most mistakes will render the message completely unreadable, so it only consists of strings of symbols. In addition, distortions in the sender's or receiver's electronic device do not constitute errors in transmission. For these reasons, the application of section 32 paragraph 2 for electronic transactions is probably limited.[541]

Mistakes about the content of an expression are, however, possible when it comes to electronic messages, so the general rule of section 32 paragraph 2 Swedish Contracts Act applies, binding the sender to her or his statement unless the receiver noticed or should have noticed the mistake.

267. In this regard, one can also discuss Article 11(2) Directive on Electronic Commerce, which stipulates an obligation for service providers to make available 'appropriate, effective and accessible technical' measures that allow the user 'to identify and correct input errors, prior to the placing of the order'. It can be argued that this could lead to users not being bound by input errors and mistakes when ordering if the service provider did not introduce appropriate technical means to correct them.[542] This potential effect of Article 11 was, however, not taken into consideration when transposing the Directive on Electronic Commerce; and sanctions

538. Sections 28 and 29 Contracts Act.
539. Section 30 Contracts Act.
540. Section 31 Contracts Act.
541. *See* Ramberg & Ramberg, 125; and Christina Hultmark, *Elektronisk handel och avtalsrätt* (Stockholm: Norstedts Juridik, 1997), 56.
542. Ramberg & Ramberg, 122; Christina Hultmark Ramberg, 'The E-commerce Directive and Formation of Contract in a Comparative Perspective', *European Law Review* 26(5) (2001): 429–450.

are restricted to orders by the Patent and Market Court (*Patent- och marknadsdomstolen*),[543] and do not include any effects from a civil law point of view.

III. Form Requirements

268. In general, Swedish contract law does not stipulate any form requirements in order for contracts to gain legal effect. Corresponding expressions of intent are, in other words, sufficient for the conclusion of a contract. There are, however, two exceptions to this rule. First, the parties can agree on certain form requirements and second, the law may stipulate a specific form, such as for real estate agreements as well as within the field of family law. The difference between the two exceptions lies in the fact that the latter requirements are mandatory, and cannot be disregarded by the parties, whereas the former are part of the freedom of contract principle.[544]

269. The two main form requirements include a document having to be in writing and/or requiring a signature. The legal effects of a missing form requirement can range from invalidity of the contract or an obligation for one party to fulfil the requirement, to invalidity against third parties (e.g., the creditor, authorities, etc.).[545]

270. As the Directive on Electronic Commerce allows for exceptions regarding contracts that create or transfer rights in real estate, though not counting rental rights,[546] the Swedish legislator decided not to remove form requirements for the purchase of real property. Therefore Chapter 4 section 1 Land Code (*jordabalken (1970:994)*) still requires the 'drawing up of a document of purchase signed by the seller and buyer'.

In addition, Sweden did not change the form requirements regarding the purchase of tenant-ownership apartments (*bostadsrätter*)[547] nor regarding time-shared real property. As the regulation on rental contracts does not explicitly stipulate that a document has to be in writing,[548] no change was made to Chapter 12 section 2 Land Code (*jordabalken*) in this regard.

271. When transposing the Directive on Electronic Commerce, Sweden changed the rules for consumer credits, which required the credit agreement to be in writing and signed by the consumer.[549] It allowed for advanced electronic signatures in

543. Previously the Market Court (*Marknadsdomstolen*).
544. Ramberg & Ramberg, 125 et seq.
545. *Ibid.*
546. Article 9(2) point a Directive on Electronic Commerce.
547. The Swedish system of ownership of apartments is mainly built upon housing cooperatives (*bostadsrättsföreningar*), and the fact that individuals own a right to inhabit an apartment for an unlimited time, as members of the cooperative.
548. A tenancy agreement shall be drawn up in writing *if* the landlord or tenant so requests.
549. Section 9 Consumer Credit Act.

accordance with section 2 of the previously in force Act on Qualified Electronic Signatures (*lag (2000:832) om kvalificerade elektroniska signaturer*).[550] With the latest amendments to the Consumer Credit Act, however, any formal requirements have been taken away.[551] In other words, no signature is required anymore, consumer credit contracts only have to be documented and contain the information required by the Consumer Rights Directive. According to section 8 Consumer Credit Act, the information has to be provided in the standardized European consumer credit form.

The other statute amended with regards to its form requirements was the Financial Instruments Trading Act (*lag (1991:980) om handel med finansiella instrument*). Its Chapter 3 section 1 was clarified to the extent that 'written' now entails a document, which is accessible to the parties in a readable and lasting format.

272. The Swedish legislators as well as legal academia distinguish between the form requirements of 'written form' and 'handwritten signature'. 'Written' can, at least in the majority of cases, include electronic documents and therefore the term would be equivalent to non-oral expression of intent, instead of the opposite of paper.[552] The reasons for the form requirements have, however, to be taken into consideration. If a paper document is needed in order to secure evidence or if the form requirement stems from traditions and historical reasons, electronic means might not be possible. The term 'handwritten signature', however, will in most cases require some sort of physical signing, and therefore exclude electronic signatures. Again, this will depend on the reason behind the requirement,[553] for example the presence of witnesses for somebody's last will.

Swedish law requires handwritten signatures on very few occasions.[554] Examples include the already above stated real estate contracts,[555] transfer of the dwelling in owner-occupied housing associations,[556] and family related legal matters, such as pre-marital agreements,[557] and last wills.[558] In these examples, electronic means will not be possible, unless explicitly stated in the Act.

IV. Electronic Contracts

273. Sweden does not have any specific legislation for contracts that are concluded via electronic means. The Swedish Contracts Act applies to contracts in

550. *See* more on electronic signatures in Ch. 2 *infra*.
551. Government Bill (*Proposition*) 2009/10:242, 'Ny konsumentkreditlag', 60.
552. Ministry Publications Series (Ds) 2001:13, 'E-handelsdirektivet – genomförande av direktivet 2000/31/EG om vissa rättsliga aspekter på informationssamhällets tjänster', 104–105; Ministry Publications Series (Ds) 2003:29, 'FORMEL – Formkrav och elektronisk kommunikation', 12.
553. Ministry Publications Series (Ds) 2003:29, 88.
554. Government Bill (*Proposition*) 2001/02:150, 'Lag om elektronisk handel och andra informationssamhällets tjänster, m.m.', 78; Ministry Publications Series (Ds) 2001:13, 103; Ramberg & Ramberg, 130.
555. Chapter 4 s. 1 Land Code.
556. Chapter 6 s. 4 Act on Owner-occupied housing (*bostadsrättslag (1991:614)*).
557. Chapter 7 s. 3 Marriage Code (*äktenskapsbalk (1987:230)*).
558. Chapter 10 s. 1 Inheritance Code (*ärvdabalk (1958:637)*).

general, irrelevant of the means of transmission. All types of contracts are therefore binding, no matter whether they are concluded orally, in writing, on paper or via electronic messages.[559]

Also the previously mentioned Consumer Sales Act, Consumer Services Act and Consumer Credit Act, as well as the Act on Terms of Contract between Undertakings and the Act on Terms of Contract in Consumer Relations apply to all types of contracts, irrespective of how they are concluded, orally, in paper or by any electronic means, and there is no specific regulation which applies purely to electronic contracts.

274. Article 9 Directive on Electronic Commerce obliges all Member States to 'ensure that their legal system allows contracts to be concluded by electronic means'. In particular this means to 'ensure that the legal requirements applicable to the contractual process neither create obstacles for the use of electronic contracts nor result in such contracts being deprived of legal effectiveness and validity on account of their having been made by electronic means'.

As the Swedish legal system only stipulates form requirements in a limited number of situations, Article 9 did not lead to any major changes in Swedish contract law. In the Government Bill leading to the implementation of the Electronic Commerce Act,[560] the Government suggested that the requirement of 'in writing' mainly means 'not orally' and that the contract has to be in some sort of 'permanent and readable format'.

§2. Electronic Documents

I. General Framework

275. A report by the Swedish Ministry of Finance and the Government Offices from 2003 dealt with the question of the legal recognition of electronic documents. The report included a review of about approximately 2,000 statutes in all areas of law, and investigated to what extent electronic documents were explicitly mentioned or excluded due to certain requirements.[561]

One of the conclusions of the report was that the majority of the statutes (around 1,200) do not prevent electronic means, as certain terms and definitions do not per se exclude the use of electronic means. For example, the terms *application, registration, message, request* are not equivalent to paper documents and therefore allow for electronic means.

Around 190 of the statutes were considered to contain potential obstacles to electronic means, and therefore require amendments in order to allow for a technological neutral application. The remainder of the Swedish laws do not require any changes at the moment.

559. Government Bill (*Proposition*) 2001/02:150, 37–38.
560. *Ibid.*
561. Ministry Publications Series (Ds) 2003:29.

276. The report also concluded that the introduction of a general rule stipulating the legal effectiveness of electronic documents or their equivalency to paper-based documents was not to be recommended, as it would lead to more confusion. By not specifically mentioning electronic means, the implication could then be that they are not admissible.[562]

277. Swedish public authorities are, in fact, encouraged to promote the use of secure and efficient electronic exchange of information among public administrations.[563] Larger agencies are even expected to handle orders of goods and services electronically.[564] The authority overseeing the financial activities of public authorities – the Swedish National Financial Management Authority (*Ekonomistyrningsverket*)[565] – has issued complementary guidelines on the information exchange between public agencies.[566]

II. Electronic Invoicing

278. A specific type of electronic documents, namely electronic invoices, has been used in Swedish businesses for a long time. Despite a generally high IT usage within Swedish companies, the overall use of electronic invoices is not yet that wide-spread.[567] In 2016, only 12% of all invoices were issued directly through an electronic system. When including pdf invoices in the term 'electronic invoice', a third of all Swedish companies were using e-invoicing in 2016.[568] The techniques that have been employed include EDI-invoice,[569] e-invoice, self-billing, invoice-files via email, online services (web-EDI, etc.) and scanning of paper invoices.[570] Standard contracts are often used in order to ensure interoperability between the computer system of the seller and that of the buyer.

562. *Ibid.*, 43.
563. Section 2 Ordinance on the Electronic Information Exchange by Public Authorities (*förordning (2003:770) om statliga myndigheters elektroniska informationsutbyte*).
564. Section 3 Ordinance.
565. www.esv.se.
566. Ekonomistyrningsverkets föreskrifter och allmänna råd till förordning (2003:770) om statliga myndigheters elektroniska informationsutbyte, 13 Jun. 2018.
567. One of the government initiatives that supports small and medium-sized companies in their digitalisation efforts is organized by Swedish Agency for Economic and Regional Growth (*Tillväxtverket*) tillvaxtverket.se/english/digitalization.html.
568. Swedish Agency for Economic and Regional Growth (*Tillväxtverket*), *Åtgärder för en ökad användning i företagen av elektroniska fakturor och kvitton* (Dnr 4.1.6-Ä 2016-000911), 28 Feb. 2017, tillvaxtverket.se/download/18.7b2b44bc15a9374dc0ead572/1489578353922/%C3%84%20 2016-000911-03%20Slutrapp%20e-faktura%20och%20kvitton.pdf%20262073_1_1.pdf.
569. EDI stands for Electronic Data Interchange.
570. The Swedish Alliance for Electronic Business (*Nätverket för Elektroniska Affärer*/NEA), 'Report on electronic invoices (*GEAs rapport Elektroniska fakturor*)', October 2006, www.nea.nu. *See also* 'Good Practices in the adoption and promotion of e-invoicing in Europe: An ACCA Discussion Paper', prepared for Activity Group 2 of the European Multistakeholder Forum on e-invoicing, August 2012, www.nea.nu/wp-content/uploads/2013/09/Activity-2-Consultation-Report1.pdf, 13.

The legal framework that applies to invoices, both electronic and paper-based, and accounting in general includes the Swedish Bookkeeping Act (*bokföringslag (1999:1078)*), the Swedish Companies Act (*aktiebolagslag (2005:551)*), the VAT Act (*mervärdeskattelag (1994:200)*) and the Tax Procedure Act (*skatteförfarandelag (2011:1244)*).[571]

279. Chapter 7 Swedish Bookkeeping Act deals with the archiving of accounting information, including electronic invoices. According to Chapter 7 section 1, accounting information shall be archived either:

(1) in normal readable format (document);
(2) in micro format; or
(3) in any other form that can be read, listened to or otherwise comprehended only using technical aids.

According to Chapter 7 section 2 Bookkeeping Act, accounting information shall be stored for seven years. Computer equipment that is necessary in order to retrieve this accounting information shall be accessible in Sweden during this time.

In 2012, the VAT Act was amended to include archiving provisions for invoices in general, including electronic invoices. According to the new Chapter 11a VAT Act the authenticity of the invoice as well as the integrity of the content have to be ensured during the period it is stored (section 2). In addition, the invoice has to be readable during this time. According to Chapter 11a section 2 the term 'authenticity' refers to ensuring the identity of the supplier, the service provider or the issuer of the invoice.

280. The Directive 2001/115/EC amending Directive 77/388/EEC with a view to simplifying, modernizing and harmonizing the conditions laid down for invoicing in respect of value added tax (VAT) (hereinafter 'Directive on Electronic Invoices') was transposed into Swedish national law in 2003 by amending the Bookkeeping Act, the VAT Act and the previous in force Tax Payment Act. Council Directive 2006/112/EC of 28 November 2006 on the common system of VAT was transposed into Swedish law in 2007 by amending the VAT Act and the Tax Procedure Act.

Following the 2003 amendments, a new section 17a was introduced in Chapter 1 of the VAT Act defining the term 'transmission of invoices or other documents electronically' which correlates with Article 2(2) point (e) Directive on Electronic Invoices. This provision was amended in 2012 and now defines electronic invoices as invoices that are 'issued and received in an electronic format'. The VAT Act also includes a provision that electronic invoices only may be issued if the receiver has approved it.[572]

---

571. The Act replaced the previously in force Tax Payment Act (*skattebetalningslag (1997:483)*).
572. Chapter 11 s. 6 VAT Act.

The VAT Act does not state any additional requirements regarding invoices that are being sent electronically. This means that even other methods than advanced electronic signatures and EDI have been accepted from a security point of view.[573]

In 2012 a provision was introduced in the VAT Act that allows public authorities in another EU Member State immediate electronic access to invoices stored by a business if the VAT has to be paid in that country (Chapter 11a section 3).[574]

281. The legal framework with regards to electronic invoices seems rather undisputed at this stage. The discussions rather circuit about which standards should be used for electronic invoices. The Swedish Alliance for Electronic Business (*Nätverket för Elektroniska Affärer* – NEA),[575] the Swedish National Board of Trade (*Kommerskollegium*)[576] as well as the Swedish Banker's Association (*Svenska Bankföreningen*)[577] are all involved in different initiatives. At the moment, many standards are based on EDI, e.g., UN/EDIFACT standard messages, and XML at the moment.[578] These discussions will, however, be affected by the implementation of an EU e-invoicing standard for the public sector.[579]

282. In 2014 the EU adopted Directive 2014/55/EU of the European Parliament and of the Council of 16 April 2014 on electronic invoicing in public procurement. The goal of the Directive was to establish a European standard for electronic invoicing. The Directive was transposed into Swedish law by adoption of the Act on electronic invoicing in public procurement (*lag (2018:1277) om elektroniska fakturor till följd av offentlig upphandling*). Swedish public authorities were, however, already expected to use electronic invoicing according to section 21f Regulation on Public Authorities' Accounting (*förordning (2000:606) om myndigheters bokföring*).

The standard that was mainly used for e-invoices by public authorities was Svefaktura, developed by Single Face To Industry,[580] a forum lead by SALAR (*SKL*). Since November 2018, authorities are also required to use the PEPPOL (Pan-European Public Procurement On-Line)[581] infrastructure to send and receive electronic messages. With the adoption of Directive on Electronic Invoicing in Public Procurement, authorities within the EU are required to use the standard CEN/TC

573. Report on electronic invoices, 55–56.
574. *See also* Government Bill (*Proposition*) 2011/12:94, 'Nya faktureringsregler för mervärdeskatt m.m.', 1.
575. www.nea.nu.
576. www.kommers.se.
577. www.swedishbankers.se. In Sweden many B2C services regarding electronic invoices are provided by banks; *see* Good Practices in the adoption and promotion of e-invoicing in Europe: An ACCA Discussion Paper, 20.
578. 'Good Practices in the adoption and promotion of e-invoicing in Europe: An ACCA Discussion Paper', 22 and 24. *See also* the EU initiative 'Connecting Europe Facility Building Blocks' ec.europa.eu/cefdigital/wiki/display/CEFDIGITAL/eInvoicing, accessed 15 Jan. 2020. UN/EDIFACT stands for the United Nations rules for Electronic Data Interchange for Administration, Commerce and Transport.
579. *See* next paragraph.
580. www.sfti.se.
581. peppol.eu.

434 – Electronic Invoicing,[582] which was developed by the CEN.[583] Based on this, the Agency for Digital Government in Sweden (DIGG) recommends companies and public authorities to use PEPPOL BIS Billing 3 in order to fulfil the requirements of the Act on electronic invoicing in public procurement.[584]

§3. Evidence

283. In Swedish law, there are no exclusionary rules regarding evidence.[585] Any evidence is therefore admissible in court.[586] The procedural law rules are laid down in the Swedish Code of Judicial Procedure (*rättegångsbalk (1942:740)*), which covers both criminal and civil procedural law.

In accordance with this principle, proving that a contract exists can be done in any possible way, with the exception of contracts that require a certain form. The burden of proof is usually placed on the party that has the best possibility to secure the evidence.[587]

582. standards.cen.eu/dyn/www/f?p=204:32:0::::FSP_ORG_ID,FSP_LANG_ID:1883209,25&cs=126F1BDBC8D6D6141F550EB578B4A9CF4, accessed 4 Jan. 2020. The standard differs from the previous Swedish standard only slightly.
583. CEN is one of three European Standardization Organizations (together with CENELEC and ETSI) that are responsible for developing and defining voluntary standards at European level, cen.eu.
584. For an overview in English, *see* the website of the European Commission, ec.europa.eu/cefdigital/wiki/display/CEFDIGITAL/eInvoicing+in+Sweden, accessed 4 Jan. 2020. For more information in Swedish, *see* the website of the Agency for Digital Government: www.digg.se/nationella-digitala-tjanster/e-handel-och-e-faktura/obligatorisk-e-faktura-till-offentlig-sektor, accessed 4 Jan. 2020.
585. Chapter 35 s. 1 Code of Judicial Procedure (*rättegångsbalk (1942:740)*).
586. Carlson, 230.
587. Hultmark, 87 et seq.

Chapter 2. Regulation of Electronic Signatures and Certification Services

§1. Legislative Framework

I. General Statement

284. The original Directive 1999/93/EC of 13 December 1999 on a Community framework for electronic signatures (hereinafter 'Directive on Electronic Signatures') was transposed into Swedish legislation through the Act on Qualified Electronic Signatures (*lag (2000:832) om kvalificerade elektroniska signaturer*). As the Act mainly stipulates rules regarding certificate providers established in Sweden and issuance of qualified certificates to the public, it was suggested that 'qualified' be included in its name.[588] The Directive further led to the enactment of the Ordinance on Qualified Electronic Signatures (*förordning (2000:833) om kvalificerade electroniska signaturer*) and the Ordinance on the financing of the National Post and Telecom's operations (*förordning (2003:767) om finansiering av Post- och telestyrelsens verksamhet*).

In 2014, the EU replaced the Directive on Electronic Signatures with Regulation (EU) No. 910/2014 of the European Parliament and of the Council of 23 July 2014 on electronic identification and trust services for electronic transactions in the internal market and repealing Directive 1999/93/EC (hereinafter 'eIDAS Regulation'). The two main goals of the regulation are to create a European internal market for electronic Trust Services (eTS) and ensure that people and businesses can use their national electronic identifications schemes (eIDs) to access public services in other EU Member States.[589]

As a result of the new EU regulation, the Swedish Act on Qualified Electronic Signatures was repealed, and a new Act with Additional Provisions to the EU Regulation on Electronic Identification (*lag (2016:561) med kompletterande bestämmelser till EU:s förordning om elektronisk identifiering*) was adopted in order to, *inter alia*, assign a supervisory authority and introduce rules on supervision of providers of trusted services.[590] A few articles in the eIDAS Regulation did not require any additional national rules, such as temporary suspension of a qualified certificate for electronic signature (Article 28(5)) or trust infrastructure (Article 17(5)) as neither the suspensions nor the model of a trust infrastructure by a supervisory authority are being used in Sweden.[591]

588. Government Bill (*Proposition*) 1999/2000:117, 'Lag om kvalificerade elektroniska signaturer, m.m.', 34.
589. *See* for more information the website of the European Commission, ec.europa.eu/digital-single-market/en/trust-services-and-eid, accessed 5 Jan. 2020.
590. Government Bill (*Proposition*) 2015/16:72, ' Kompletterande bestämmelser till EU:s förordning om elektronisk identifiering', 42.
591. *Ibid.*

II. Definitions

285. The eIDAS Regulation is broader in scope than the previously in force Directive on Electronic Signatures. Though the Regulation integrates the rules of the Directive, it also encompasses electronic identification and trust services (in Swedish: *betrodda tjänster*) in general, which includes electronic signatures (eSignature), electronic seals (eSeal), time stamping (eTimestamp), registered electronic delivery (eDelivery) and website authentication (Website Authentication Certificates/WACs).

According to Article 3 point 10 eIDAS Regulation, electronic signature means 'data in electronic form which is attached to or logically associated with other data in electronic form and which is used by the signatory to sign'.[592] One of the main differences in this regard is, therefore, that e-signatures are now regarded as a means to express consent on the data by a natural person. According to Article 3 point (9) eIDAS Regulation a signatory is 'a natural person who creates an electronic signature'.[593] Identification of the sender and the addressee can be done electronically or by notified eID means under the regulation.[594]

In adapting to the new EU framework, Sweden changed the wording of electronic signature in its legislation. Previously, in accordance with the Directive on Electronic Signatures the Swedish term '*elektronisk signatur*' was used in the legislation. This was changed now into '*elektronisk underskrift*' in order to emphasize the signing process and adapt the terminology more to everyday use of the language. The government suggested, therefore, to replace the term '*elektronisk signatur' with 'elektronisk underskrift*' in all relevant legislation.[595]

286. With the adoption of the eIDAS Regulation, legal persons cannot receive certificates for electronic signatures anymore, but have to use electronic seals whose aim is to ensure the integrity and origin of data.[596] According to Article 3 point 25 eIDAS Regulation, electronic seal means 'data in electronic form, which is attached

592. In contrast, the previous in force Directive included an authentication element according to Art. 2(1): electronic signature 'means data in electronic form which are attached to or logically associated with other electronic data and which serve as a method of authentication'. The relevant Swedish legislation included both authentication and integrity requirements; according to s. 2 of the previously in force Swedish Act on Qualified Electronic Signatures, electronic signatures were 'data in electronic form attached to or logically associated with other electronic data, and used to verify that the content originates from the alleged issuer, and has not been altered'.

593. This is in strong contrast to the previous Art. 2(3) Directive on Electronic Signatures, where signatory meant 'a person who holds a signature creation device and acts either on her or his own behalf or on behalf of the natural or legal person or entity she or he represents.'

594. The conformity assessment report is used to show that the identification process set by the qualified trust service provider meets the requirements of the regulation and the supervisory authority. *See* European Commission, Questions & Answers on Trust Services under eIDAS, 29 Feb. 2016, ec.europa.eu/digital-single-market/en/news/questions-answers-trust-services-under-eidas, accessed 7 Jan. 2020.

595. Government Bill (*Proposition*) 2015/16:72, ' Kompletterande bestämmelser till EU:s förordning om elektronisk identifiering', 53.

596. European Commission, Questions & Answers on Trust Services under eIDAS.

to or logically associated with other data in electronic form to ensure the latter's origin and integrity'. The seal ensures origin and integrity of data, but is not an electronic signature of the legal person.[597]

An eTimestamp proves that a document existed at a specific time (Article 3 point 33). According to Article 3 point 36 eIDAS Regulation, eDelivery is a service that permits the electronic transfer of data between companies, public authorities and private individuals and provides proof of sending and receiving the data as well as protection against the risk of loss, theft, damage or unauthorized alterations. WACs are electronic certificates that are issued to prove to users that a natural or legal person owns a website (Article 3 point 38) and help avoid data phishing.

287. The eIDAS Regulation generally distinguishes between qualified and non-qualified trust services. Qualified means that a trust service providers fulfils all the requirements of the eIDAS Regulation. Qualified trust service providers are included on the European Commission's Trusted List Browser,[598] and can use the EU trust mark to identify themselves.[599] Non-qualified services have not gone through an official process to ensure that they comply with the eIDAS Regulation. So, while they are not less trustworthy, they have a weaker legal certainty and technical security.

Electronic signatures and electronic seals can be advanced or qualified. An advanced electronic signature (Article 3 point 11) is one that meets the requirements of Article 26 eIDAS Regulation. Qualified electronic signature means that the signature was created by a qualified creation device and is based on a qualified certificate (Article 3 point 12).

According to Article 26 eIDAS Regulation, an advanced electronic signature is 'an electronic signature' that:

- is uniquely linked to a signatory;
- is capable of identifying the signatory;
- is created using means that are under the signatory's sole control; and
- is linked to other electronic data in such a way that any alteration to the said data can be detected.[600]

Qualified electronic signatures have to meet the requirements in Annex I of the eIDAS Regulation, pursuant to Article 28.

597. *Ibid.*
598. The Trusted List Browser is a tool to browse the national Trusted Lists and the European List of Trusted Lists (LOTL), webgate.ec.europa.eu/tl-browser/#/, accessed 15 Jan. 2020.
599. European Commission, *EU trust mark*, ec.europa.eu/digital-single-market/en/eu-trust-mark, accessed 15 Jan. 2020.
600. The definition is more or less the same as in the previous Directive on Electronic Signatures. The most commonly used electronic identifications on the Swedish market can be considered advanced electronic signatures; *see* Government Bill (*Proposition*) 2015/16:72, ' Kompletterande bestämmelser till EU:s förordning om elektronisk identifiering', 53.

As mentioned above, some legislation might allow for electronic means or electronic signatures in general, some might stipulate the use of a specific type of electronic signature, though the latter is less common.[601] When enacting the Act with Additional Provisions to the EU Regulation on Electronic Identification, several Swedish statutes that included explicit references to the previous in force Act on Qualified Electronic Signatures had to be amended. These included the Social Insurance Code (*socialförsäkringsbalken*), the Act on Foundations (*stiftelselagen (1994:1220)*), and the Annual Report Act (*årsredovisningslagen (1995:1554)).*[602]

Trust services (Article 3 point 17), trust service providers (Article 3 point 20), electronic time stamps (Article 3 point 34) and certificates for website authentication (Article 3 point 39) can be qualified. Chapter III section 3 of the eIDAS Regulation specifies the requirements for trust services (Articles 13–24), section 5 regulates electronic seals, section 6 electronic time stamps and section 8 website authentication.

§2. Electronic Identification

288. While there previously was no specific legislation that described the basic requirements for electronic identifications (eIDs) in Sweden, the adoption of the eIDAS Regulation introduced an EU-wide framework for businesses and consumers to identify who they are (identification process) and prove that they are who they say they are (authentication process). Since September 2018 it has also been mandatory to recognize notified eID systems from other EU countries.

The reason for the previous lack of a definition for eIDs in Swedish laws and regulations is that traditionally, Swedish eIDs have been issued by the private sector, mainly banking institutions and electronic communications providers.[603] Until 2011, eIDs were selected in a public procurement process, organized by the Swedish Legal, Financial and Administrative Services Agency (*Kammarkollegiet*).[604]

In 2011, the Swedish e-Identification Board (*E-legitimationsnämnden*)[605] was established as an authority under the Swedish Ministry of Enterprise, Energy and Communications.[606] Its task is to promote and coordinate electronic identification and electronic signatures for e-services provided by the public sector. The

601. *See* Ch. 1 §1 III *supra* (para. 271).
602. For a complete list, *see* (in Swedish) Government Bill (*Proposition*) 2015/16:72.
603. Despite or because of this most citizens and residents in Sweden have an eID. One of the largest providers of eIDs in Sweden, Finansiell ID-teknik BID AB, which is owned by seven banks, offers the eID BankID (bankid.com). According to their statistics, their number of users in 2018 was almost 8 million and the amount of times a BankID was used was 3.3 billion in 2018. There are three types of BankID, but the most common one (around 7 million users) is the mobile BankID which means the eID is stored in an app on the user's mobile phone or tablet device. *See* Government Official Report SOU 2019:14, 'Ett säkert statligt ID-kort – med e-legitimation', 136.
604. The Swedish Legal, Financial and Administrative Services Agency (*Kammarkollegiet*) is the responsible authority for the public procurement, *see* www.kammarkollegiet.se.
605. www.elegnamnden.se.
606. Ordinance with Instructions for the e-Identification Board (*förordning (2010:1497) med instruktion för E-legitimationsnämnden*).

e-Identification Board issued a regulatory framework that described the identify federation and technical specifications for eIDs in Sweden.[607] The goal was, *inter alia*, to develop a new infrastructure for eIDs in Sweden, and introduce a standardized identity assertion (based on the SAML standard). As the pilot EU framework STORK[608] was also based on SAML, this development hoped to increase cross-border interoperability.

With the adoption of the eIDAS Regulation, the EU established the eIDAS Network which consists of a number of interconnected eIDAS-Nodes, one per Member State. Each node can either request or provide cross-border authentication.[609] Connecting Europe Facility (CEF), a key EU funding instrument, supports and develops services that Member States can use when building their eIDAS-Nodes.[610] It also keeps a list of Member States' notified eID schemes under the eIDAS Regulation.[611] Sweden does not have a notified scheme at the moment; it does, however, use SAML 2.0 as its technical framework.[612] The e-Identification Board (*E-legitimationsnämnden*) is now a part of the Agency for Digital Government (DIGG), which is now the responsible authority for electronic identification. It is also the Single Point of Contact for Sweden.[613]

289. Any physical person with a Swedish personal identity number can obtain an eID. Legal persons can also use an eID, but it must be linked to a user with a Swedish personal identity number. A legal person as such cannot have an eID, but some companies offer eIDs for their employees – 'employment eIDs' (*e-tjänstelegitimation*).[614] 'Employment eIDs' have been used within the public sector for a while; for example, SITHS is a smart card solution with the Swedish healthcare sector.[615]

---

607. www.elegnamnden.se/regelverket11.4.77dbcb041438070e039a8b6.html, accessed 5 Apr. 2014.
608. STORK stands for Secure idenTity acrOss boRders linKed and aims at establishing a European eID Interoperability Platform that will allow citizens to establish e-relations across borders, just by using their national eID; www.eid-stork.eu.
609. CEF Digital, European Commission, *eID Documentation – What is eID*, ec.europa.eu/cefdigital/wiki/display/CEFDIGITAL/What+is+eID, accessed 6 Mar. 2020.
610. CEF Digital, European Commission, *eID Documentation – Background of eID*, ec.europa.eu/cefdigital/wiki/display/CEFDIGITAL/Background+of+eID, accessed 6 Mar. 2020.
611. CEF Digital, European Commission, *eID Documentation – Country overview*, ec.europa.eu/cefdigital/wiki/display/CEFDIGITAL/Country+overview, accessed 6 Mar. 2020.
612. Agency for Digital Government (DIGG), *Om e-legitimeringssystemet*, www.elegnamnden.se/elegitimeringssystemet/omelegitimeringssystemet.4.4498694515fe27cdbcf235.html, accessed 6 Mar. 2020.
613. CEF Digital, European Commission, *eID Documentation – Country overview*, ec.europa.eu/cefdigital/wiki/display/CEFDIGITAL/Country+overview, accessed 6 Mar. 2020.
614. Government Official Report SOU 2019:14, 'Ett säkert statligt ID-kort – med e-legitimation', 137; and Government Official Report SOU 2010:104, 'E-legitimationsnämnden och Svensk e-legitimation', 26.
615. SITHS (*Nationell identifieringstjänst*) is a national security solution for electronic identification and secure communication of information. The company Inera (inera.se), owned by the Swedish county councils, is responsible for the implementation. *See* more at www.inera.se/TJANSTER--PROJEKT/SITHS/, 5 Apr. 2014.

In order to create cooperation and trust in eIDs, the Swedish government developed a quality seal called Swedish eID (*Svensk e-legitimation*).[616] Based on the trust framework, the Agency for Digital Government (DIGG) assesses providers of eIDs in Sweden and assigns them different trust levels.

In March 2019, the Swedish government proposed a new act and ordinance on government identity documents with provisions for government identity cards and government electronic identification.[617] The government identity card is planned to include a government electronic identification, which can also be used to create an electronic signature. The suggestion is to issue the card and identification to Swedish citizens and Swedish residents aged 13 or over.[618] The report proposes the Swedish Police Authority as the issuing body and the storage of fingerprints and facial images on the government identity cards. The legislation is planned to enter into force on 1 January 2022, in order to allow the responsible authorities to prepare the transition.

§3. Technical and Organizational Framework in Sweden

290. The eIDAS Regulation distinguishes between three different levels of assurance (LoAs) defined by the electronic identification scheme. The LoAs refer to the degree of confidence that eID means provide in the claimed identity of a person taking into account processes, management activities, and technical controls implemented.[619] EU Regulation 2015/1502[620] mentions the minimum technical specifications and procedures for the different levels along with the different key elements (Annex I). The different LoAs offer a low, substantial or high degree of confidence in the claimed or asserted identity of a person; and refer to technical specifications, standards and procedures.

A low LoA refers to only a limited degree of confidence in the claimed identity of a person, and the assumption that a person possesses genuine evidence recognized by a Member State. A substantial LoA equals a substantial degree of confidence and requires, in addition to the low LoA requirements, the verification of the possession of evidence and a check of the evidence and if the evidence is genuine. The high LoA requires all of the previous mentioned as well as, e.g., the possession of a photo or biometric identification evidence, and a check of the claimed identity through a comparison with one or more physical characteristic; or that the eID is

616. *See* more details in §3 *infra* (para. 290).
617. Government Official Report SOU 2019:14, 'Ett säkert statligt ID-kort – med e-legitimation'. The report includes an English summary.
618. SOU 2019:14, 31.
619. EU Publication Office, 'Study on EID and Digital On-Boarding – Mapping and Analysis of Existing on-Boarding Bank Practices across the EU, Final Report' (2018), op.europa.eu:443/en/publication-detail/-/publication/8da08249-49cd-11e8-be1d-01aa75ed71a1/language-en/format-PDF, 18 et seq.
620. Commission Implementing Regulation (EU) 2015/1502 of 8 Sep. 2015 on setting out minimum technical specifications and procedures for assurance levels for electronic identification means pursuant to Art. 8(3) of Regulation (EU) No. 910/2014 of the European Parliament and of the Council on electronic identification and trust services for electronic transactions in the internal market.

issued on the basis of a notified electronic identification.[621] Article 6 eIDAS Regulation stipulates that Member States have to recognize other notified Member States' means that are qualified 'high' or 'substantial'.

291. The Swedish trust framework for the quality mark is regulated by Agency for Digital Government (DIGG). The framework is based on ISO/IEC 29115 and builds upon 4 different levels of trust.[622] Level 1 can be a user account that a person registers without proving their identity. This level is not included in the framework. Levels 2, 3 and 4 require multi-factor authentication.

There are three categories of authentication factors; 'something one knows' (codes such as passwords or one-time passwords and codes), 'something one is' (biometrics) and 'something one has' (e.g., computer, mobile phone or card). The basis of the Swedish trust framework is that codes are combined with possession of a stored data structure. An eID on trust levels 2 or 3 has to be based on a two-factor authentication, which consists of electronically stored information held by the user, as well as something the individual has to use to activate the eID. An example is an eID on a mobile phone which is activated through a pincode. Such eIDs can be issued after remote identification of the user which is described in detail in the framework.

An eID on level 4 is based on two-factor authentication as well and consists of a personal security module which the user has to have control over, and something that the user activates the module with. The device protects the data stored on the eID and is often found on a card. Activation is done with a code. Issuing eIDs on level 4 requires a personal visit of the user.

DIGG regards the Swedish trust level 3 to match the substantial LoA of the eIDAS Regulation, and trust level 4 to be equivalent to the high LoA. According to DIGG, both the LoAs of the eIDAS Regulation and the Swedish trust levels are based on the same international standard. Article 6 eIDAS Regulation is therefore applied in Sweden to comprise levels 3 and 4 of the Swedish trust framework.

The trust seal is not obligatory in Sweden and it is up to every provider to apply for the seal. At the moment, only two of the main four providers in Sweden have received the seal: AB Svenska Pass (trust level 4) and Freja eID+ (trust level 3). The more commonly used BankID/Mobilt BankID and Telia eID have not been assessed by DIGG but are considered to reach trust level 3. When it comes to employment eIDs, SITHS, e.g., has a trust seal (level 3).[623]

292. For trusted services besides eIDs, PTS is the responsible authority. PTS' guidelines for trusted services from 2017[624] describe the process to establish a provider of qualified trusted services, the requirements for non-qualified trust services,

621. *See* Regulation (EU) 2015/1502 for more details.

622. Agency for Digital Government (DIGG), ' Välj tillitsnivå inom eIDAS', www.elegnamnden.se/eidas/anpassaetjansttilleidas/valjtillitsnivainomeidas.4.4498694515fe27cdbcf1ff.html, accessed 11 Jan. 2020.

623. Agency for Digital Government (DIGG), *Om e-legitimeringssystemet.*

624. *See* for an overview, PTS, Betrodda tjänster enligt eIDAS, pts.se/sv/bransch/internet/betrodda-tjanster-eidas, accessed 15 Jan. 2020.

routines for incident reporting and the use of alternative standards to the ones suggested by the EU. The guidelines are both aimed at providers of qualified trust services and providers of non-qualified trust services.[625]

293. Conformity of qualified electronic signature creation devices with the requirements laid down in Annex II of the eIDAS Regulation shall be certified by appropriate public or private bodies designated by Member States (Article 30 eIDAS Regulation). In Sweden, the Swedish Civil Contingencies Agency[626] is assigned to issue specific regulation on security requirements, while the Swedish Defence Materiel Administration[627] certifies qualified electronic signature creation devices.[628]

The national accreditation body for Sweden is Swedac.[629] In accordance with the previously in force Directive,[630] Sweden introduced a voluntary accreditation scheme for certification bodies. The existing Technical Conformity Assessment Act (*lag (1992:1119) om teknisk kontroll*) already established a framework for a voluntary accreditation scheme. Accreditation is seen as a tool to create trust in the services that accredited bodies provide, which in turn creates trust in the certificates themselves, especially in an international context.[631] The 1992 Act was replaced in 2011 by the Act on Accreditation and Technical Conformity Assessment (*lag (2011:791) om ackreditering och teknisk kontroll*).[632] A conformity assessment body which wants to be accredited according to the eIDAS Regulation has to file an application with Swedac. The national accreditation authority then assesses whether the body fulfils the requirements of EU Regulation 765/2008[633] and the Act on Accreditation and Technical Conformity Assessment.

As the Swedish National Financial Management Authority (*Ekonomistyrningsverket/ESV*) works with e-commerce and s-sense, its mission was widened to

625. *See* more at, pts.se/eidas.
626. Myndigheten för samhällsskydd och beredskap (MSB), msb.se.
627. Försvarets materielverk (FMV/CSEC), fmv.se.
628. PTS, 'Vägledning För Betrodda Tjänster i Sverige Enligt EIDAS' (2017), No. 1650–9862, pts.se accessed 8 Jan. 2020; and Government Bill (Proposition) 2015/16:72, 'Kompletterande bestämmelser till EU:s förordning om elektronisk identifiering', 46.
629. www.swedac.se.
630. Article 3(2): 'Without prejudice to the provisions of paragraph 1, Member States may introduce or maintain voluntary accreditation schemes aiming at enhanced levels of certification-service provision. All conditions related to such schemes must be objective, transparent, proportionate and non-discriminatory.'
631. Government Bill (Proposition) 1999/2000:117, 45.
632. According to its s. 1 the Act complements Regulation (EC) No. 765/2008 of the European Parliament and of the Council of 9 Jul. 2008 setting out the requirements for accreditation and market surveillance relating to the marketing of products.
633. Regulation (EC) No. 765/2008 of the European Parliament and of the Council of 9 Jul. 2008 setting out the requirements for accreditation and market surveillance relating to the marketing of products and repealing Regulation (EEC) No. 339/93.

include CEF eDelivery.[634] ESV has since been participating in EU meetings and arranged pilot projects and conferences on the topic.[635]

294. SignGuard Europe AB[636] was the first Swedish company to offer qualified electronic signatures to public authorities and private companies in accordance with section 8 of the previously in force Swedish Act on Qualified Electronic Signatures. However, SignGuard terminated this service in 2016. According to EU's Trusted List Browser TrustWeaver AB is currently the only active trust service provider in Sweden.[637]

§4. SUPERVISION

295. Article 17 eIDAS Regulation stipulates that Member States shall designate a supervisory authority that, *inter alia*, supervises qualified trust service providers, as well as other trust service providers. The supervisory authority shall, *inter alia*, analyse conformity assessment reports (Articles 20(1) and 21(1)), carry out audits, and cooperate with data protection authorities. The Swedish government decided not to introduce any fines or sanctions on a national level.[638]

296. PTS was chosen as the National Regulatory Authority, as stipulated in section 4 Ordinance with Additional Provisions to the EU Regulation on Electronic Identification (*Förordning (2016:576) med kompletterande bestämmelser till EU:s förordning om elektronisk identifiering*). Decisions by PTS can be appealed to the Administrative Court in Stockholm.

Providers of trusted services who want to offer qualified trusted services have to register with PTS, who assesses whether they fulfil the requirements in the eIDAS Regulation. Providers of non-qualified trusted services have to report security and personal data breaches.[639]

§5. LEGAL RECOGNITION

I. General Recognition by Law

297. As mentioned above, Swedish private law contains relatively few rules on form requirements, especially regarding rules requiring a signature. The fact that a

634. CEF, eDelivery, ec.europa.eu/cefdigital/wiki/display/CEFDIGITAL/eDelivery, accessed 11 Jan. 2020.
635. The Swedish National Financial Management Authority (ESV), 'E-delivery – statusrapport 2017 (2018), www.esv.se//publicerat/publikationer/2018/e-delivery--statusrapport-2017/ accessed 11 Jan. 2020.
636. www.signguard.se.
637. webgate.ec.europa.eu/tl-browser/#/tl/SE, accessed 8 Jan. 2020.
638. Government Bill (Proposition) 2015/16:72, ' Kompletterande bestämmelser till EU:s förordning om elektronisk identifiering', 48.
639. Section 8 Act on Qualified Electronic Signatures.

signature can have significance as evidence to support a certain statement should of course be taken into consideration; however, in Swedish law, signatures are rarely mentioned as a form requirement in order for a statement to receive legal recognition.

Instead of being a legal requirement, signatures have become important from a practical point of view within everyday life for both individuals and businesses. Signing has become an established method for confirmation, control and proof of any statement. In this regard, Chapter 15 section 13 Swedish Penal Code (*brottsbalk (1962:700)*) should be mentioned, stating:

> A person who denies her or his signature on a document, shall, if the act jeopardises proof, be sentenced for denial of signature to a fine or imprisonment for at most six months or, if the crime is gross, imprisonment for at most two years.

In other words, non-repudiation, as one of the purposes of a signature, is, in the context of evidence, punishable by criminal law.

In addition, unauthorized use of somebody else's identity (*olovlig identitetsanvändning*) is punishable by criminal law since 2016. Pursuant to Chapter 4 section 6 b Swedish Penal Code, a person who uses another person's identification information in order to claim her or his identity and causes damage or inconvenience, shall be sentenced to a fine or imprisonment for a maximum of two years.

298. Article 5(1) point a of the previously in force Directive on Electronic Signatures, stated that Member States shall ensure that qualified electronic signature 'satisfy the legal requirements of a signature in relation to data in electronic form in the same manner as a handwritten signature satisfies those requirements in relation to paper-based data'. The eIDAS Regulation widens this principle of non-discrimination of the legal effect and admissibility as evidence in legal proceedings to electronic signatures, electronic seals, electronic time stamps, electronic registered delivery services and electronic documents. The non-discrimination clause does not stipulate an obligation to use electronic means, but simply means that courts and other public bodies have to assess electronic tools in the same way as their paper equivalent.

When transposing the previously in force Directive on Electronic Signatures, it was not considered appropriate to introduce a general rule that gives electronic signatures the same legal value as handwritten signatures.[640] Section 17 of the previously in force Swedish Act on Qualified Electronic Signatures explicitly stated that if a requirement of a handwritten signature may be fulfilled by electronic means, a qualified signature will always meet this requirement. This rule did, however, not prevent other types of electronic signatures with a lower level of security, such as advanced or 'normal' electronic signatures from being accepted by law or business practice.[641]

640. Government Bill (*Proposition*) 1999/2000:117, 58.
641. *Ibid.*

Section 17 also allowed for the origin of the electronic signature to be questioned, that is, whether the right person signed a specific document. As for handwritten signatures, the origin can always be questioned if there is reason to doubt it.[642]

Swedish legislation that includes formal requirements regarding electronic signatures does not contain any requirements for qualified electronic signatures. The form requirements regarding electronic signatures refer to either advanced electronic signatures or in most cases electronic signatures in general.[643] The currently available Swedish eIDs, such as BankID, are considered to fulfil the requirements of advanced electronic signatures.[644]

299. In certain cases, Swedish public authorities set up form requirements. Examples for this include the regulations of the National Tax Agency (*Skatteverket*) and the Social Insurance Agency (*Försäkringskassan*) where an explicit reference is made to eIDs and not only to electronic signatures in general, for example, Regulation SKVFS 2009:8 by the Swedish National Tax Agency (*Skatteverkets föreskrifter om e-tjänsten Inkomstdeklaration*).

II. Evidence Value

300. Even in situations where a signature is not required by law, it can have significance with regards to proof. Signing a document can mean that a specific person is the signer and has approved the terms and conditions of the written contract.

Swedish law, as mentioned previously, has no exclusionary rules regarding evidence. This principle means on one hand that all sorts of sources can be used as evidence in a court trial, and on the other hand that the judge is not bound by any legal rules when it comes to evaluating the evidence and its weight. In other words, electronic signatures or any other electronic documents can be used as evidence in Swedish courts.[645] This also means that Article 5(1) point b of the previously in force Directive on Electronic Signatures requiring Member States to ensure that qualified electronic signatures 'are admissible as evidence in legal proceedings' did not need specific legislative measures in Sweden. The same applies for Article 5(2) stipulating that electronic signatures should not be 'denied legal effectiveness and admissibility as evidence in legal proceedings'.[646]

301. One rule that does exist, however, both in statute and case law is burden of proof. Even though there is no statutory rule regarding the situation where somebody denies having signed a contract and claiming that the signature is a forgery, the Swedish Supreme Court has established some guidelines in a case from

642. *Ibid.*
643. Government Bill (*Proposition*) 2015/16:72, ' Kompletterande bestämmelser till EU:s förordning om elektronisk identifiering', 52 et seq.
644. *Ibid.*
645. Government Bill (*Proposition*) 1999/2000:117, 17.
646. *Ibid.*

1976.[647] According to this decision, if a party claims not to have signed a document, the other party has to prove that the signature is not a forgery. If one party claims, however, that although the signature is genuine (i.e., not a forgery), the content was changed, it is that party who has to prove any change in the document content.

302. The Governmental report preceding the bill[648] stated that admissibility of evidence should never be restricted and there should be no special rules when it comes to electronic evidence as opposed to any other sort of evidence. Neither should there be any specific rules concerning burden of proof when it comes to electronic evidence.

§6. Liability and Burden of Proof

303. Article 6 of the previously in force Directive on Electronic Signatures and section 14 Swedish Act on Qualified Electronic Signatures specified a liability for damages for qualified certificates. Article 13 eIDAS Regulation stipulates that 'trust service providers shall be liable for damage caused intentionally or negligently to any natural or legal person due to a failure to comply with the obligations under this Regulation'. Paragraph 2 of the same Article adds a burden of proof for the natural or legal person in case the provider offers non-qualified trust services.

In addition to Article 13, the general rules on damages in tort law apply.[649]

647. Decision by Supreme Court from 3 Dec. 1976, NJA 1976 s. 667.
648. Ministry Publications Series (Ds) 1998:14, 'Digitala signaturer – en teknisk och juridisk översikt'.
649. *Ibid.*, 75.

Chapter 3. Legal Aspects of Electronic Banking

§1. General Legal Framework

I. General Statement

304. The Swedish banking system is not covered by a single payment systems Act. Instead, there are a number of separate Acts forming the legal framework for the payment and settlement systems infrastructure.[650]

Chapter 9 Article 13 Instrument of Government appoints the Riksbank as the central bank of Sweden that is responsible for the monetary policy, and has the sole right to issue coinage and banknotes. The Swedish Riksbank Act (*lag (1988:1385) om Sveriges riksbank*) stipulates in Chapter 1 section 2 that the Riksbank shall 'promote a safe and efficient payments mechanism'.

The Banking and Financing Business Act (*lag (2004:297) om bank- och finansieringsrörelse*) contains regulations on banking and financing and lays down, *inter alia*, licensing requirements for the conduct of such operations and guidelines governing the supervision of credit institutions.

The Payment-Service Act (*lag (2010:751) om betaltjänster*) implemented large parts of the previously in force EU Payment Services Directive (PSD)[651] and regulates rights and obligations of end users and payment-service providers.[652] The Act stipulates operational requirements for payment services providers and rules concerning market access for new providers. The second EU Payment Service Directive (PSD 2)[653] was adopted in 2015 in order to adapt the existing rules to new digital payment services. PSD 2 was fully transposed into Swedish law in 2019.[654]

The Act on the Securities Market (*lag (2007:528) om värdepappersmarknaden*)[655] transposes the EU Investment Services Directive[656] into Swedish national law, stipulates licensing requirements for securities firms and offers guidelines governing the supervision of such firms, and the types of business such firms

650. For detailed information on the banking sector, *see* European Central Bank, 'Payment and Securities Settlement Systems in the European Union', Blue Book, 4th edn, vol. 2 (Non-Euro area countries), 331 et seq.
651. Directive 2007/64/EC of the European Parliament and of the Council of 13 November 2007 on payment services in the internal market amending Directives 97/7/EC, 2002/65/EC, 2005/60/EC and 2006/48/EC and repealing Directive 97/5/EC (Text with EEA relevance).
652. An overview of EU legislation is available at European Commission, 'Payment Services', ec.europa.eu/info/business-economy-euro/banking-and-finance/consumer-finance-and-payments/payment-services/payment-services_en, accessed 11 Jan. 2020.
653. Directive (EU) 2015/2366 of the European Parliament and of the Council of 25 November 2015 on payment services in the internal market, amending Directives 2002/65/EC, 2009/110/EC and 2013/36/EU and Regulation (EU) No. 1093/2010, and repealing Directive 2007/64/EC.
654. Government Bill (*Proposition*) 2017/18:77, 'Nya regler om betaltjänster'. *See also* the website of the Financial Inspection Board (FI) (*Finansinspektionen*) for their instructions, fi.se.
655. The Act replaced the Securities Business Act (*Lag (1991:981) om värdepappersrörelse*).
656. Directive 2004/39/EC of the European Parliament and of the Council of 21 April 2004 on markets in financial instruments amending Council Directives 85/611/EEC and 93/6/EEC and Directive 2000/12/EC of the European Parliament and of the Council and repealing Council Directive 93/22/EEC.

may engage in. In addition, several other Acts regulate the financial market and are applicable to specific types of financial instruments or financial services.[657]

The previously in force Act on cross-border payments within the EU (*lag (1999:268) om betalningsöverföringar inom Europeiska ekonomiska samarbetsområdet*) transposed the EU Directive on Cross-border Credit Transfers[658] into Swedish law. In 2010, it was incorporated into the Payment-Service Act (*lag (2010:751) om betaltjänster*) which now covers payment services provided in Sweden and performed in the EEA. Sweden has, furthermore, decided to apply Regulation (EC) No. 924/2009 of the European Parliament and of the Council of 16 September 2009 on cross-border payments in the Community.[659]

Sweden is also actively involved in the EU project – Single Euro Payments Area (SEPA).[660] SEPA consists of three main parts: credit transfer, direct debits and card payment and is based on. At the moment the majority of national Euro credit transfers are being processed as SEPA Credit Transfers. Cross-border Euro payments are also compliant with SEPA Credit Transfer. SEPA direct debit is optional for non-Euro countries, and therefore it is up to the banks to offer this possibility, which only a few banks in Sweden chose.

International payments are mostly sent over SWIFT's network for secure financial messages. Most payments in Sweden are currently settled in the Riksbank's settlement system for large-value payments (known as RIX). Riksbank plans to eventually uses the Eurosystem's and European Central Bank's (ECB's) platform for instant settlements, Target Instant Payment Settlement.[661]

II. Electronic Banking

305. There is no specific legislation dealing with electronic banking as such. Most Acts stated above are technology-neutral, and apply to any form of banking.

One of the first national acts dealing to some extent specifically with electronic banking was the Swedish Act on the issuing of electronic money (*lag (2002:149) om utgivning av elektroniska pengar*), which transposed the previous EU Directive

657. More information at the website of Swedish Banker's Association (*Svenska Bankföreningen*), www.swedishbankers.se/.
658. Directive 97/5/EC of the European Parliament and of the Council of 27 January 1997 on cross-border credit transfers.
659. Sveriges Riksbank, 'The Swedish retail-payment market', Riksbank Studies, June 2013, www.riksbank.se/Documents/Rapporter/Riksbanksstudie/2013/rap_riksbanksstudie_The_Swedish_retailpayment_market_130605_eng.pdf, 89.
660. *See* more at the website of the European Central Bank (ECB) www.ecb.europa.eu/paym/sepa/html/index.en.html, accessed 11 Jan. 2020.
661. Sveriges riksbank, 'Payments in Sweden 2019' (7 Nov. 2019) riksbank.se/payments-in-sweden-2019.

on Electronic Money.[662] The Act was replaced in 2011 with the Electronic Money Act (*lag (2011:755) om elektroniska pengar*), which is based on the 2009 E-Money Directive.[663]

The current in force Electronic Money Act states requirements for issuers of electronic money and guidelines governing the supervision of such issuers. Electronic money is defined in Chapter 1 section 2, in accordance with Article 1(2) 2009 e-Money Directive, as 'electronically stored monetary value':

- as represented by a claim on the issuer;
- which is issued on receipt of funds for the purpose of making payment transactions as defined in point 5 of Article 4 of Directive 2007/64/EC; and
- which is accepted by a natural or legal person other than the electronic money issuer.

Electronic money is, according to this definition, not the same as virtual currency.[664]

Issuing of electronic money in Sweden requires a permit by the Financial Inspection Board (*Finansinspektionen* – FI)[665] unless the issuer is a bank. Only Swedish limited companies (*aktiebolag*) or Swedish economic associations (*ekonomisk förening*) can apply for a permit and have to prove, *inter alia*, a sufficient minimum start-up capital and operating capital base. The Electronic Money Act also stipulates other requirements for issuers of electronic money, for example, issuers may not receive deposits or other repayable funds from the general public.[666]

The Act is applicable to all issuers of electronic money, but only a few of its provisions are applicable to banks and credit market companies as they fall within the scope of specific legislation, according to section 1.

The Swedish national bank (*Sveriges riksbank*) is currently investigating whether it would be possible to issue a central bank digital currency, an 'e-krona'. The e-krona project started in 2017 and in December 2019 the national bank started a public procurement for a potential supplier.[667]

662. Directive 2000/46/EC of the European Parliament and of the Council of 18 September 2000 on the taking up pursuit of and prudential supervision of the business of electronic money institutions.
663. Directive 2009/110/EC of the European Parliament and of the Council of 16 September 2009 on the taking up, pursuit and prudential supervision of the business of electronic money institutions amending Directives 2005/60/EC and 2006/48/EC and repealing Directive 2000/46/EC.
664. Sveriges Riksbank, 'The Swedish retail-payment market', 92.
665. www.fi.se.
666. *See* more at Sveriges Riksbank, 'The Swedish retail-payment market', 92 et.sequ.
667. Sveriges Riksbank, 'Riksbank develops an e-krona in a test environment', 13 Dec. 2019, www.riksbank.se/en-gb/press-and-published/notices-and-press-releases/notices/2019/riksbank-develops-an-e-krona-in-a-test-environment/, accessed 12 Jan. 2020.

III. Supervision

306. In general, FI is the supervisory authority for the banking sector, and also the authority granting the licence to provide certain banking or financing services. Within its capacity, it also issues regulatory code (*Finansinspektionens författningssamling, FFFS*) further defining provisions stated by law.

In its capacity as the Swedish Financial Supervisory Authority, FI supervises and monitors companies and organizations operating in financial markets. In many cases, companies offering financial services in Sweden have to acquire a permit issued by FI.

According to Chapter 2 section 1 Electronic Money Act, FI authorizes the issuing of electronic money.

§2. Consumer Protection

307. In general, the Swedish Consumer Credit Act regulates the granting of credit to consumers and contains, *inter alia*, provisions on marketing and information.

308. As stated above, the PSD was transposed into Swedish national law by enactment of the Payment-Service Act (*lag (2010:751) om betaltjänster*) in 2010. The Act, *inter alia*, stipulates the type of information that providers of payment services must present to their customers, how quickly a payment transaction is to be performed and the fees that may be charged to the user for payment services. Regarding the time frame, electronic payments in SEK or EUR must reach the payee no later than the day after the payment was initiated (Chapter 5 section 18).

Regarding liability for unauthorized transactions with a payment instrument, the Act on Unauthorized Transactions with Payment Instruments (*lag (2010:738) om obehöriga transaktioner med betalningsinstrument*) used to regulate the responsibility of the account holder. When transposing PSD 2, the Act was repealed and the provisions were moved into the Payment-Service Act. Chapter 1 section 4 Payment-Service Act defines payment instrument as a bank card or any other personalized device or personal routine that, based on contract, is used to electronically initiate a payment transaction. Chapter 5 section 6 stipulates the account holder's obligation to, *inter alia*, protect the authentication information (e.g., personal code) and to report to the payment-service provider as soon as possible if the payment instrument has been mislaid or been used in an unauthorized manner. Chapter 5 a sections 2, 3 and 4 state the liability of the account holder. If the account holder did not protect the personal code, the liability covers the amount that has been debited up to SEK 400. In case of gross negligence the account holder is liable for the full amount; however, if the account holder is a consumer, this amount is limited to a maximum of SEK 12,000, except in extremely reprehensible cases.

309. In addition, the Act on Distance Contracts and Contracts Outside a Place of Business (*lag (2005:59) om distansavtal och avtal utanför affärslokaler*),[668] transposing, *inter alia*, the Directive on Distance Contracts for Financial Services and Financial Instruments,[669] covers in its Chapter 3 obligations for providers of distance contracts for financial services and financial instruments.

668. Explained more in Ch. 4 §3 *infra* (paras 326 et seq.).
669. Directive 2002/65/EC of the European Parliament and of the Council of 23 September 2002 concerning the distance marketing of consumer financial services and amending Council Directive 90/619/EEC and Directives 97/7/EC and 98/27/EC.

Chapter 4. Protection of Users of Electronic Services

§1. General Statement

310. Though the term 'electronic services' is neither used nor defined in any of the relevant Directives or statutes mentioned below, this chapter will focus on the protection of users of information society services as well as distance contracts.

In general, the legal framework of consumer protection applies, including the Consumer Sales Act (*konsumentköplag (1990:932)*), the Consumer Services Act (*konsumenttjänstlag (1985:716)*), the Consumer Credit Act (*konsumentkreditlag (1992:830)*), as well as the Act on Terms of Contract in Consumer Relations (*lag (1994:1512) om särskilda avtalsvillkor i konsumentförhållanden*), and the Price Information Act (*prisinformationslag (2004:347)*).

Regarding marketing practices, the Swedish Marketing Act (*marknadsföringslag (2008:486)*) covers Business-To-Consumer (B2C) as well as Business-To-Business (B2B) relations, and is applicable in all situations where advertisement is used, not only towards consumers, but also towards competitors of the advertising company. The Competition Act (*konkurrenslag (2008:579)*) further aims at eliminating and counteracting obstacles to effective competition in the production of, and trade in, goods and services. In this respect, it can protect both consumers and competitors from unfair trade practices.

§2. Information Society Services

I. General Statement

311. The Directive on Electronic Commerce[670] was transposed into Swedish national law by passing the Act on Electronic Commerce and other information society services (*lag (2002:562) om elektronisk handel och andra informationssamhällets tjänster*; hereinafter 'Electronic Commerce Act'), as well as amending the then in force Marketing Act (*marknadsföringslag (1995:450)*),[671] the Financial Instruments Trading Act (*lag (1991:980) om handel med finansiella instrument*) and the Consumer Credit Act, among others.

312. The Directive[672] as well as the Electronic Commerce Act in section 1 exempts certain services from their application. The Swedish Act does not reflect the Directive word-for-word, but mentions as services that do not fall within its scope:

670. Directive 2000/31/EC of the European Parliament and of the Council of 8 June 2000 on certain legal aspects of information society services, in particular e-commerce, in the Internal Market (hereinafter 'Directive on Electronic Commerce').

671. Now replaced by the Marketing Act (*marknadsföringslag (2008:486)*).

672. Article 1(5) points a–d Directive on Electronic Commerce.

(1) taxation;
(2) processing of personal data;
(3) cooperation between companies that limits competition;
(4) activities of notaries or equivalent professions to the extent that they involve an exercise of public authority;
(5) activities that involve representation or defence of a client's interests before the courts; or
(6) gambling activities which involve wagering a stake with monetary value in games of chance.

The reason for exempting these activities is a result of the lack of competence of the EU within those fields.[673] This means, that the national legislator can enact laws within these areas, which do not necessarily have to be harmonized within the EU.[674]

Another reason for the Electronic Commerce Act not to be applicable is activities which fall under the Freedom of the Press Act (*tryckfrihetsförordning (1949:105)*) or the Fundamental Law on Freedom of Expression (*yttrandefrihetsgrundlag (1991:1469)*), which both have constitutional status. This is in line with Recital 9 Directive stating that the 'Directive is not intended to affect national fundamental rules and principles relating to freedom of expression.'

313. The Directive in Article 3(1), as well as Electronic Commerce Act, section 3 establishes the country of origin principle (*ursprungslandsprincip*) in relation to rights and obligations of service providers. In other words, a provider of information society services has to comply with the rules of the Member State that it is established and registered in, but not with the rules of every Member State in which the service can be received (the effects doctrine – *effektlandsprincip*). The country of origin principle only concerns, however, rules regarding the taking up and pursuit of information society services ('coordinated field') and not requirements applicable to goods or their delivery.

314. The Act, in accordance with the Directive, stipulates certain rules for information society services. As will become clear from the definitions mentioned below, in particular the fact that both the Directive and the Act speak about recipients of the service and not consumers, these rules apply both in B2B as well as B2C relations.

---

673. Recital 12 Directive on Electronic Commerce: 'It is necessary to exclude certain activities from the scope of this Directive, on the grounds that the freedom to provide services in these fields cannot, at this stage, be guaranteed under the Treaty or existing secondary legislation; excluding these activities does not preclude any instruments which might prove necessary for the proper functioning of the internal market.'

674. As an example, the previously in force Swedish Lotteries Act (*lotterilag (1994:1000)*) required an undertaking to apply for a permit (from the Government) to organize gambling or lottery activities on the Swedish market. The law was technology-neutral and therefore applied to online gambling as well. The responsible supervisory authority was the Gaming Board for Sweden (*Lotteriinspektionen*, www.lotteriinspektionen.se).

More specifically, the Swedish Electronic Commerce Act covers provisions relating to the internal market, the establishment of service providers, commercial communications, electronic contracts, the liability of intermediaries, codes of conduct, out-of-court dispute settlements as well as court actions.[675] In the following mainly the obligations of service providers will be covered, as liability of intermediaries is discussed in Part V Chapter 3 *infra*, and out-of-court dispute settlements are included in Part I Chapter 5 *supra* as well as Part II Chapter 6 *supra* with regards to domain name disputes.

II. Definitions

315. The definitions in section 2 Electronic Commerce Act reflect the definitions of Article 2 Directive on Electronic Commerce to a large extent.

Information society services are defined as 'services normally provided for remuneration and at a distance, by electronic means and at the individual request of a recipient of services'. All four criteria have to be fulfilled in order for a service to be covered by the Electronic Commerce Act. This reflects section 2 Swedish Ordinance on Technical Rules (*förordning (1994:2029) om tekniska regler*) which in turn builds upon the previously in force Directive on Technical Standards and Regulations,[676] and which the Directive on Electronic Commerce refers to in its Article 2 point a. Annex V of the Directive on Technical Standards and Regulations mentioned a list of activities that were not covered by the term 'information society services'.[677] This list is now contained in Annex I of the 2015 Directive on Technical Standards and Regulations.

The term 'service' is not further explained, neither in the Electronic Commerce Act nor in any other Swedish legislation, and does not have an established meaning as such. There was no discussion of this term in the Swedish preparatory works; however, the Governmental Bill[678] referred to Article 57[679] TFEU which defines services as performances that 'are normally provided for remuneration, in so far as they are not governed by the provisions relating to freedom of movement for goods, capital and persons'.

The preparatory works further mention the following examples of information society services: marketing and sale of goods and services, online newspapers, financial services and video-on-demand, under the assumption that they all are provided online. Concerning sale of goods and services, including computer programs,

675. *See* Art. 1(2) Directive on Electronic Commerce.
676. Directive 98/34/EC of the European Parliament and of the Council of 22 June 1998 laying down a procedure for the provision of information in the field of technical standards and regulations (hereinafter 'Directive on Technical Standards and Regulations'). This EU Directive was replaced in 2015 by Directive (EU) 2015/1535 of the European Parliament and of the Council of 9 September 2015 laying down a procedure for the provision of information in the field of technical regulations and of rules on Information Society services.
677. Recital 17 Directive on Electronic Commerce explicitly refers to that list.
678. Government Bill (*Proposition*) 2001/02:150, 'Lag om elektronisk handel och andra informationssamhällets tjänster, m.m.', 56.
679. Ex Art. 50.

real estate agents, and accounting services, the Electronic Commerce Act only applies to the steps of the ordering process that are provided online. In other words, if the computer program is bought online, but delivered in physical form offline, only the ordering is covered by the Act.[680] Marketing by email is also covered as an information society service. Email or other direct personal messages between individuals outside their profession do not fall within the scope, however. This also applies if the contract is concluded via exchange of emails.[681]

316. Section 2 Swedish Electronic Commerce Act further defines *service provider* as any natural or legal person providing an information society service. This can include ISPs, providers of search engines, owners of servers and companies offering goods and services online. To the extent that some economic goal exists, public authorities and universities can also fall under the definition. Typical private websites with no economic purpose are, however, not considered as service providers.[682]

The Swedish Electronic Commerce Act describes the term 'country of establishment', which in substance transposes Article 2 point c Directive on Electronic Commerce, as the Member State where the service provider has its fixed establishment. The country of origin is, in other words, the main place of business for the company, and not where the technology or website is located.[683]

The term 'recipient of the service' covers any natural or legal person who uses an information society service. This includes more or less everybody who takes advantage of such a service, individuals who publish information on public networks as well as individuals who search for information on the Internet for private or professional purposes. A person or company can be both a provider and a recipient of an information society service, for example, the owner of a website is both service provider as well as recipient if a web hotel is used for the storage of the website.[684]

Section 2 describes the term 'regulated profession' as a profession which according to law or ordinance requires authorization of some sort. It furthermore also defines *coordinated field* as provisions with requirements for information society services applicable to service providers regarding the taking up and pursuit of activities concerning such services.

III. Obligation to Provide Information

317. Section 8 Electronic Commerce Act, implementing Article 5 Directive on Electronic Commerce, stipulates an obligation for service providers to render certain information to the recipients of the service. This information includes, *inter alia*, data about the name, address and email address of the service provider, as well

680. Government Bill (*Proposition*) 2001/02:150, 110.
681. *See also* Recital 18 Directive on Electronic Commerce.
682. Government Bill (*Proposition*) 2001/02:150, 110.
683. *See also* Recital 19 Directive on Electronic Commerce.
684. Government Bill (*Proposition*) 2001/02:150, 110.

as the registration number for the company and, if applicable, the relevant supervisory authority. The information should be easily, directly and permanently accessible to the recipients and public authorities.

If the information society service concerns a regulated profession, the published information should also include the professional title and the Member State where it has been granted, the professional body or similar institution with which the service provider is registered, and the applicable professional rules in the Member State of establishment and the means to access them.[685]

If the service provider refers to prices of goods or services, they should be indicated clearly and unambiguously. If tax or delivery costs are added, this should also be stated explicitly.[686]

IV. Requirements for the Online Ordering Process

318. Section 10 Swedish Electronic Commerce Act, reflecting Article 11(2) Directive on Electronic Commerce, stipulates an obligation for service providers to make available appropriate and effective technical means allowing the recipient to identify and correct input errors, prior to the placing of the order. This obligation does not include a duty for the service provider itself to correct or verify the information given by the recipient, but to provide the means for the user to notice mistakes.

319. In addition, the provider of an information society service has to render certain information in the ordering process. More specifically, according to section 11, the service provider has to inform the recipient about:

(1) the technical means according to section 10 as well as the different technical steps to follow when concluding the contract;
(2) which languages the contract is available in;
(3) whether the concluded contract will be archived by the service provider and whether it will be accessible;
(4) the relevant codes of conduct to which the service provider subscribes to and information on how these codes can be consulted electronically.

The information has to be provided clearly and unambiguously prior to the order being placed.[687]

685. Section 8 para. 2 Electronic Commerce Act.
686. Section 9 Electronic Commerce Act.
687. Section 11 Electronic Commerce Act, transposing Art. 10(1) and (2) Directive on Electronic Commerce.

320. After the order has been placed, the service provider has to acknowledge the receipt of the order without undue delay and by electronic means. Orders and acknowledgements of receipt are deemed received when the parties to whom they are addressed are able to access them.[688]

321. General terms and conditions of a contract must be made available in a way that allows the recipient to store and reproduce them.[689]

V. Possible Sanctions

322. If the provider of an information society service fails to adhere to the obligations to provide certain information or appropriate technical measures, it faces sanctions according to the Swedish Marketing Act (*marknadsföringslag (2008:486)*). Section 15 Swedish Electronic Commerce Act follows the examples of other related legislation, such the Act on Distance Contracts and Contracts Outside a Place of Business (*lag (2005:59) om distansavtal och avtal utanför affärslokaler;* hereinafter 'Distance Contracts Act') as well as the Price Information Act (*prisinformationslag (2004:347)*), which both refer to the Marketing Act in relation to possible sanctions.

Section 15 Electronic Commerce Act allows for sanctions under the Marketing Act for not meeting the requirements according to sections 8 and 9 (obligation to provide certain information) as well as sections 11–13 (requirements when ordering online) and section 10 (not providing technical measures). The Swedish Marketing Act stipulates in sections 24–27 and 37 the sanctions for non-compliance with the rules of the Electronic Commerce Act.

323. According to section 24 Marketing Act, a provider of an information society service, its employee or any person acting on its behalf can be ordered to provide the necessary information. This order may include providing information in advertisements or other presentations used by the company in the course of marketing, through labelling of the goods at the point of sale, or in another form to a consumer who requests such information. Similar to this provision, section 25 Marketing Act stipulates an order to provide technical aids.

In both cases, the order issued by the relevant authority can be combined with a conditional fine unless special reasons render it unnecessary.[690] If the service provider intentionally or negligently violates an order that has been issued pursuant to section 24 or 25, it shall compensate a recipient for any damage suffered thereby.[691]

688. Section 12 Electronic Commerce Act, transposing Art. 11(1) Directive on Electronic Commerce.
689. Section 13 Electronic Commerce Act, transposing Art. 10(3) Directive on Electronic Commerce.
690. Section 26 Marketing Act.
691. Section 37 Marketing Act.

324. The proceedings for an order according to section 24 or 25 Marketing Act shall be brought before the Patent and Market Court (*Patent- och marknadsdomstolen*)[692] They can be initiated by:[693]

(1) the Consumer Ombudsman (*Konsumentombudsmannen*);[694]
(2) the company affected by the marketing practices; or
(3) an organization of consumers, companies or employees.

In cases of minor importance, the Consumer Ombudsman may issue orders directly, in accordance with sections 24 and 25 Marketing Act. These orders shall be combined with a conditional fine. In order to be valid, an information order must be accepted by the service provider immediately or within a specific period of time. If the order has been accepted, it shall apply as if it were a final judgment of the Market Court.[695]

325. There are no other possible sanctions for not meeting the requirements stated in the Electronic Commerce Act. For example, fines for disruptive marketing practices[696] cannot be issued in such cases.[697] It was also not deemed necessary to introduce specific rules on civil or criminal liability for not following the requirements stipulated above.[698]

§3. Distance Contracts

I. General Statement

326. Directive 97/7/EC of the European Parliament and of the Council of 20 May 1997 on the protection of consumers in respect of distance contracts (hereinafter 'Distance Contracts Directive') was transposed into Swedish law with the Distance and Doorstep Sales Act (*distans- och hemförsäljningslag (2005:59)*).[699] When transposing the Consumer Rights Directive[700] the Swedish Act was amended and

692. www.marknadsdomstolen.se.
693. Section 47 Marketing Act.
694. The Swedish Consumer Ombudsman is part of the Swedish Consumer Agency (*Konsumentverket*), www.konsumentombudsmannen.com.
695. Section 28 Marketing Act.
696. Sections 29–36 Marketing Act.
697. Section 15 Electronic Commerce Act.
698. Government Bill (*Proposition*) 2001/02:150, 75.
699. This Act replaced the previous Act on Consumer Protection in respect of Distance Contracts and Doorstep Sales Contracts (*lag (2000:274) om konsumentskydd vid distansavtal och hemförsäljningsavtal*).
700. Directive 2011/83/EU of the European Parliament and of the Council of 25 October 2011 on consumer rights, amending Council Directive 93/13/EEC and Directive 1999/44/EC of the European Parliament and of the Council and repealing Council Directive 85/577/EEC and Directive 97/7/EC of the European Parliament and of the Council. The latest amendment to the Directive – Directive (EU) 2019/2161 of the European Parliament and of the Council of 27 November 2019 amending

restructured and its name changed to Act on Distance Contracts and Contracts Outside a Place of Business (*lag (2005:59) om distansavtal och avtal utanför affärslokaler*; hereinafter 'Distance Contracts Act'). The Act contains provisions for consumer protection with regards to distance contracts for goods and non-financial services (Chapter 2) and distance contracts for financial services and financial instruments (Chapter 3).

II. Definitions

327. Entering into a distance contract is not necessarily the same as providing an information society service. Chapter 1 section 2 Distance Contracts Act defines it as a contract entered into within the undertaking's organized system for concluding contracts at a distance if where communication exclusively takes place at a distance. It is important that the undertaking has established a system for entering into contracts online, a simple advertisement to facilitate customer relations that does not include the possibility to sell goods or services at a distance, does not fulfil the criteria for a distance contract according to the definition. The threshold of 'organized' is, however, rather low; an advertisement with a telephone number that allows ordering of goods and services would constitute an organized system. Examples of such distance contracts include any type of offering of goods and services on the Internet that allows a consumer to order directly via the website or email or telephone. Services not included are, however, ordering of goods in a physical store, or using a telephone number in a newspaper advertisement to make an appointment with a dentist, lawyer or hairdresser. The Distance Contracts Act is, in other words, not applicable if the undertaking and the consumer meet face-to-face.[701]

In accordance with Article 2(4) Distance Contracts Directive, the techniques used for the system or the communication are any means that can be used for a conclusion of a contract without the parties being simultaneously physically present. The preparatory works refer to the list in Annex I of the Distance Contracts Directive[702] that states, *inter alia*, the following examples of means of distance communication: addressed and unaddressed printed matters, press advertising with order form, catalogues, telephone with or without (automatic calling machine) human intervention, radio, email, television (teleshopping). An important other means of communication is, of course, the Internet,[703] and nowadays also SMS.

328. The definitions of consumer and undertaking in the Swedish Act reflect the Distance Contracts Directive as well as most other legislation within business law.

Council Directive 93/13/EEC and Directives 98/6/EC, 2005/29/EC and 2011/83/EU of the European Parliament and of the Council as regards the better enforcement and modernization of Union consumer protection rules – has not yet been incorporated into Swedish law.

701. Government Bill (*Proposition*) 2004/05:13, 'Distans- och hemförsäljningslag m.m.', 122.
702. *Ibid.*
703. *Ibid.*, 123.

The term 'consumer' includes 'any natural person who is acting primarily for purposes which are outside her or his commercial activities', while *trader* covers 'any natural or legal person trading for purposes connected with her or his own commercial activities'.

As most other consumer legislation, contract terms or conditions that are 'to the disadvantage of the consumer shall be unenforceable against such consumer'.[704]

329. As is the case for information society services, some contracts are explicitly exempted from the scope of the Distance Contracts Act. Specifically, this concerns contracts that relate to the construction of buildings, are entered into by means of an automatic vending machine or other similar automatic machines or automated commercial premises, concern public pay phones, or regard auctions that allow other means of participation.[705]

330. The Distance Contracts Act sets up certain obligations for the service provider, to some extent similar to the Electronic Commerce Act, which will be described more in detail below.

III. Information

331. The duty to provide information is more detailed than the one stipulated in the Electronic Commerce Act and includes two parts. Certain information has to be provided both before[706] and after the contract has been entered into.[707]

The information that shall be provided, according to Chapter 2 section 2 Distance Contracts Act, in reasonable time prior to the conclusion of the contract, includes, *inter alia*:

- the name and address of the undertaking;
- the main characteristics of the goods or services;
- the price of the goods or services including taxes and charges;
- delivery costs;
- the arrangement for payment and delivery or performance in any other manner;
- the terms of the right of withdrawal in accordance to this Act and a reference to the model withdrawal form available at the Swedish Consumer Agency (*Konsumentverket*);
- the cost of using means of distance communication, where it is calculated other than at the basic rate;
- the period for which the offer remains valid;
- the minimum term of the contract, where the contract relates to the recurrent supply of goods or a service to be performed permanently;

704. Chapter 1 s. 4 Distance Contracts Act.
705. Chapter 2 s. 1 Distance Contracts Act.
706. Chapter 2 s. 2 Distance Contracts Act.
707. Chapter 2 s. 4 Distance Contracts Act.

- the possibility of having recourse to an out-of-court complaint and redress mechanism; and
- the functionality and interoperability of digital content.

The law does not specify what 'before the contract is entered into' means but only states 'within a reasonable time prior to entering into a distance contract'. Article 8(1) Consumer Rights Directive states, however, that information should be provided 'directly before the consumer places his order'. Chapter 2 section 3 Distance Contracts Act also stipulates that the information be 'provided in a clear and comprehensible manner and in a manner appropriate to the means of distance communication used'.

Pursuant to Chapter 2 section 4 (and Article 8 Consumer Rights Directive), the trader has to provide the consumer with a confirmation of the contract concluded, on a durable medium, within a reasonable time *after* the conclusion of the distance contract. That confirmation shall include the information stated in Chapter 2 section 2 Distance Contracts Act, unless the trader has already provided that information to the consumer on a durable medium. In the event the consumer agreed to not use the right of withdrawal with regards to digital content, the confirmation should include that information.

Chapter 2 section 9 (transposing Article 8(2) Consumer Rights Directive) stipulates that a consumer is only bound by an order placed via a website if the binding nature was made clear before the order was placed and the consumer explicitly acknowledged the obligation to pay.

IV. Right of Withdrawal

332. A right only applicable in distance consumer contracts is the right of withdrawal, which means that the consumer can withdraw from a concluded contract by 'submitting or sending notice thereof to the undertaking within fourteen days'[708] of the delivery of goods or the day on conclusion of the contract in case of services.[709] While Article 6 of the previously in force Distance Contracts Directive only stipulated seven working days, Article 9 Consumer Rights Directive now explicitly states fourteen days.

According to Article 11 Consumer Rights Directive, to exercise the right of withdrawal, the consumer may either use a model withdrawal form[710] or 'make any other unequivocal statement'.

In case the information according to Chapter 2 section 2 Distance Contracts Act was not provided together with delivery of the goods, or the conclusion of the

708. Chapter 2 s. 10 Distance Contracts Act.
709. Chapter 2 s. 12 Distance Contracts Act.
710. The model form is set out in Annex I(B) of the Directive.

contract regarding a service, the withdrawal period shall commence on the day it was provided[711] and ends the latest 'one year after the day on which the withdrawal period should have commenced'.[712]

333. A withdrawal means a cancellation of the contract, which is why the consumer has to return the goods to the supplier.[713] The consumer shall reimburse the trader for any diminished value of the goods resulting from the handling of the goods other than what is necessary to establish the nature, characteristics and functioning of the goods. As the consumer has to return the goods, the trader has to refund any payments made by the consumer.[714]

334. No right of withdrawal exists for the following types of contracts, pursuant to Chapter 2 section 11 Distance Contracts Act (transposing Article 16 Consumer Rights Directive):[715] accommodation; serving, catering or any other similar services; cultural events, sporting events, or any other similar leisure activities, if the service shall be provided 'on a specified day or during a specified period of time'. In addition, the right of withdrawal does not apply to distance contracts regarding:[716]

- a service, the performance of which has begun with the consumer's consent during the withdrawal period;
- goods which, by their nature, are liable to deteriorate or expire rapidly;
- supply of personalized goods;
- a sealed audio or video recording or sealed computer software, where the seal has been broken;
- public auctions;
- the supply of digital content; or
- a newspaper or periodical unless it concerns a subscription.

V. Performance of the Contract

335. In accordance with Article 18 Consumer Rights Directive, section 5 Consumer Sales Act[717] stipulates a right for consumers that performance of a contract shall be carried out within thirty days after the placement of the order, unless otherwise agreed by the partners in the contract.

According to section 13 Consumer Sales Act, the consumer can terminate the contract if the time of delivery is of great importance to the consumer or if both parties agreed upon a specific time. The consumer may also terminate the contract if

711. Chapter 2 s. 12 Distance Contracts Act.
712. Chapter 2 s. 12 Distance Contracts Act.
713. Chapter 2 s. 13 Distance Contracts Act.
714. Chapter 2 s. 14 Distance Contracts Act.
715. For a full list, *see* Art. 16 Consumer Rights Directive.
716. Chapter 2 s. 4 Distance Contracts Act.
717. Previously Art. 7(1) and (2) Distance Contracts Directive, and Ch. 2 s. 17 Swedish Distance Contracts Act.

the trader informs that there will be no delivery. If the consumer asks for delivery within an additional period of time, the consumer may also terminate the contract if delivery does not occur within that additional time period.

336. If the consumer terminates the contract, the trader has to refund any sums already paid by the consumer, without undue delay, according to section 43 Consumer Sales Act, transposing Article 18(3) Consumer Rights Directive.[718]

337. Chapter 2 section 17 paragraph 3 of the previously in force Distance and Doorstep Sales Act stipulated an exemption from the right to performance for certain distance contracts, in accordance with Article 3(2) Distance Contracts Directive. In transposing the Consumer Rights Directive, the provisions on performance of contract were added to the Consumer Sales Act and therefore apply to contracts regarding goods, but not explicitly services.

VI. Choice of Law

338. For choice of law regarding consumer contracts, Article 6 of the Regulation (EC) No. 593/2008 of the European Parliament and of the Council of 17 June 2008 on the law applicable to contractual obligations (Rome I) applies. This is also emphasized in Recital 58 Consumer Rights Directive. For financial services, Chapter 3 section 14 Distance Contracts Act stipulates that a term in a contract assigning the law of a country outside the EEA is not valid under certain circumstances.

VII. Possible Sanctions

339. The sanctions for not meeting the information requirements in Chapter 2 sections 2–5 Distance Contracts Act are stipulated in the Marketing Act.[719] As for information society services, the Marketing Act provides the possibility to issue orders to provide information,[720] which can be combined with a conditional fine unless special reasons render this unnecessary.[721] Under certain circumstances, the undertaking can be liable for damages as well.[722] Fines for disruptive marketing practices are, however, not covered by possible sanctions.[723]

The Consumer Ombudsman (*Konsumentombudsmannen*) can initiate proceedings before the Market Court (*Marknadsdomstolen*),[724] or in minor cases issue orders itself.[725]

718. Previously, Ch. 2 s. 17 Distance and Doorstep Sales Act stipulated thirty days of receipt of notice from the consumer.
719. Chapter 2 s. 6 Distance Contracts Act.
720. Section 24 Marketing Act.
721. Section 26 Marketing Act.
722. Section 37 Marketing Act.
723. Chapter 2 s. 6 Distance Contracts Act.
724. Section 47 Marketing Act.
725. Section 28 Marketing Act.

§4. Other Information Requirements

340. As is clear from above, providing consumers with reliable and relevant information has been one of the focus areas of EU legislation. In this context, section 9 Marketing Act can be mentioned, stipulating a duty to identify commercial communications as well as to clearly state the sender of the advertisement. Not following this provision intentionally or negligently can lead to fines for disruptive marketing practices according to section 29 Swedish Marketing Act.

The Price Information Act (*prisinformationslag (2004:347)*) stipulates information obligations, concerning mainly, as the name implies, the prices of products. Failure to provide information according to this Act can lead to sanctions according to the Marketing Act.[726]

In addition, several other Swedish Acts contain provisions regarding information requirements, such as the Swedish Companies Act (*aktiebolagslag (2005:551)*). Chapter 28 section 5 stipulates that a company's letters, invoices, order forms, and websites shall state the company's name, the place where the Board is registered as well as the company's registration number.

§5. Unsolicited Communication

341. Article 7 Directive on Electronic Commerce, dealing with unsolicited commercial communication, was not explicitly transposed into the Swedish Electronic Commerce Act in 2002, mainly because an opt-out solution did not require any specific legislative measures.

However, in transposing the Directive on Privacy and Electronic Communications, Sweden had to introduce an opt-in solution into national law, which was done in the previously in force Marketing Act (*marknadsföringslag (1995:450)*), and was transferred into the current Marketing Act (*marknadsföringslag (2008:486)*). The below-mentioned provision on unsolicited advertisement also implements Article 10 Distance Contracts Directive into Swedish law.

342. Section 6 point 1 Swedish Electronic Commerce Act exempts the question of direct unsolicited marketing from the country of origin principle.[727] Therefore, the effects doctrine applies and the Swedish Marketing Act is applicable on commercial communications that are aimed at the Swedish market. Factors that can help determine if the target market is Sweden are if the advertisement is in Swedish, if prices are in Swedish kronor, or if a Swedish address is provided.[728]

---

726. The same rules apply as failure to meet information requirements according to ss 8 and 9 Electronic Commerce Act, *see* §2 V *supra* (paras 322 et seq.) or Ch. 2 ss 2–5 Distance Contracts Act, *see* §3 VII *supra* (para. 339).
727. Sections 3–5 Swedish Electronic Commerce Act.
728. Henrik Bengtsson, 'Marknadsföring med hjälp av elektroniska meddelanden', *Ny Juridik* 3 (2009): 42–43.

The Swedish Marketing Act defines email as an electronic text, voice, sound or image message which is addressed or otherwise individualized and sent over a public communication network, and which can be stored in the network or in the recipient's terminal equipment until the recipient collects it.[729]

As this definition is rather broad, the term 'email' also includes SMS,[730] MMS and other types of messages that can be sent via instant message services such as Skype or ICQ. In addition, messages left on answering machines as well as communication within a network addressed directly to an IP-address can be considered email.[731]

343. Section 19 Marketing Act deals with unsolicited commercial communications and stipulates that an undertaking may only use email, telefax, automated calling systems or other similar automated systems that allow individual communication, and do not involve a natural person, in their marketing to natural persons, if prior consent has been given.

The consumer's consent is, however, not necessary if the company has acquired the contact details in the context of the sale of a product to that person and:

- the natural person has not refused that the electronic address is used for marketing purposes;
- the marketing concerns the undertaking's own products; and
- the natural person clearly and distinctly is given the opportunity to object, free of charge and in an easy manner, to use the contact details for marketing purposes when they were collected, and on the occasion of each following message.[732]

344. Last, but not least, the general rules of the General Data Protection Regulation (GDPR) apply.[733] While marketing purposes have been considered a valid interest on the side of the company, an individual's expressed wishes not to receive advertisements will balance the interest in favour of the individual's privacy.

345. To conclude, Swedish law clearly applies an opt-in solution, as shown by section 19 Marketing Act, which means that undertakings and service providers have to receive the consent of their potential customers in order to be able to send out direct commercial communications to them.

---

729. Section 3 Marketing Act in accordance with Art. 2 Directive on Privacy and Electronic Communications.
730. As also mentioned in Recital 40 Directive on Privacy and Electronic Communications.
731. Bengtsson, *Marknadsföring*, 37. Art. 29 Data Protection Working Party, 'Opinion 5/2004 on unsolicited communications for marketing purposes under Art. 13 of Directive 2002/58/EC', MARKT/11601/03/EN – WP 90.
732. The Swedish Market Court decided on 18 Jun. 2006 in MD 2006:18 that the possibility to object can be given by clicking a button on a website and also by unselecting an already checked box. *See also* Bengtsson, *Marknadsföring*, 48–49.
733. *See* Part VI *infra* (para. 385).

The sanctions of not abiding by section 19 are, however, not very strong. In the preparatory works to the new Marketing Act,[734] it was decided that fines for disruptive marketing practices[735] cannot be issued for any unsolicited advertisements.[736] However, in the case of failure to abide by section 20 Marketing Act, which stipulates that an email used for advertisement purposes has to contain a valid contact address where the natural or legal person can object to the marketing, a fine for disruptive marketing practices can be issued by the Market Court.[737]

734. Government Bill (*Proposition*) 2007/08:115, 'Ny marknadsföringslag'.
735. Sections 29–36 Marketing Act.
736. Government Bill (*Proposition*) 2007/08:115, 121.
737. Section 29 para. 1 Marketing Act.

Part V. Non-contractual Liability

Chapter 1. Negligence

§1. General Statement

346. The Tort Liability Act (*skadeståndslag (1972:207)*) is the primary regulation of Swedish tort law. According to Chapter 1 section 1 of the said Act, the principles set forth in the Act apply unless another statute provides otherwise. As far as non-contractual liability is concerned, the main rule is that a person or a company is only liable for personal injury or property damage, if the damage is caused intentionally or through negligence. In general, one is only liable for damages caused by means of actions, but under certain conditions, liability can be extended to include damages caused by omission.

In a non-contractual relationship, liability for purely financial loss – that is, loss not connected to personal injury or property damage – arises in exceptional cases such as situations where the loss is caused by a criminal act, the loss is caused by a public agency in the exercise of public authority, and in some specific cases, by negligent information.[738] There are also specific statutes, such as the GDPR[739] and the Copyright Act (*lag (1960:729) om upphovsrätt till litterära och konstnärliga verk*), that include provisions that extend liability to cover purely financial loss in certain situations.

347. The purpose of compensation for damages under Swedish tort law is that of repair. As a general principle, the compensation shall put the injured in the same financial situation as before the injury or damage occurred. As far as non-pecuniary damages are concerned, such damages are only covered when stipulated in law, for example compensation for pain and suffering according to Chapter 5 section 1 Tort Liability Act. However, compensation for non-pecuniary damage rarely tends to reach any substantial amounts. It should also be noted that the system of social and collective insurance plays an important role in Swedish tort law.[740] For example, compensation can be mitigated pursuant to Chapter 3 section 6 Tort Liability Act

738. Chapter 2 s. 2 and Ch. 3 ss. 2 and 3 Tort Liability Act.

739. Regulation (EU) 2016/679 of the European Parliament and of the Council of 27 Apr. 2016 on the protection of natural persons with regard to the processing of personal data and on the free movement of such data, and repealing Directive 95/46/EC.

740. *See* Jan Hellner & Marcus Radetzki, *Skadeståndsrätt*, 7th edn (Stockholm: Norstedts Juridik, 2006), 357.

with account to insurance. Furthermore, Chapter 6 section 2 Tort Liability Act provides for mitigation of liability in cases where the burden of liability is considered unreasonably heavy.

As stated above, special liability provisions supersede the general rules in the Tort Liability Act. However, such provisions rarely deal with every aspect involved in tort law. For instance, the specific liability provision in the GDPR does not give guidance on how to determine the compensation for violation of personal integrity. As to the calculation of damages, the courts apply the general principles set forth in the Tort Liability Act.

348. The fundamental question when determining whether a person has been negligent or not is if the person challenged with negligence has deviated in a blameworthy manner from what can be expected from her or him. Naturally, you can expect more from an expert in a certain field than from a novice. The assessment of a deviant behaviour or action is made primarily from any law or regulation that may exist governing the specific area, court precedents and established customary practices. If none of the above gives guidance on how to act in a certain situation, the assessment of a deviant behaviour or action has to be made on a case-by-case basis. The test performed by the Swedish courts is similar to what is often called 'the Learned Hand formula', after a famous American judge.[741]

In short, the test is performed by assessing the likelihood that a certain conduct will injure others (including property damage), the seriousness of the injury if it happens, balanced against the interest which she or he must sacrifice to avoid the risk, taking into account the person's subjective possibility to foresee the damage. These different factors are weighed against one another in an overall assessment to determine whether the circumstances called for a different behaviour than the one that occurred. Swedish courts tend to pay regard to the likelihood of damage, for example, the greater the likelihood of damage, and the greater the damages that might occur, the higher the demands on the person performing the action. It should be stressed that to a large extent the meaning and scope of the notion negligence in Swedish tort law is based on case law.[742]

349. As far as the employer's liability for damages caused by her or his employees is concerned, the general starting point, *see* Chapter 3 section 1 Tort Liability Act, is that the employer is liable for personal injury and property damage that an employee has caused within the course of her or his employment. Damage caused by an employee unrelated to the employment is consequently not covered by this rule. Only under extraordinary circumstances is the employer free from liability for damages caused by employees through fault or negligence in the course of the employment.

741. Hellner & Radetzki, 133–134.

742. *See*, e.g., Decision by Supreme Court from 10 May 1984, NJA 1984 s. 323; Decision by Supreme Court from 10 May 1995, NJA 1995 s. 274; and Decision by Supreme Court from 5 Nov. 1998, NJA 1998 s. 617.

The rules on complicity in crime in Chapter 23 Swedish Penal Code should also briefly be mentioned, since liability may be extended in accordance with the provision. Chapter 23 section 4 Penal Code states that a punishment in accordance with the Code shall be imposed not only on the person who committed the act, but also on anyone who furthered it by advice or deed. The same applies to any other act punishable with imprisonment under another law; for example, copyright infringement in accordance with the Copyright Act. Each accomplice is judged according to the intent or the negligence attributable to her or him.

§2. Financial Loss and Property Damage

350. In the Information and Communications Technology (ICT) sector, the legal classification of the damage is essential since liability for purely financial loss typically arises only when the loss is caused by a criminal act or where a specific statutory regulation extends the liability.

The distinction between purely financial loss and property damage is not always as obvious as it would seem. For example, loss of data on a hard drive without destroying the hard drive per se is often categorized as property damage.[743] Under Swedish law, this is due to the fact that the loss of data is a consequence of altering the hard drive in a negative way, but there are many examples in the ICT sector where the damage might be categorized as purely financial. For example, if valuable data on a hard drive is copied, the hard drive is still in the same condition as before. If damage is caused by the disposition the damage is considered to be purely financial, since it is not connected with either property damage or personal injury.

§3. Jurisdiction

351. Much can be said on the often complex legal aspects as to the rules on jurisdiction and choice of law in the ICT sector. These aspects will, however, not be covered here. Nevertheless, it should be noted that the main rule stipulated in Chapter 2 section 1 Swedish Penal Code (*brottsbalk (1962:700)*), which is relevant in many cases concerning non-contractual liability, is that crimes committed in Sweden are to be judged in accordance with Swedish law and by a Swedish court. The same applies when it is uncertain where the crime was committed but grounds exist for assuming that it was committed in Sweden. The main rule in the Swedish Code on Judicial Procedure (*rättegångsbalk (1942:740)*) concerning tortuous actions stipulates that action for recovery of damages may be brought to the court at the place where the tortuous act was committed or where the injury or damage occurred,[744] or in the court where the defendant resides.[745]

743. *See* Lindberg & Westman, 109.
744. Chapter 10 s. 8 Code on Judicial Procedure.
745. Chapter 10 s. 1 Code on Judicial Procedure.

Chapter 2. Liability of Network Operators

352. In the Electronic Communications Act (*lag (2003:389) om elektronisk kommunikation*), which is the result of the implementation of the EU Regulatory Framework for electronic communications into Swedish law,[746] a distinction is made between: (i) an operator of an electronic communications network; and (ii) an electronic communication service provider. An operator is defined as the owner of an electronic communications network. An electronic communications network is in brief a transmission system in the wired or wireless arena. In this Chapter, the notion 'network operator' is understood as corresponding to the notion 'operator' in the said Act. An *electronic communication service provider* is an undertaking that, normally for remuneration, conveys signals on electronic communications networks.[747]

In short, the Electronic Communications Act obliges undertakings to give notice to PTS[748] of activities involving the providing of public communications networks and publicly available communications services. The aim of the regulation is to assure private and public needs for electronic communication, and to ensure efficient competition. PTS is the central administrative authority with overall responsibility in the field of electronic communications.

353. Network operators, as well as most other natural or legal persons, are subject to the general rules of the Tort Liability Act and must subsequently repair personal injury and damage to property caused intentionally or through negligence. In addition, liability is in some cases extended by the Electronic Communications Act.

According to Chapter 7 section 13a Electronic Communications Act, an operator with significant influence on the market that deliberately or as a result of negligence takes a measure that is in breach of, or fails to take a measure that is necessary in order to comply with, an obligation under Chapter 4 section 4 or Chapter 5 section 13 of said Act, shall compensate for the damage thereby incurred.

The requirements referred to in Chapter 7 section 13a have as their objective to ensure just competition, such as obligations not to apply discriminatory terms and conditions or obligations as to pricing policies. Requirements include obligations towards (i) other operators, Chapter 4 section 4 and (ii) consumers, Chapter 5 section 13.

According to Chapter 8 section 7, a company is considered to have a significant influence on a specified market if it, alone or in cooperation with other companies, is able to act independently of its competitors, its customers and the consumers. This latter prerequisite corresponds to a large extent to the notion of dominance found in national and EU competition law.[749] In addition, the Government or PTS gives guidance on how to evaluate whether a company is considered to have a significant

746. *See* Part I Ch. 1 *supra* (para. 42).
747. The liability of service providers is dealt with in Ch. 3 *infra* (paras 355 et seq.).
748. The Swedish Post and Telecom Authority.
749. Article 102 Treaty on the Functioning of the European Union.

influence on a specified market under Chapter 8 section 7. For example, the Swedish telecom operators Telia and Tele2 have been considered to have a significant influence on the Swedish telecommunications market for interconnection and other markets.[750]

354. The liability rule stipulated in Chapter 7 section 13a covers, according to the preparatory works, not only damage caused by means of actions, but also damage caused by omission.[751] Subsequently, network operators with significant influence on a market, must actively make sure that they honour the obligations that are applicable to them. For example, if a network operator is obliged by PTS to make its technical specifications public and fails to do so, that network operator is liable for damages caused to other operators by the omission.

As have been accounted for in the previous chapter, liability for purely financial loss is limited under Swedish law and typically only arises when the loss is caused by a criminal act. As has also been mentioned in the previous chapter, liability may be extended to cover purely financial loss in certain situations. The most important consequence of Chapter 7 section 13a is that the liability, through the provision, is extended to include purely financial loss, which should be the damage most likely to be caused to competitors by unfair competition.[752]

The provision in Chapter 7 section 13a has been imposed to ensure that other operators, which do not have a contractual relationship with the operator accused of causing damage, can be compensated for purely financial losses. However, the relatively new rule has not, to the author's knowledge, yet been applied in civil proceedings against a network operator.

750. *See* PTS Decision of 21 Feb. 2002, No. 00-14849/23, PTS Decision of 20 Feb. 2017, No. 17-1106 and PTS Decision of 19 Feb. 2015, No. 11-9306.

751. Government Bill (*Proposition*) 2006/07:119, 'En effektivare lag om elektronisk kommunikation', 45.

752. *Ibid.*

Chapter 3. Liability of Service Providers

§1. General Statement

355. Service providers – the notion here is understood as providers of services by electronic means – in the ICT sector are subject to the general liability rules of the Tort Liability Act. Consequently, service providers must repair personal injury and damage to property caused intentionally or through negligence. However, as stated above, it is possible for the legislator to derogate from the general rules of the Tort Liability Act by enacting specific statutory provisions. We outline in this chapter the most important special liability statutes for service providers in the ICT sector.

§2. Liability in Accordance with the Electronic Commerce Act

I. Background

356. The Swedish Act on Electronic Commerce and Other Information Society Services (*lag (2002:562) om elektronisk handel och andra informationssamhällets tjänster*; hereinafter 'Electronic Commerce Act') is based on the EU Directive on Electronic Commerce.[753] The main objective of the Directive is to ensure the free movement of information society services between the Member States. The term 'information society service' is defined in the Directive on Technical Standards and Regulations[754] as *any service normally provided for remuneration, at a distance, by electronic means and at the individual request of a recipient of services.* As far as non-contractual liability is concerned, the Electronic Commerce Act lays down rules on freedom from liability in certain cases. However, as accounted for below, the exemptions from liability are far from absolute and are dependent on several requirements and conditions.

II. Mere Conduit

357. Section 16 Electronic Commerce Act (corresponding to Article 12 Directive on Electronic Commerce), stipulates that an *information society service provider* shall not be liable for the content of the information, if the service only consists of the transmission of information, provided by a recipient of the service, in a communication network, or if the service provider only gives access to a communication network.

753. Directive 2000/31/EC of the European Parliament and of the Council of 8 June 2000 on certain legal aspects of information society services, in particular e-commerce, in the Internal Market.

754. Article 1(2) of Directive (EU) 2015/1535 of the European Parliament and of the Council of 9 September 2015 laying down a procedure for the provision of information in the field of technical regulations and of rules on Information Society services.

This exemption from liability applies only if the service provider: (i) has not initiated the transmission; (ii) does not select the receiver of the transmission; and (iii) does not select or modify the information contained in the transmission.

358. In contrast, service providers that are the sources of the information, select recipients of the transmission or modify the information transmitted, with exception of mere technical manipulation during the transmission,[755] can be liable for the damage caused.

Further, in accordance with Recital 42 Directive on Electronic Commerce, the exemptions from liability only cover cases where the activity of the service provider is of a mere technical, automatic and passive nature. The service provider must neither have knowledge of nor control over the information which is transmitted or stored.

359. The question of an ISP's responsibility for its customers' communication was discussed in two Swedish court cases in 2011 and 2012. In both cases the plaintiffs demanded injunctions to prohibit the ISPs to provide Internet service for BitTorrent trackers – that is, servers that assist in the communication between peers using the BitTorrent protocol – accused of copyright infringement. However, one of the cases (The *Portlane* case) did not regard liability per se, but a temporary injunction.

A. *The* Black Internet *Case*[756]

360. In the first case, copyright holders filed a request for an injunction to prohibit the Swedish ISP Black Internet from providing Internet service for the well-known Pirate Bay.[757] The copyright holders also requested a temporary injunction, until the case was finally adjudicated or otherwise is decided. Such injunction and temporary injunction are provided for under section 53b Copyright Act.

The grounds for the injunction (as well as the temporary injunction) was that Black Internet, by providing Internet service for The Pirate Bay, objectively was considered aiding and abetting the copyright infringements taking place with the help of the file sharing service provided for by The Pirate Bay. Black Internet disputed the motions and held that their role as an ISP could not be considered aiding and abetting copyright infringement.

B. *The* Portlane *Case*[758]

361. In the second case, copyright holders filed a similar temporary injunction to prohibit the Swedish ISP Portlane, to provide Internet service to one or more BitTorrent trackers connected with the domain name tracker.openbittorrent.com. In this

755. *See* Recital 43 Directive of Electronic Commerce.
756. Decision of the District Court of Stockholm from 21 Aug. 2009, No. T 11712–09.
757. *See* §2 IV A *infra* (para. 368).
758. Decision of the District Court of Stockholm from 1 Dec. 2009, No. T 17127–09.

case, however, the district court came to the conclusion that an ISP cannot be burdened with such far-reaching responsibility that they can be regarded as contributors to the copyright infringement. Hence, the petition for temporary injunction was denied.

The decision was appealed by the copyright holders. The Court of Appeal overruled the aforesaid decision and held that the copyright holders had shown a probable cause that Portlane had objectively contributed to the copyright infringement. Thus, the Court of Appeal temporarily prohibited by penalty of a fine Portlane to provide Internet services to the BitTorrent trackers.[759]

Portlane thereafter went bankrupt and the parties entered into a settlement. The case was therefore dismissed.[760]

362. The position in Swedish law following the two cases was that an ISP could only be held liable if it had objectively contributed to the copyright infringements taking place on the illegal file sharing website. This position was however changed by the Swedish Patent and Market Court of Appeal following the CJEU's decision in Case C-314-12, *UPC Telekabel.*[761] The case was not brought before the CJEU by a Swedish Court, but it is mentioned here since it changed the position of Swedish law.

C. *Case 314-12,* UPC Telekabel

363. Two copyright holders filed an order enjoining the ISP 'UPC Telekabel' to block the access of its customers to a website where copyright-protected films were available to download or 'stream'. In contrast with the *Black Internet* and *Portlane* cases, the action was not brought against the ISP of the illegal file sharing website. It had not even been established that the ISP's own customers had visited the site. The court referred to the CJEU for a preliminary ruling and asked whether Article 8(3) of Directive 2001/29[762] should be interpreted as meaning that a person who makes protected subject matter available to the public on a website without the agreement of the rightholder, for the purpose of Article 3(2) of that directive, is using the services of the Internet service provider of the persons accessing that subject matter, which is to be regarded as an intermediary within the meaning of Article 8(3) of Directive 2001/29.

The court held that an ISP which allows its customers to access protected subject matter made available to the public on the Internet by a third party is an intermediary within the meaning of Article 8(3) of Directive 2001/29. Consequently, such an ISP could be subject to an injunction. The Court held that there is no requirement of a specific relationship between the ISP and the person infringing copyright

759. Decision of Svea Court of Appeal from 21 May 2010, No. Ö 10146-09.
760. Decision of the District Court of Stockholm from 8 Mar. 2011, No. T 17127-09.
761. Judgement of 27 Mar. 2014, UPC Telekabel Wien, C-314/12, ECLI:EU:C:2014:192.
762. Directive 2001/29/EC of the European Parliament and of the Council of 22 May 2001 on the harmonization of certain aspects of copyright and related rights in the information society.

or a related right, or of the copyright holders showing that the ISP's customers have actually accessed the protected subject matter.

D. The B2 Bredband *Case*[763]

364. Shortly after the decision in *UPC Telekabel*, the Swedish Patent and Market Court ruled in a similar case, where several copyright holders had filed an order enjoining the ISP B2 Bredband to block its customer's access to two illegal file-sharing websites.

The Swedish Copyright Act does not lay out a specific statutory provision enabling a court to order an ISP to block its customer's access to illegal file-sharing websites. Section 53b of the Swedish Copyright Act only states that whoever contributes to copyright infringement may be ordered to stop its contribution.

The Patent and Market Court found that the CJEU's judgment in the *UPC Telekabel* case did not necessitate an interpretation of Swedish Copyright law to include contribution by means of providing Internet access. The District Court therefore gave its judgment in accordance with the findings in the *Black Internet* and *Portlane* cases. The District Court found that B2 Bredband had not objectively contributed to the copyright infringements simply by providing Internet access and dismissed the claim for an injunction.[764]

The copyright holders appealed to the Patent and Market Court of Appeal. The Court of Appeal took the opposite view, and found that the Swedish Copyright Act must be interpreted in light of the CJEU's decision. The Court of Appeal therefore concluded that the ISP did not have to objectively contribute to the infringements in order for an injunction to be ordered against the ISP. Instead – in accordance with the CJEU's judgment – the court found that an injunction can be ordered against any ISP that provides Internet access that enables its customers to access illegal file-sharing websites. Thus, the Patent and Market Court of Appeal ordered B2 Bredband by penalty of a fine to block their customer's access to the illegal file-sharing websites.[765]

III. Caching

365. Section 17 Electronic Commerce Act, corresponding to Article 13 Directive on Electronic Commerce, provides for a rule on freedom from liability regarding caching. In brief, caching is the process where information is temporarily stored by, for example, ISPs or other intermediaries, for the purpose of reducing the amount of resources that otherwise would be involved in the transmission of data. For example, ISPs regularly store parts of popular websites on their servers, thus increasing the access speed and freeing bandwidth for its subscribers. From a legal

763. Judgement of the Patent and Market Court of Appeal from 13 Feb. 2017, No. PMT 11706-15.
764. Judgement of the Patent and Market Court from 27 Nov. 2015, No. T 15142-14.
765. Judgement of the Patent and Market Court of Appeal from 13 Feb. 2017, No. PMT 11706-15.

point of view, caching primarily raises questions regarding copying under the law on copyright, but also other branches of law may be concerned.

For caching to be legally possible without infringing copyright or other rights, section 17 Electronic Commerce Act stipulates that a Service Provider is not liable for transmissions of information provided by a recipient of the service in a communication network if the storage of information is automatic, intermediate and temporary, and the storage is made for the sole purpose of making the transmission to other recipients of the service more efficient.

Further, for freedom from liability, it is required that the provider (i) does not modify the information, (ii) complies with conditions on access to the information, (iii) complies with rules recognized and used by the industry regarding updating of the information, (iv) does not interfere with the lawful use of technology widely recognized and used by the industry, and, finally, (v) without delay intervenes to remove or to disable access to the information it has stored upon obtaining actual knowledge that the information at the initial source of the transmission has been removed from the network, or access to it has been disabled, or that a court or an administrative authority has ordered such removal or disablement.

366. As far as copyright is concerned, it is necessary to mention the limitations of reproduction rights stipulated in section 11a Copyright Act.[766] The provision in the aforesaid section excludes from the rights of the copyright holder any temporary acts of reproduction which are an integral and essential part of a technological process, and where the reproductions only are transient or incidental. Further, the reproductions must not have any independent economic significance, the purpose of the reproduction must be to enable transmission in a network between third parties and the use must be lawful.

The consequence of the aforesaid provision in the Copyright Act is that section 17 Electronic Commerce Act regarding caching to some extent loses its importance, at least in the area of copyright. The Electronic Commerce Act is only applicable in situations where the intermediary is liable according to the Copyright Act. Since section 11a Copyright Act excludes liability for temporary acts of reproduction, the Electronic Commerce Act is not applicable. Thus, the importance of section 17 Electronic Commerce Act has been reduced by section 11a Copyright Act.

IV. Hosting

367. The rule in the Electronic Commerce Act limiting liability for various hosting services is found in section 18, and corresponds to Article 14 Directive on Electronic Commerce. Examples of hosting services covered by the provision are web

766. Section 11a Copyright Act is the result of the implementation of Directive 2001/29/EC of the European Parliament and of the Council of 22 May 2001 on the harmonization of certain aspects of copyright and related rights in the information society. *See* Part II Ch. 1 §6 I *supra* (paras 170–171).

hotels, electronic bulletin boards, guest books and other interactive online services.[767] In accordance with section 18, service providers which store information provided by a recipient of the service are not liable for the information stored. However, to have the benefit of freedom from liability, the service provider must not have actual knowledge of the illegal information or activity, and must not be aware of facts or circumstances from which the illegal activity or information is apparent. As soon as the service provider obtains such knowledge or awareness, the service provider must, without delay, prevent further access to the information.

The question of freedom from liability for hosting services has recently been subject to two judgments in the Svea Court of Appeal and the District Court of Stockholm.

A. *The* Pirate Bay *Case*[768]

368. In the first case, the question of freedom from liability for hosting services arose in the criminal proceedings against the people behind the Swedish file sharing website The Pirate Bay (thepiratebay.org).

In the case, the prosecutor charged the defendants with complicity in copyright infringement. It was argued that copyright-protected material was made available to the general public in a way which was to be regarded as a breach of the Copyright Act. The defendants pleaded not guilty. In accordance with the Swedish Code on Judicial Procedure, civil claims of copyright holders were also addressed in the case.

Regarding liability for hosting services, the Court of Appeal confirmed the finding of the district court, and held that the file sharing service provided by The Pirate Bay was considered an information society service covered by the Electronic Commerce Act. However, referring to the CJEU's judgment in Cases C-236/08–C-238/08,[769] the court stated that a person providing a search engine service can very well be a service provider within the meaning of the EU Directive on Electronic Commerce, without being covered by any of the provisions regarding limitations of liability. In order for a release from liability for damages according to sections 16–18 Electronic Commerce Act, the service provided must be limited to either forwarding, caching or hosting services only. The court found that although the website did not involve a pure transmission service or caching, it did in certain aspects correspond to hosting services covered by section 18 Electronic Commerce Act. However, this release of liability provision focuses on liability for the *content* of stored information. The damages claim was not based on liability for the content of the information stored on the website, but on the *functions* which were provided and that had furthered copyright exploitation by users. Therefore, the court found that

767. Government Bill (*Proposition*) 2001/02:150, 'Lag om elektronisk handel och andra informationssamhällets tjänster, m.m.', 21.

768. Judgment of the Svea Court of Appeal from 26 Nov. 2010, No. B 4041-09.

769. Judgement of 23 Mar. 2010, Google France and Google, Joined Cases C-236/08–C-238/08, ECLI: EU:C:2010:159.

the service on the website was not covered by any of the provisions set forth in sections 16–18 Electronic Commerce Act and the rules of freedom from liability could not be applied. The Court of Appeal found the defendants guilty of complicity in copyright infringement. It should be noted that, in accordance with Swedish penal law, to be convicted for complicity in crime it is not a requirement that the perpetrators behind the main crime are identified, provided that an actual crime has been committed. It should also be noted that the court found Swedish law applicable in accordance with the above-mentioned rules on jurisdiction and choice of law. The defendants were sentenced to four to twelve months imprisonment (each defendant was punished only for the act he had committed himself) and ordered to pay damages in the range of SEK 46 million (approximately EUR 4.4 million).

The sentence was appealed to the Supreme Court by the defendants, who also requested that a preliminary ruling be obtained from the CJEU. The Supreme Court denied this request and also denied leave to appeal.[770]

B. The Matklubben.se *Case*[771]

369. In the second case, a copyright holder claimed damages for copyright infringement from the companies behind the Swedish website Matklubben.se.[772] The website offers a database which contains thousands of recipes and photographs of each dish. All recipes and photographs are uploaded and shared by the Internet users themselves and not by any of the companies behind the website. Regarding liability for hosting services, the district court held that the file sharing services provided by Matklubben.se was considered an information society service covered by the Electronic Commerce Act. It was clear that the services were provided at a distance by electronic means and at the individual request of the recipients of the services (*see* the definition above).

Even though the recipients of the service did not pay for the service (*see* the requirement normally provided for remuneration), the court found that since it was partly funded by advertising revenue, the service was covered by the Electronic Commerce Act. Further, the court stated that since the website contained only uploaded recipes and photographs, discussion forums and adverts, and no editorial material, the service was to be regarded as a hosting service covered by section 18 Electronic Commerce Act. As stated above, for freedom from liability, the service provider must not be aware of the illegal information or activity and is obliged to prevent further access to the information when such knowledge is obtained. In the case, it was established that Matklubben.se was used mainly for legal purposes. It was further established that the defendants had offered to immediately prevent access to files uploaded on Matklubben.se, as soon as requests had been made by copyright holders. Thus, the defendants had fulfilled its obligations under section 18 Electronic Commerce Act and were released from liability. The copyright holders did not appeal and the ruling has gained legal force.

770. Decision of Supreme Court from 1 Feb. 2012, No. B 5880-10.
771. Judgment of the District Court of Stockholm from 27 Jun. 2013, No. T 10848-09.
772. www.matklubben.se.

§3. Electronic Bulletin Boards

370. An Electronic Bulletin Board is, in accordance with the legal definition in the Act on Responsibility for Electronic Bulletin Boards (*lag (1998:112) om ansvar för elektroniska anslagstavlor*), a service for the electronic transmission of messages. According to the Act, a message is text, pictures, sound or other information. However, the law does not apply to network operators, or to mediation of messages within a public authority, between public authorities, within an enterprise or between a legal group of enterprises. Further, the law does not apply to services that are covered by the regulations in the Freedom of the Press Act or the Fundamental Law on Freedom of Expression, such as the rule regarding databases found in Chapter 1 section 9 Fundamental Law on Freedom of Expression, or to email.[773]

Examples of Electronic Bulletin Boards are services where users can perform functions such as uploading and downloading software and data, reading news and exchanging messages with other users. There are no special liability rules in the Act of Responsibility for Electronic Bulletin Boards. The supplier of an electronic bulletin board is of course not exempted from the general principles of the Tort Liability Act. However, since electronic bulletin boards fall under the definition of hosting services in section 18 Electronic Commerce Act, the provisions on freedom from liability regarding hosting in that Act must also be taken into account.[774]

371. The main principles on liability in the Act on Responsibility for Electronic Bulletin Boards are found in sections 3–5.

First, according to section 3, the supplier of an electronic bulletin board must notify each person who connects to the service of the identity of the supplier and to what extent messages posted will be available to other users.

Second, according to section 4, the supplier has an obligation to supervise the service to a reasonable extent, considering the scope and objective of the service.

Third, according to section 5, the supplier must remove a message, or in some other way make it inaccessible, if it is obvious that the message is in breach of certain sections of the Swedish Penal Code. Such obligations arise if a message is an unlawful threat[775] or an unlawful encroachment on personal integrity,[776] is inciting rebellion,[777] agitates against an ethnic group or another group of persons with allusion to race, colour, national or ethnic origin, religious belief or sexual orientation,[778] portrays or in any other way makes pornographic pictures of children available to others,[779] is an unlawful depiction of violence,[780] or is instigating

773. *See* Government Bill (*Proposition*) 1997/98:15, 'Ansvar för elektroniska anslagstavlor', 12.
774. Government Bill (*Proposition*) 2001/02:150, 121.
775. Chapter 4 s. 5 Penal Code.
776. Chapter 4 s. 6c Penal Code.
777. Chapter 16 s. 5 Penal Code.
778. Chapter 16 s. 8 Penal Code.
779. Chapter 16 s. 10a Penal Code.
780. Chapter 16 s. 10b Penal Code.

terrorism.[781] Further, the supplier must also remove messages if it is obvious that the user, by submitting the message, has committed copyright infringement.

372. The obligation to remove messages concerning agitation against a group with certain sexual orientation has been subject to a ruling by the Swedish Supreme Court.[782] Certain negative remarks concerning persons with homosexual preferences were posted on an electronic bulletin board (in this case a guestbook on a website) with reference to the Bible. The Court held that even if the messages objectively constituted agitation against an ethnic group in accordance with Chapter 16 section 8 Penal Code, this was not obvious to the supplier of the electronic bulletin board and thus the supplier was freed of all charges.

373. As stated above, there are no special rules on liability in the Act on Responsibility for Electronic Bulletin Boards. The responsibilities set forth in the Act – for example, the omission to remove certain postings – are sanctioned by fine or imprisonment. This, however, does not exclude liability in accordance with the Tort Liability Act. As accounted for in section 1, the fundamental question when determining whether a person has been negligent or not is if the person accused of being negligent has deviated in a blameworthy manner from what can be expected from her or him. The assessment of a blameworthy deviant behaviour is made primarily based on any law or regulation governing a specific area. The rules in the Act on Responsibility for Electronic Bulletin Boards stipulate a certain way of conduct, for example an obligation to remove certain messages. Hence, damage caused by deviance from this way of conduct, unless the circumstances provide otherwise, is generally a basis for liability. The consequence of the fact that it is a criminal act not to remove, for instance, copyright-protected material, is that the liability also covers purely financial loss.

§4. Personal Data Protection

374. Many companies in the ICT sector process personal data in the course of their business. The Personal Data Act (*personuppgiftslag (1998:204))* which regulated the processing of personal data in Sweden was repealed on the 25 May 2018 and replaced by the GDPR.

The GDPR aims to protect people against the violation of their personal integrity by processing of personal data. According to Article 2 GDPR, the Regulation applies to all processing of personal data that is, wholly or partly, performed with the aid of computers. The Regulation also applies to other processing of personal data that form part of a filing system or are intended to form part of a filing system. Processing of personal data that a natural person performs in the course of activities of a purely personal or household activity is, however, excluded.

781. Section 3 Act on Criminal Responsibility for Public Provocation, Recruitment and Training concerning Terrorist Offences and other Particularly Serious Crimes.
782. Decision by Supreme Court from 7 Nov. 2007, NJA 2007 s. 805.

Processing means everything one does with personal data, whether performed through a computer or not. For example, collection, registration, storage and compilation of personal data are all considered processing in the meaning of the GDPR.

Article 5 prescribes that personal data shall be processed lawfully, fairly and in a transparent manner in relation to the data subject. In addition, personal data shall only be collected and further processed for a specified, explicit and legitimate purpose. No more personal data than is necessary may be processed and the personal data may not be kept for a longer period than necessary with regard to the purpose of the processing. Lastly, personal data shall always be accurate and, where necessary, kept up to date and only be processed in a manner that ensures appropriate security of the personal data.

375. As far as liability is concerned, Article 82 provides a specific liability provision. As previously stressed, specific provisions supersede the general liability rules of the Tort Liability Act. However, general tort law principles apply to the extent that the specific liability provision does not give guidance in a certain question, for instance on how to determine the compensation.

Article 82 grants registered persons a right to recover damages from the data controller or data processor for any material or non-material damage caused by processing in breach of the GDPR. Liability is strict and the right to damages therefore arises regardless of any intent or negligence attributable to the person violating the rules. All damages, including personal injury, property damage, purely financial loss and violation of personal integrity, can be recovered under the Regulation.

The GDPR does not provide for any guidance on how to calculate damages. Instead, this follows from the general principles laid down in the Tort Liability Act. As stated above, the general principle is that the compensation shall put the injured in the same financial situation as before the injury or damage occurred.

§5. Liability under the Fundamental Law on Freedom of Expression

376. In Sweden, there are two separate constitutional laws concerning freedom of speech. The Freedom of the Press Act (*tryckfrihetsförordning (1949:105)*) regulates the printed word, such as books and newspapers, whereas the Fundamental Law on Freedom of Expression (*yttrandefrihetsgrundlag (1991:1469)*) regulates certain other types of mass media, such as television, certain web sites, radio, and films. This chapter will briefly deal with the Fundamental Law on Freedom of Expression and the specific liability provisions therein.

In accordance with Chapter 1 Article 1 Fundamental Law on Freedom of Expression, every Swedish citizen is guaranteed the right, vis-à-vis the public institutions, to publicly express thoughts, opinions and sentiments, and in general to communicate information on any subject whatsoever on sound radio, television and certain like transmissions, films and video recordings. The only restrictions permitted are the ones stated in the Fundamental Law on Freedom of Expression itself. For example, the general rule in Chapter 1 Article 3, stating that censorship prior to publication is not allowed, is restricted in the same Article for movies intended for public showing.

The purpose of the Fundamental Law on Freedom of Expression is to protect the freedom of expression in the media forms covered by the law. Therefore, only certain offences are punishable under the Fundamental Law on Freedom of Expression. Furthermore, the law specifies exactly who may be held responsible.

Chapter 4 Fundamental Law on Freedom of Expression stipulates that all radio programmes and technical recordings shall have a responsible editor empowered to supervise the publication. According to Chapter 6 of the aforesaid law, the liability for freedom of expression offences (e.g., defamation) rests with the responsible editor, or if a deputy is acting in place of the editor, liability rests with the deputy. If none of those persons are traceable, someone else steps in, in a sort of chain of responsible persons. Hence, in these situations undertakings involved in the provision of information society services, such as ISPs, are exempted from liability by statutory provisions in the Swedish constitution.

Chapter 4. Product Liability

§1. General Statement

377. The primary regulation of product liability in Sweden is found in the Product Liability Act (*produktansvarslag (1992:18)*). The Act is a result of the implementation of the EU Directive on Liability for Defective Products[783] in Swedish law. However, liability may also follow from principles developed in Swedish case law.[784] The existence of the Product Safety Act (*produktsäkerhetslag (2004:451)*) concerning the safety of products should also be noted. However, the Act will not be dealt with further in this chapter, since it does not concern liability per se.

In accordance with section 1 Product Liability Act, the main rule is that personal injury caused due to a defect in a product shall be compensated. This also applies to property damage, if the damage is caused by a defect in the product, provided that the product is of a type that is intended for private purposes and the damage was caused when the product was used mainly for the purpose intended for such products. Hence, property damages caused by products used in the course of business are not covered by the Product Liability Act. Liability for such damages may, however, follow from general principles developed in Swedish case law.[785] Furthermore, the Swedish Supreme Court has established that the notion property damage shall have the same meaning as in the Tort Liability Act.[786]

There is no requirement of intent or negligence, consequently the liability is strict.

To be compensated, damages must exceed SEK 3,500 (approximately EUR 340). This unusual regime is due to a general deduction from any compensation to be paid under the Act.[787] Even though the Directive on Liability for Defective Products provides the possibility to set a threshold for the producer's total liability, such a limitation has not been implemented in the Swedish Product Liability Act. It should be noted that purely financial losses are not compensated under the Product Liability Act.

---

783. Council Directive 85/374/EEC of 25 July 1985 on the approximation of the laws, regulations and administrative provisions of the Member States concerning liability for defective products (hereinafter 'Directive on Liability for Defective Products'). The Directive 1999/34/EC of the European Parliament and of the Council of 10 May 1999 amending Council Directive 85/374/EEC on the approximation of the laws, regulations and administrative provisions of the Member States concerning liability for defective products did not give rise to any changes of the Product Liability Act.
784. Lindberg & Westman, 125.
785. Government Bill (*Proposition*) 1990/91:197, 'Regeringens proposition om produktskadelag', 76–78.
786. *See* Decision by Supreme Court from 20 Feb. 1996, NJA 1996 s. 68.
787. Section 9 Product Liability Act.

§2. Movables, Hardware and Software

378. In accordance with section 2 Product Liability Act, the notion product includes all movables. It also includes movables that are incorporated into or in some other way have become a component part of another movable or an immovable. If damage has occurred due to a defect in a product that has become a component part of another movable or an immovable, both products shall be deemed to have caused the damage. However, in contrast to the Directive on Liability for Defective Products, the Product Liability Act does not include electricity. The discrepancy is explained in the Government Bill.[788] According to Swedish law electricity is not recognized as a movable. Instead, the provisions on strict liability in relation to electricity are included in sections 28–35 of the Electrical Safety Act (*elsäkerhetslag (2016:732)*).

It is evident that hardware, such as a computer, is covered by the notion product, and thus falls within the scope of the Product Liability Act. In contrast, software is typically not considered a product under the Product Liability Act. In accordance with the preparatory works, software is merely considered to be a series of instructions that make hardware perform certain actions.[789]

If damage is caused by a product, in the sense of the Product Liability Act, and the damage is due to a defect in software integrated in the product, it is still the product that shall be deemed to have caused the damage. However, the legislator provides some possibilities for the courts to make other interpretations of the notion product with account to technical development.[790] It has been argued that software should fall under the notion product, and thus the strict liability in the Product Liability Act.[791] The uncertainty is noteworthy considering how common it is that software controls important occurrences and defects may cause a great deal of damage. However, it should also be noted that liability for defective software still may follow from the general principles of the Tort Liability Act.

§3. Defective Products

379. The notion defect is defined in section 3 Product Liability Act. A product is considered defective when it does not provide the safety that a person is entitled to expect. When determining the safety of the product, account must be taken of the use to which it could reasonably be expected that the product would be put and how it was marketed. Furthermore, account must be taken of the directions for use, the time when the product was put into circulation and all other circumstances. In Article 6(2) Directive on Liability for Defective Products, it is stated that a product shall not be considered defective for the sole reason that a better product is subsequently put into circulation. No such provision is included in the Product Liability

788. Government Bill (*Proposition*) 1990/91:197, 14.
789. *Ibid.*, 93.
790. *Ibid.*, 94.
791. Lindberg, Westman, 125.

Act. Nevertheless, the preparatory works state that a rule with the same meaning may be applicable under the Product Liability Act.[792] To the author's knowledge, it has yet to be tried by a Swedish court.

§4. Persons Liable for Damages

380. With the given definition of the notion product,[793] it is also evident that services are excluded from the strict liability of the Product Liability Act. For example, ISPs are not liable under the Product Liability Act for damages caused to a computer in connection with the service. However, they may be liable for providing hardware causing damage.

In accordance with sections 6 and 7 Product Liability Act, liability is vested with the manufacturer, the creator or the collector of the tortuous product, the importer of the product into the EU, or any person who has marketed the product as her or his own by putting her or his trademark or other distinguishing feature on the product. When none of the above can be identified, each supplier of the product will be liable in accordance with the Product Liability Act.

The supplier may escape liability if she or he, within one month from a claim of compensation or request for information about the producer of the product, informs the claimant of the identity of the producer or of the person who supplied her or him with the product.

Contractual derogation from liability is declared null and void in accordance with section 5 Product Liability Act.

381. The persons liable for damages in accordance with sections 6 and 7 Product Liability Act may, however, escape liability under certain circumstances as specified in section 8 of the Act. No liability is inflicted to the person normally liable in accordance with the above, if that person:

- shows that she or he did not put the product into circulation in the course of business; or
- makes it probable that the defect which caused the damage did not exist at the time when the product was put into circulation; or
- shows that the defect is due to compliance of the product with mandatory regulations issued by the public authorities; or
- shows that the state of scientific and technical knowledge at the time when the product was put into circulation was not such as to enable the existence of the defect to be discovered.

Section 8 Product Liability Act corresponds to a large extent to Article 7 Directive on Liability for Defective Products. However, section 8 Product Liability Act

792. Government Bill (*Proposition*) 1990/91:197, 108.
793. *See* §2 *supra* (para. 378).

does not include a defence for manufacturers of a component. According to the preparatory works, no divergence is intended.[794] The situation is considered to be covered by the above-mentioned rule in section 2 Product Liability Act, which states that the component manufacturer as well as the manufacturer of the finished product shall be liable for damages caused by a defect in the component part.

382. When two or more are liable for the same damage, the general principle in the Tort Liability Act is joint and several liability.[795] Since the principle is generally applicable, the legislator did not find it necessary to include an explicit provision on this in the Product Liability Act, even though such provision is found in Article 5 Directive on Liability for Defective Products.

§5. Reduction of Liability, Limitation of Actions

383. Under section 10 Product Liability Act, the liability may be reduced having regard to what is reasonable, when negligence on the part of the injured person has contributed to the damage. Compared to the general rules of the Tort Liability Act, under which liability may only be mitigated due to gross negligence or intent on the part of the injured person, the Product Liability Act provides a less consumer friendly approach in this respect. Nevertheless, in accordance with the preparatory works, the injured person still has the possibility to claim damages under the Tort Liability Act, provided that the injured person can establish that the producer was negligent. Thus the person liable for the tortuous product has to show gross negligence on the part of the injured person for the liability to be mitigated.[796]

384. Section 12 Product Liability Act provides a statutory rule limiting the time within which proceedings can be brought. Actions must be launched within three years from the day on which the plaintiff became aware, or should reasonably have become aware, of the relevant circumstances. Furthermore, section 12 Product Liability Act states that the right to compensation in accordance with the Act is extinguished after the expiry of a period of ten years from the date on which the producer put the product which caused the damage into circulation.

---

794. Government Bill (*Proposition*) 1990/91:197, 96.
795. Chapter 6 s. 4 Tort Liability Act.
796. Government Bill (*Proposition*) 1992/93:38, 'Proposition om ändring i produktansvarslagen (1992:18) m.m.', 15.

Part VI. Privacy Protection

Chapter 1. Regulation of Personal Data Processing

§1. General Statement

385. The Swedish Instrument of Government (*regeringsform (1974:152)*) is one of the four constitutional laws in Sweden. Its Chapter 2 Article 6 paragraph 2 protects privacy as a fundamental right. While privacy was previously regulated in Chapter 2 Article 3, the constitution now states in Chapter 2 Article 6:

> [e]veryone shall be protected in their relations with the public institutions against significant invasions of their personal privacy, if these occur without their consent and involve the surveillance or systematic monitoring of the individual's personal circumstances.

Though privacy is not defined as such in the constitution, Article 6 mentions surveillance and monitoring, which seems to indicate that the focus remains to be the processing of personal data.

Sweden implemented the European Parliament and Council Directive 95/46/EC of 24 October 1995 on the protection of individuals with regard to the processing of personal data and on the free movement of such data (hereinafter 'Data Protection Directive') in 1998 by enacting the Personal Data Act (*personuppgiftslag (1998:204)*). The Personal Data Act replaced the previously in force Swedish Data Act (*datalag (1973:289)*) from 1973, which had mainly focused on computer registers and not data processing in general.

With the adoption of the EU GDPR,[797] the Personal Data Act was repealed and replaced with a law that complements the GDPR. The new Data Protection Act (*lag (2018:218) med kompletterande bestämmelser till EU:s dataskyddsförordning [dataskyddslag]*) was enacted in April 2018 and contains sections that complement or regulate the GDPR in more detail.

797. Regulation (EU) 2016/679 of the European Parliament and Council of 27 Apr. 2016 on the protection of natural persons with regard to the processing of personal data and on the free movement of such data, and repealing Directive 95/46/EC (General Data Protection Regulation).

386. The Swedish legislative framework protects privacy in many different aspects.[798] Starting from criminal provisions protecting against kidnapping or unlawful deprivation of liberty,[799] defamation,[800] breach of postal or telecommunication secrecy[801] or eavesdropping,[802] privacy-related provisions can also be found within tax law (exchange of personal data between public authorities), credit information and debt collection, court proceedings and criminal procedural coercive measures, as well as police investigations (surveillance and databases with criminal records), within health and social care and in the rules relating to processing of employees' personal data. In the following, focus will be placed on the general legal framework for automated data processing, along with the mention of a few special statutory provisions.

§2. GDPR FROM A SWEDISH PERSPECTIVE

387. In accordance with Article 1 GDPR (and previously Article 1 Data Protection Directive), the EU and Swedish law protect individuals against violations of their personal integrity, in particular the right to the protection of data. As also stipulated in the Swedish constitution,[803] the protection covers data processing and not privacy in general.

According to Article 3 GDPR, the regulation applies to controllers or processors established in the EU, and to controllers and processors outside the EU who offer goods or services to individuals within the EU or monitor behaviour or individuals within the EU.[804] As the GDPR is directly applicable in all EU Member States, the GDPR does not specify a particular country's legislation. Section 5 Swedish Data Protection Act (*dataskyddslag*) stipulates that it applies to processing that is done by controllers or processors who are established in Sweden or who offer goods or services *to*, or monitor behaviour *of* individuals situated in Sweden.[805]

The GDPR regulates the processing of personal data and the requirements such processing has to fulfil, in particular Articles 5 and 6,[806] in order to be allowed. The GDPR amended the original principles of the Data Protection Directive, dealing with certain aspects in more detail as well as adding principles such as privacy by design and rules on data impact assessments. As the GDPR replaced the Data Protection Directive and subsequently the Swedish Personal Data Act, certain Swedish amendments such as the special rules for unstructured processing introduced in 2007[807] are no longer in force.

798. *See* for a complete analysis of privacy-related legislation: Government Official Report SOU 2007:22, 'Skyddet för den personliga integriteten, Kartläggning och analys Del 1'.
799. Chapter 4 ss 1 and 2 Penal Code.
800. Chapter 5 s. 1 Penal Code.
801. Chapter 4 s. 8 Penal Code.
802. Chapter 4 s. 9a Penal Code.
803. *See* §1 *supra* (para. 385).
804. *See* in particular Art. 3.2 GDPR.
805. Section 5 Swedish Data Protection Act (*dataskyddslag*).
806. Previously ss 9 and 10 Swedish Personal Data Act (*personuppgiftslag*).
807. Government Bill (*Proposition*) 2005/06:173, 'Översyn av personuppgiftslagen'.

The following structure of this chapter has been kept from previous editions, following the Swedish Personal Data Act and the Data Protection Directive, but was amended to the extent required by additional rules in the GDPR. The chapter will focus on requirements for processing of personal data, rules on sensitive personal information, information to the individual as well as the transfer of personal data to third countries.

I. Definitions

388. Article 4 GDPR,[808] defines *inter alia*, the following terms.

A. *Personal Data*

389. Personal data: any information relating to an identified or identifiable natural person ('data subject').

390. The definition of personal data excludes data on legal persons, unless the company is a sole trader. As the registration number of a sole trader consists of the personal number of the owner of the company, it is considered personal data.[809]

Any information that can be attributed to an individual is personal data, regardless of whether it concerns that person's private, work or social life.[810] The GDPR mentions as examples of identifiers 'name, an identification number, location data, an online identifier or [a reference] to one or more factors specific to the physical, physiological, genetic, mental, economic, cultural or social identity of that natural person'. Examples of personal data therefore include name, address, telephone number, personal number and car registration number. Images or sounds can constitute personal data if an individual can be directly or indirectly identified in them.[811] Biometric data, such as fingerprints, retinal patterns, facial structure and DNA, also falls within the category of personal data.[812]

In accordance with Recital 26 of the previously in force Data Protection Directive, in determining 'whether a person is identifiable account should be taken of all the means likely reasonably to be used either by the controller or by any other person to identify the said person'. This means that as long as somebody, not necessarily the controller, can link a piece of information to a natural person, it is considered personal data. Therefore encrypted data, as well as anonymous details such as IP numbers or other eIDs that require a key or access to the database of the

808. Previously Art. 2 Data Protection Directive and s. 3 Swedish Personal Data Act.
809. *See* decision by the Court of Appeal Svea hovrätt from 31 Aug. 2004, nr B 4151–04.
810. *See* Art. 29 Data Protection Working Party, 'Opinion N° 4/2007 on the concept of personal data', 01248/07/EN – WP 136, 6–7.
811. Sören Öman & Hans-Olof Lindblom, *Personuppgiftslagen – En kommentar*, 4th edn (Stockholm: Norstedts, 2009), s. 3; Sören Öman, *Dataskyddsförordningen (GDPR) m.m.*, (Stockholm: Norstedts Juridik, 2019), heading Första punkten – Personuppgifter.
812. *See* Art. 29 Data Protection Working Party, 'Opinion N° 4/2007 on the concept of personal data', 8.

ISP, fall within the scope of data protection.[813] In a decision in 2005, the Swedish Data Protection Authority (*Datainspektionen*), as well as the Stockholm Administrative Court of Appeal (*Kammarrätt*), considered IP numbers being used by a Swedish anti-pirate organization as personal data.[814] This approach was confirmed in a CJEU judgment from 2016 in the *Breyer* case where dynamic IP addresses were considered personal data.[815] In addition, Recital 30 GDPR mentions online identifiers such as Internet protocol addresses, cookie identifiers or radio frequency identification (RFID) tags as types of personal data and points out the particular risk of this data to be used for profiling of users. Recital 34 also mentions genetic data, in particular DNA and RNA analysis, as personal data.

In 2017, the CJEU decided that the definition of personal data can also include 'opinions and assessments' that relate to the individual, so information does not have to be sensitive or private in order to be considered personal data.[816] Photographs and audio recordings are personal data to the extent an individual person can be identified.[817]

Examples that do not fall within the definition of personal data are generic names of cities or streets, general descriptions of people concerning hair or eye colour, as well as the history list on a computer that contains all previously visited web pages.[818]

The requirement for the data subject to be a natural person excludes dead or unborn people such as embryos. Information about relatives of the deceased or parents of an unborn child is, however, considered to be personal data.

B. *Special Categories of Personal Data (Previously Sensitive Personal Data)*

391. Article 9 GDPR[819] regulates the processing of special categories of personal data. As examples for special categories, the article mentions data relating to:

- racial or ethnic origin;
- political opinions;
- religious or philosophical beliefs;
- trade union membership;
- genetic or biometric data for the purpose of uniquely identifying a natural person;
- health;
- a natural person's sex life or sexual orientation.

813. Öman & Lindblom, *Personuppgiftslagen*, s. 3.
814. Decision by the Data Protection Authority from 8 Jun. 2005, nr 593–2005; and Decision by the Administrative Court of Appeal (*Kammarrätt*) in Stockholm from 8 Jun. 2007, nr 285–07.
815. *See* Case C-582/14 *Breyer*, EU:C:2016:779, para. 46.
816. *See* Case C-434/16 *Nowak*, ECLI:EU:C:2017:994, para. 34.
817. *See*, e.g., Case C-345/17 *Buivids*, ECLI:EU:C:2019:122, paras 31 and 32.
818. *See* Decision by the Swedish Supreme Administrative Court from 11 Oct. 1999, RÅ 1999 ref. 18 II.
819. Previously s. 13 Swedish Personal Data Act.

Previously, several governmental reports had considered details about a name and language skills being able to indirectly reveal a person's ethnic origin.[820] It is not clear at this point to what extent this interpretation is still accepted.

Details regarding health life include all types of data concerning physical as well as psychological health of an individual, including indications of drug abuse, pregnancy, prescriptions for medicine, and possibly even information about sick leave. In accordance with a decision by the CJEU, information about somebody injuring their foot and being on sick leave constitutes sensitive data on a person's health.[821] This was also the case for details on an employee having difficulties to cooperate and being on sick leave.[822]

Compared to the previously in force Swedish Personal Data Act, the GDPR explicitly added genetic and biometric data as examples. However, genetic data was already considered sensitive data according to section 13 Swedish Personal Data Act as it could reveal both health as well as ethnic origin.[823]

A question that has been discussed is to what extent photographs reveal a person's ethnic origin, health or religious beliefs. The Swedish Government previously considered that pictures of individuals in typical contexts generally do not reveal any sensitive data. If the photographs display people in a religious or political context, however, they typically will constitute sensitive data.[824] In line with this approach, Recital 51 GDPR states that photographs are not 'systematically' considered sensitive data but considered biometric data to the extent they allow the unique identification of a natural person.

Personal data relating to criminal convictions is specifically regulated in Article 10.[825] The Swedish Data Inspection Authority has previously considered the following as data relating to criminal convictions:

- Digital pictures of graffiti if it is possible to identify the person responsible for the damage, e.g., via a tag.[826]
- IP numbers that are being used in conjunction with copyright infringement.[827]
- Data about vehicles whose tanks were filled at a gas station without payment.[828]

---

820. Government Official Report SOU 2001:32, 'Domstolarnas register och personuppgiftslagen – En rättslig anpassning', 124; Government Official Report SOU 2001:100, 'Informationshantering och behandling av uppgifter vid domstolar – En rättslig översyn', 93 et seq.; and Government Official Report SOU 2003:40, 'Utlänningsdatalag', 180.
821. *See* Case C-101/01 *Bodil Lindqvist* [2003] ECR I-12971.
822. Decision by the Swedish Supreme Court from 26 May 2005, NJA 2005 s. 361.
823. Government Bill (*Proposition*) 2005/06:64, 'Genetisk integritet m.m.', 63. *See also* the Swedish Genetic Integrity Act (*lag (2006:351) om genetisk integritet m.m.*).
824. Government Official Report SOU 1997:39, 'Integritet – Offentlighet – Informationsteknik'.
825. Previously s. 21 Swedish Personal Data Act.
826. Decision by the Swedish Data Inspection Authority 1020-2005 of 30 Aug. 2005; and Decision 352-2011 of 13 Apr. 2011.
827. For example, Decision by the Swedish Data Inspection Authority 1631-2006 and 1632-2006 of 15 Dec. 2006.
828. *See* decision by the Supreme Administrative Court (*Högsta förvaltningsdomstol*) HFD 2016 ref. 8.

The government is of the opinion that potential crimes that are caught via camera surveillance should not be considered sensitive personal data.[829]

Chapter 3 section 10 Swedish Data Protection Act (*dataskyddslag*) contains specific provisions for personal identity numbers in Sweden,[830] in accordance with Article 87 GDPR.

C. Processing

392. Processing: Any operation or set of operations which is taken as regards personal data, whether or not it occurs by automatic means, for example, collection, recording, organization, storage, adaptation or alteration, retrieval, gathering, use, disclosure by transmission, dissemination or otherwise making information available, alignment or combination, blocking, erasure or destruction.

393. Processing is defined in Article 4(2) GDPR[831] and includes any use of personal information wholly or partly by automated means 'as well as to manual processing, if the personal data are contained or are intended to be contained in a filing system'.[832] Once personal information is digitalized, all types of rendering this information fall within the law.[833] There is no general requirement; any type of automated processing is included in the definition.

Typical examples of processing would be collecting personal information in connection with the registration of customers or in applying for membership, storing personal information about patients in hospital, transferring details about one's employees to the tax authority, as well as publication of personal information in text or images on a website.[834]

394. Automated processing covers any use of personal data on a computer or network. The Swedish Data Protection Authority has in several of its decision advanced a view that any recording or collecting of personal data, even if the data is only available temporarily, falls under the definition of processing. For example, publishing pictures, taken with a digital camera, on a website without saving them, constitute processing.[835]

Recording of personal data on analogue devices such as audio- or videotapes, or mechanical time clock or cash registers is not covered by automated processing.[836]

---

829. *See* Government Bill (*Proposition*) 2017/18:105, ' Ny dataskyddslag', 99.
830. This was previously regulated in s. 22 Swedish Personal Data Act.
831. Previously s. 5 Swedish Personal Data Act.
832. Recital 15 GDPR and Art. 2.1 GDPR. Compare Recital 15 Data Protection Directive: 'Whereas the processing of such data is covered by this Directive only if it is automated.'
833. Government Official Report SOU 2003:40, 190–191.
834. *See*, e.g., Case C-101/01 *Bodil Lindqvist* [2003] ECR I-12971.
835. Decision by the Data Protection Authority from 20 Sep. 2005, No. 763–2005.
836. Government Official Report SOU 1997:39, 347.

Processing which is partly automated also falls within the application of the GDPR, according to Recital 15. This is the case, for example, if personal data is collected manually but is intended to be transferred to a digital medium at a later point, or if digital personal information is printed out or shared via the telephone.

Manual processing is covered to the extent the data is or is intended to become part of a register, i.e., 'filing system'. In order to qualify as a register, the data has to be structured 'according to specific criteria.'[837] The prevalent view in Sweden has been that the register has to be searchable by more than one criterion.[838] A manual file system with cards sorted by last name or personal number does, therefore, not fall under the scope of the law.

D. *Unstructured Processing (According to the Previously in Force Swedish Personal Data Act)*

395. Section 5a of the old Swedish Personal Data Act dealt with special rules concerning unstructured processing. This section exempted most provisions of the Personal Data Act from their application to unstructured processing.

Section 5a Personal Data Act was introduced in 2007 in an attempt to facilitate everyday processing of personal data in electronic communications and ordinary composing of texts.[839] The idea was to shift from the traditional model of regulating the processing of data to a more abuse-centred regulatory approach.[840]

Section 5a defined unstructured processing as personal data that does not or is not intended to become part of a collection of personal data which has been structured in a way that clearly facilitates searching or compiling of the data. As the definition and name indicate, the important factor is the structure of the material, not the type or format of the information.[841]

Examples of unstructured processing included the following:[842]

- mentioning personal information in any continuous text;
- sending emails containing personal details;
- publishing personal information on a website;
- individuals' images or sound recordings.

837. *See* Recital 15 GDPR:. Compare Recital 15 Data Protection Directive: 'a filing system structured according to specific criteria relating to individuals, so as to permit easy access to the personal data in question'.

838. *See* Government Official Report SOU 1997:39, 342; Decision by the Administrative Supreme Court from 25 Jun. 2001, RÅ 2001 ref. 35; and Government Bill (*Proposition*) 2005/06:64, 47.

839. Government Bill (*Proposition*) 2005/06:173, 'Översyn av personuppgiftslagen'.

840. *See* Sören Öman, *Implementing Data Protection in Law*, Scandinavian Studies in Law, vol. 47 (IT Law) (Stockholm: Stockholm Institute for Scandinavian Law, 2004), 392; Sören Öman, 'Protection of Personal Data: But How?', in *Law and Information Technology -Swedish Views (SOU 2002:112)*, ed. Peter Seipel (Stockholm: IT Law Observatory, 2002), 177–184.

841. Government Bill (*Proposition*) 2005/06:173, 58.

842. *Ibid.*, 21 et seq.

With the enactment of the GDPR and the repeal of the Personal Data Act, section 5a is no longer valid. Chapter 5 section 2 Swedish Data Protection Act (*dataskyddslag*) does, however, mention continuous text and exempts Article 15 GDPR from personal data that is contained in continuous text which has not been finalized or that is considered notes. The exemption does not apply if the personal data has been shared with third parties or has been processed for longer than one year.

E. Profiling and Pseudonymization

396. The two terms are new in the GDPR and are defined in Article 4 GDPR points (4) and (5) respectively.

Profiling: 'means any form of automated processing of personal data consisting of the use of personal data to evaluate certain personal aspects relating to a natural person, in particular to analyse or predict aspects concerning that natural person's performance at work, economic situation, health, personal preferences, interests, reliability, behaviour, location or movements;'.

Simply put, profiling involves gathering data about an individual and studying their behaviour patterns in order to categorize them into a group.[843] Profiling is mainly important for automated decision-making, mentioned in Article 22.1 GDPR. The Article 29 Working Party, *inter alia*, has issued more detailed guidelines on profiling.[844]

Pseudonymization involves using either hash functions and algorithms or code keys[845] in order to use data in a less identifiable way. According to Article 4(5):

> pseudonymisation means the processing of personal data in such a manner that the personal data can no longer be attributed to a specific data subject without the use of additional information, provided that such additional information is kept separately and is subject to technical and organisational measures to ensure that the personal data are not attributed to an identified or identifiable natural person.

While pseudonymization does not exempt a data controller from applying the GDPR, it can 'help controllers and processors to meet their data-protection obligations'.[846]

---

843. Art. 29 Data Protection Working Party, 'Guidelines on Automated individual decision-making and Profiling for the purposes of Regulation 2016/679 (wp251rev.01)', 22/08/2018, 7.
844. Art. 29 Data Protection Working Party, 'Guidelines on Automated individual decision-making and Profiling for the purposes of Regulation 2016/679 (wp251rev.01)', 22/08/2018.
845. Öman, *Dataskyddsförordningen (GDPR) m.m.*, Ch. I Art. 4 Femte punkten – Pseudonymisering.
846. Recital 28 GDPR.

F. Controller, Processor, and Data Protection Officer

397. Controller: A person who alone or together with others decides the purpose and means of processing personal data.

398. Controller (*personuppgiftsansvarig*) is the natural or legal person who de facto decides on the processing, with or without legal grounds. It is the controller who is responsible for the processing being in compliance with the GDPR. In a few cases of registers held by public authorities, the controller is appointed by law.

Where the controller is a legal person, it can, of course, appoint its employees responsible for the actual processing. This does, however, not exempt the company, organization or public authority from its civil liability according to the law.

Deciding the purpose of processing is not the same as having access to the data. Only the person being able to independently change, amend or delete the personal data will be considered the controller.[847] The Swedish Data Protection Authority declared that by linking to another website which contains personal data one does not become the controller for the site that is referred to. Where links themselves contain personal information, the website owner will be regarded as the controller of this data.[848] This was also in line with Recital 47 Data Protection Directive, which stated that the controller of personal data contained in a message transmitted by electronic communications 'will normally be considered to be the person from whom the message originates, rather than the person offering the transmission services'.

In the *Google Spain* decision, the CJEU considered search engines to be controllers as it was important to 'ensure, through a broad definition of the concept of 'controller', effective and complete protection of data subject'.[849]

Processor: A natural or legal person, public authority, agency or other body which processes personal data on behalf of the controller.

399. A processor[850] (*personuppgiftsbiträde*) is a natural or legal person to whom the data controller outsourced the personal data processing. Employees of the controller do not fall within this definition.[851]

Article 28 regulates processors more in detail and stipulates that the contract between the data controller and the processor has to be in writing[852] and specifically include provisions, *inter alia*, that the processor 'processes the personal data only on documented instructions from the controller', and 'makes available to the controller all information necessary to demonstrate compliance with the obligations laid down in this Article and allow for and contribute to audit'.

847. *See* Swedish Data Protection Authority, 'Datainspektionens informationsblad om personuppgiftsansvar'.
848. Answer of the Swedish Data Protection Authority in Case No. 785–2000.
849. *See* Case C-131/12 *Google Spain*, ECLI:EU:C:2014:317, para. 34.
850. Previously called personal data assistant.
851. *See* Swedish Data Protection Authority, 'Datainspektionens informationsblad om personuppgiftsansvar'.
852. Previously regulated in s. 30 para. 2 Personal Data Act and Art. 17(3) Data Protection Directive.

Personal data representative: A natural person, appointed by the controller of personal data, who shall independently assure that the personal data is processed in a correct and lawful manner.

400. A data protection officer (*personuppgiftsombud*) can only be a natural person, so companies and organizations cannot be considered. The function of the data representative as such is not stated in Article 2 Data Protection Directive, but mentioned in Article 18(2).[853] Article 37 regulates the designation of the data protection officer, while Articles 38 and 39 specify the obligations and rights of the data protection officer. Sections 38–40 Swedish Personal Data Act regulate the obligations of a personal data representative, including 'ensuring that the controller processes personal data in a lawful and correct manner and in accordance with good practice', pointing out any inadequacies to the controller, as well as maintaining 'a register of the processing that the controller of personal data implements'.

G. The Data Subject

401. The data subject:[854] A person to whom the personal data relates.

402. In accordance with the definition of personal data[855] the registered person has to be a living individual; legal persons are therefore excluded from the definition. The term 'data subject' is as such not defined in Article 4 GDPR but can be gathered from the definition of personal data.

II. Requirements When Processing Personal Data

403. Article 5 GDPR[856] stipulates several requirements which have to be met when personal data is being processed. Most of these requirements refer to the purpose of processing and all of them are applicable regardless of the legal grounds for the processing. In particular, the controller has to ensure that personal data is:

(a) processed lawfully, fairly and in a transparent manner ('lawfulness, fairness and transparency');
(b) collected for specified, explicit and legitimate purposes and not further processed in a manner that is incompatible with those purposes ('purpose limitation');

853. Article 18(2) Data Protection Directive: '[W]here the controller, in compliance with the national law which governs him, appoints a personal data protection official, responsible in particular: – for ensuring in an independent manner the internal application of the national provisions taken pursuant to this Directive; – for keeping the register of processing operations carried out by the controller, containing the items of information referred to in Art. 21(2).'
854. Previously called registered person.
855. *See* A *supra* (para. 389).
856. Previously s. 9 and Art. 6 Data Protection Directive. The numbering and wording of the specific points (a)–(f) below has changed, but the main principles are the same.

(c) adequate, relevant and limited to what is necessary in relation to the specified purposes ('data minimization');
(d) accurate and kept up to date; and if necessary erased or rectified without delay ('accuracy');
(e) not kept in a form which permits identification of data subjects for longer than is necessary for the specified purposes ('storage limitation');
(f) processed with appropriate security ('integrity and confidentiality').

A. *Lawfulness, Fairness and Transparency*

404. The assessment of whether processing is lawful according to point a is made with reference to the provisions of the GDPR in general, as well as other national legislation such as the Swedish Penal Code (e.g., intrusion into a safe depository);[857] as well as eavesdropping,[858] breach of data secrecy[859] and the Marketing Act (e.g., provisions on unsolicited commercial communication). Some decisions by Swedish Administrative Courts of Appeal, applying the previously in force Swedish Personal Data Act, considered sending of emails to teachers at a certain school, without prior consent, not an unsolicited communication according to the Marketing Act and therefore the processing of personal data was lawful.[860] In 2016, the Supreme Administrative Court decided that lawful only referred to the previously in force Swedish Personal Data Act and not any other legislation.[861] It is not clear at this point if this interpretation will hold in the future.[862]

According to Recital 39 GDPR, the principle of transparency requires that information about the processing should be 'easily accessible and easy to understand, and that clear and plain language be used'. The Article 29 Working Party issued more detailed guidelines on the principle in 2016.[863]

B. *Purpose Limitation*

405. Article 5 point b[864] requires specific, explicitly stated and justified purposes for any collecting of personal data. It is important that the purposes are explicit and determined when the personal data is collected.[865] The word specific presumes a certain level of explicitness and precision in the purposes, which is also

857. Chapter 4 s. 9 Penal Code.
858. Chapter 4 s. 9a Penal Code.
859. Chapter 4 s. 9c Penal Code.
860. *See* Decision by the Administrative Court of Appeal (*Kammarrätt*) in Stockholm from 8 Feb. 2006, No. 6624–05; and Decision by the Administrative Court of Appeal (*Kammarrätt*) in Jönköping from 20 Jan. 2006, No. 3162–05.
861. Decision by the Supreme Administrative Court from 3 Jun. 2016, HFD 2016 ref. 40.
862. *See* Öman, *Dataskyddsförordningen (GDPR) m.m.*, Ch. II Art. 5 Led a.
863. Article 29 Working Party, Guidelines on Transparency under Regulation 2016/679, 22 Aug. 2018, WP 260, ec.europa.eu/newsroom/article29/item-detail.cfm?item_id=622227, accessed 17 Dec. 2019.
864. Previously s. 9 para. 1 point c Swedish Personal Data Act.
865. Recital 39 GDPR.

necessary for determining if the information is adequate and relevant (point c). The Swedish Data Protection Authority did not consider control a specific enough purpose for logging and surveillance, but also demanded the intention behind the control, for example, to follow up on compliance with internal technical and security measures.[866]

The term 'justified' has been interpreted by the Swedish government[867] as directly related to the legal grounds for processing in Article 6 GDPR. In other words, if the requirements of Article 6 are not met, the purposes are not justified either. The Article 29 Working Party considers the term also to encompass other legislation.[868]

Although there is no direct requirement for the purposes to be in writing,[869] several other provisions such as Articles 13 and 14 (information to the data subject) as well as Article 30 (stipulating records to be kept with certain information) lead to a recommendation to document the purposes in writing.[870]

With regards to the second part of point b, if the controller wants to process personal data for other purposes than they were initially collected, the 'new' purposes have to be compatible with the original ones. According to Recital 50 GDPR, archiving in the public interest along with research and statistical purposes are considered compatible. In order to determine compatibility, Article 6.4 and Recital 50 list a few points to assess, such as any link between the original and the 'new' purposes, context of collection, 'the reasonable expectations of data subjects based on their relationship with the controller as to their further use', and the nature of the data, e.g., if the data is sensitive or not. Earlier cases where the equivalent provision in the previously in force Swedish Personal Data Act[871] were applied and where the 'new' purposes were *not* considered compatible include the following: evaluating employees' performance by using data collected in the context of control of compliance with security measures in the workplace;[872] collecting information on employees for human resources administration and later using it to assess employee performance;[873] Last, but not least, registering the personal identification number of children at a school for administration purposes and subsequently using it to publish the pupils' individual schedules on the Internet was not compatible with the original purposes.[874]

866. Swedish Data Protection Authority, 'Monitoring in working life', Report 2005:3.
867. Government Bill (*Proposition*) 2017/18:105, 'Ny dataskyddslag', 47.
868. Article 29 Working Party, Opinion 03/2013 on purpose limitation, 2 Apr. 2013, WP 203, ec.europa.eu/justice/article-29/documentation/opinion-recommendation/files/2013/wp203_en.pdf.
869. Compare the previously in force s. 36 Swedish Personal Data Act stipulating registration with the supervisory authority and ss 23–25 and 42 obliging the controller to render information to the individual.
870. Öman, *Dataskyddsförordningen (GDPR) m.m.*, Ch. II Art. 5 Led b – Ändamålsbegränsning.
871. Section 9 point d Personal Data Act.
872. Government Official Report SOU 2002:18, 'Personlig integritet i arbetslivet', 136 and 297.
873. Swedish Data Protection Authority, 'Behandling av personuppgifter för kontroll av anställda', Report 2003:3, 9.
874. Decision by the Swedish Data Protection Authority from 1 Oct. 2008, No. 898–2008.

C. Data Minimization

406. The requirement of data minimization limits the types and amount of personal data processed to what is necessary with regards to the specified purposes. In accordance with Recital 39 GDPR this refers to both the duration of storage and an assessment whether the purposes can be fulfilled with other means. The general assessment of adequate and relevant data is, at first, left for the controller.

A case in 2005 discussed the question of whether a fingerprint requirement for school children to ensure the lunch fee had been paid to the school was adequate according to the equivalent provision in the previously in force Swedish Personal Data Act. While the Swedish Data Inspection Authority and the first instance court considered the data to fall outside the adequate and relevant criteria, both the appeal court and the Supreme Administrative Court confirmed the processing as in line with data minimization.[875] The same interpretation was held for palm prints of school children.[876] The same applies to requiring fingerprints of school children to log into the school computers and processing travellers' fingerprints to check in luggage at the airport, i.e., these types of processing *were* considered adequate and relevant.

Cases where processing was *not* deemed adequate and relevant include: registering the birth date of all customers buying alcoholic drinks in order to ensure that they are above 18 years old;[877] and processing fingerprints of employees in order to ensure attendance at work.[878]

D. Accuracy

407. The general assessment of adequate and relevant data is, at first, left for the controller. In some cases, however, processing of certain data is not deemed adequate or relevant.

408. The term 'accurate' is linked to the purpose of the processing and encompasses both processing correct data as well as keeping personal data up-to-date where necessary. Keeping up-to-date can involve both rectifying the data as well as erasing it.

The controller has an active duty to adjust incorrect and out-of-date information, as well as to rectify, block or erase such personal data at the request of the individual.[879]

875. Decision by the Supreme Administrative Court from 16 Dec. 2008, RÅ 2008 ref. 83.
876. Decision by the Administrative Court (*Kammarrätt*) in Stockholm from 16 Jun. 2006, No. 652-06.
877. Decision by the Swedish Data Protection Authority from 9 Mar. 2005, No. 1978–2004; *see also* Decision of the District Administrative Court (*Länsrätten*) in Stockholm from 9 Jun. 2006, No. 7055–2005.
878. Opinion by the Swedish Data Protection Authority from 17 Dec. 2003, No. 731–2003.
879. Articles 16 and 17 GDPR; previously s. 28 Personal Data Act.

E. Storage Limitation

409. The time for storing personal information depends, as many of the other requirements, on the purpose of the processing. According to Recital 39, the controller should establish time limits for erasure or for periodic reviews. The Swedish Data Protection Authority has previously published guidelines and recommendations on the period of time necessary for different purposes.[880]

For direct marketing purposes, information about previous customers may be kept for a period of one year after the client relationship has ended, or the product or service has been delivered. Personal details of members in a club or association, after they terminated their membership, should be erased immediately but may be kept for up to one year in order to encourage them to rejoin the organization. In the event of dismissal of employees, any personal data should be deleted immediately unless necessary for purposes stipulated by the law, for example, rules on taxes or pensions.[881]

Personal data collected in the context of control of employee email or Internet use should be anonymized or erased as soon as it is not of value for the control anymore. In the event of camera surveillance or alike, information should be deleted daily or weekly.[882]

According to the Swedish Data Protection Authority, a public transport company storing data on its customers' travel may keep the information for up to sixty days.[883] The Swedish Rail Administration SJ (*Statens järnvägar*) was allowed to keep information about its passengers for three months as this corresponded to the recommended objection period.[884]

In accordance with Articles 13.2 a and 14.2 a, the data subject should receive information on the period for which the personal data will be stored, or at least the criteria used to determine that period, already at the time of collection of the data. In practice, this means that the controller has to decide on the time of storage before personal data is collected.[885]

Article 5(1) point e allows for storage for longer periods if the data is processed 'solely for archiving purposes in the public interest, scientific or historical research purposes or statistical purposes in accordance with Article 89(1)'. In this case the controller has to implement 'appropriate technical and organisational measures'.

880. Swedish Data Protection Authority, 'Hur länge får personuppgifter bevaras?', Datainspektionen informerar, No. 10, Nov. 2008.
881. *Ibid.*
882. Swedish Data Protection Authority, 'Monitoring in working life', 19 and 24.
883. Decisions by Swedish Data Protection Authority from 30 Oct. 2007, nos 183–2007, 550–2007 and 1356–2007.
884. Decision by the Swedish Data Protection Authority from 22 Dec. 2008, No. 711–2008.
885. Öman, *Dataskyddsförordningen (GDPR) m.m.*, Chapter Art. 5 Led e – Lagringsminimering.

F. Integrity and Confidentiality

410. The controller has to ensure 'appropriate security of the personal data, including protection against unauthorized or unlawful processing and against accidental loss, destruction or damage, using appropriate technical or organizational measures'. Article 32 deals with security in more detail and suggests the following measures, taking into account the state of the art, costs of implementation as well as purposes of the processing:

(a) pseudonymizing and encrypting personal data;
(b) measures to ensure 'confidentiality, integrity, availability and resilience of processing systems and services';
(c) the ability to restore access to personal data after a technical incident;
(d) regular testing and evaluating of the measures.

III. When Processing Is Allowed

411. Article 6 GDPR[886] stipulates the conditions under which processing is allowed and therefore lawful. Besides consent of the individual, processing can be permitted if it is necessary for one of the stated six reasons. The list in Article 6 is exhaustive, that is processing is not lawful for other reasons than specified in this provision:

a. The consent of the individual always leads to the processing being allowed. Consent is defined in Article 4(11) GDPR[887] as:

> Any freely given, specific, informed and unambiguous indication of the data subject's wishes by which he or she, by a statement or by a clear affirmative action, signifies agreement to the processing of personal data relating to him or her.[888]

This definition still stipulates four conditions for an act of consent to be accepted by the law: voluntary, specific, unambiguous and informed. In addition, Article 7 GDPR specifies further details about consent.

With regards to *unambiguous*, the consent does not have to be in writing, though the burden of proof is on the controller.

The condition of *freely given* typically means that the individual agreed to the processing without being forced or in fear of certain consequences. According to Recital 42 the individual should have a genuine and free choice without the risk of

886. Previously s. 10 Personal Data Act, which transposed Art. 7 Data Protection Directive.
887. Previously s. 3 Personal Data Act.
888. Previously: 'Every kind of voluntary, specific and unambiguous expression of will by which the registered person, after having received information, accepts processing of personal data concerning her or him.'

detriment. In employment relationships this has been considered a difficult question, as consent by an employee to certain data processing involving control and surveillance might not be completely optional.[889] The consent of flight passengers to use their fingerprints for check-in was considered voluntary, as it was also possible to use manual identity controls.[890] Recital 43 GDPR points out challenges for the requirement of freely given consent in cases where the controller is a public authority or where there is a clear imbalance between the controller and the individual.

Specific expression of acceptance concerns the type of processing and is therefore also related to Article 5 GDPR, requesting explicit purposes for the use of personal data. Last, but not least, informed consent requires the controller to inform the individual of the purpose and type of processing before any valid consent is possible. Recital 42 GDPR also mentions that the data subject should be informed of the identity of the controller. Even though not explicitly stipulated, the registered person has to accept processing before it starts, and consent cannot be given in retrospect.[891]

412. Without consent pursuant to point a, and even against the wishes of an individual, personal data may be processed if this is necessary pursuant to one of the remaining points in Article 6:

b. for the performance of a contract to which the data subject is party;
c. for compliance with a legal obligation to which the controller is subject;
d. in order to protect the vital interests of the data subject or of another natural person;
e. for the performance of a task carried out in the public interest or in the exercise of official authority vested in the controller;
f. processing is necessary for the purposes of the legitimate interests pursued by the controller or by a third party.

The first requirement is that processing is necessary. In a judgment[892] the CJEU held that 'the concept of necessity laid down by Article 7(e) of the [Data Protection] Directive cannot have a meaning which varies between the Member States. It follows that what is at issue is a concept which has its own independent meaning in Community law'. The Court did, however, not particularly define the term 'necessity' in general. The common perception in Sweden is that the requirement of 'necessary' is met if the processing obviously facilitates a task or legal obligation.[893] Recital 39 GDPR adds that personal data should only be processed 'if the purpose of the processing could not reasonably be fulfilled by other means'.

Point b is commonly considered to cover any type of contract, including sales of goods, employment, rental or service contracts. A contract to purchase goods online

889. Government Official Report SOU 2009:44, 'Integritetsskydd i arbetslivet', 237 et seq.

890. *See* Decision by the Swedish Data Protection Authority from 30 Mar. 2006, No. 84–2006.

891. *See* Decision by the Supreme Court from 26 May 2005, NJA 2005 s. 361.

892. Case C-524/06 *Huber* [2008] ECR I-0000.

893. Öman & Lindblom, *Personuppgiftslagen*, s. 10. *See also* Öman, *Dataskyddsförordningen (GDPR) m.m.*, Chapter Art. 6 Nödvändighetskravet.

may contain clauses that the seller will process the surfing behaviour of the individual or provide personalized advertising. According to guidelines by the European Data Protection Board (EDPB), this will not be covered by point b unless these measures are necessary for the performance of the contract.[894] In most cases personalized advertising or profiling will not be necessary for the performance of the contract and therefore will not be covered by point b.[895]

A legal obligation pursuant to point c is usually presumed if the duty stems from a statutory provision or decision by a public authority. According to Recital 41 the legal basis does not require a legislative act but the 'legislative measure should be clear and precise and its application should be foreseeable to persons subject to it'. Member States are allowed to regulate legal obligations in more detail based on Article 6(2) GDPR. According to Chapter 2 section 1 Swedish Data Protection Act (*dataskyddslag*), a legal basis can encompass legislation, collective agreements (*kollektivavtal*) or decisions by authorities. Article 6(3) GDPR stipulates that the legal obligation has to be regulated either by EU law or by the Member State to which the controller is subject. Obligations based on foreign national law are therefore not covered by point b.[896] Processing of personal data in the context of public administration is covered by point e.

'Vital interests' of point d includes use of personal data which is essential for the data subject's life or that of another natural person.[897] A typical example of such a situation is if the data subject is unconscious and the hospital uses their personal data to check the blood type or contact next-of-kin.

Public interest of point e has to be regulated either in EU or in Member State law, due to Article 6(3). The requirement for the legal basis to be 'clear and precise' (Recital 41 GDPR) has to be decided on a case-by-case basis according to the Swedish Government, depending on the character of the processing and the activity.[898] If the nature of the processing is harmless, e.g., names of school children in regular school activities, the legal basis can be held rather general. If the processing concerns health-related data, for example, the legal basis has to be very precise in order for the processing to be predictable.

Public interest is not defined as such in the GDPR. Recital 45 mentions public healthcare as an example. Examples of public interest have previously included

894. European Data Protection Board (EDPB), Guidelines 2/2019 on the processing of personal data under Art. 6(1)(b) GDPR in the context of the provision of online services to data subjects, 16 Oct. 2019, paras 28–26, edpb.europa.eu/our-work-tools/our-documents/guidelines/guidelines-22019-processing-personal-data-under-article-61b_en.

895. *Ibid.*, paras 31–36.

896. *See also* Art. 29 Data Protection Working Party, 'Opinion 1/2006 on the application of EU data protection rules to internal whistleblowing schemes in the fields of accounting, internal accounting controls, auditing matters, fight against bribery, banking and financial crime', 00195/06/EN WP 117, 8: 'By contrast, an obligation imposed by a foreign legal statute or regulation which would require the establishment of reporting systems may not qualify as a legal obligation by virtue of which data processing in the EU would be made legitimate. Any other interpretation would make it easy for foreign rules to circumvent the EU rules laid down in Directive 95/46/EC. As a result, SOX whistleblowing provisions may not be considered as a legitimate basis for processing on the basis of Art. 7(c).'

897. Recital 46 GDPR, previously Recital 31 Data Protection Directive.

898. Government Bill (*Proposition*) 2017/18:105, ' Ny dataskyddslag', 51.

archiving for historical purposes, research, compilation of statistics, surveys concerning questions of interest for society, and statistics of salaries in certain industries.[899]

413. The balance of interest argument is an omnibus clause for allowing processing of personal data in accordance with the GDPR. The legitimate interest of the controller or the third party is weighed against the interest of the data subject to be protected against privacy violation. Again, the requirements of Article 5 have to be met here too. This means that a legitimate interest of the controller or third party first has to be established, and then weighed against the privacy interest of the individuals. The question on the legitimacy of the interest has to be decided on a case-by-case basis. The Swedish Data Protection Authority confirmed a legitimate interest to archive data in a system of identification and attendance control for a period of two years in order to allow the handover of the data to the Tax Authority.[900] It was also considered legitimate to hand over data collected in an electronic access control system to the police in the context of filing a report.[901] The Data Protection Authority did, however, not recognize as legitimate an interest of a private company providing an online service where electronic police reports could be filed by individuals, which were automatically passed on to the police.[902]

Preventing fraud is considered a legitimate interest according to Recital 47 GDPR, whereas direct marketing purposes *may* be regarded as a legitimate interest. In general, legitimate purposes concerning security measures[903] have been considered as weighing more heavily than economic interests.[904] When balancing economic interests against privacy of an individual, the former have to weigh considerably more in order for processing to be allowed according to Article 6(1)(f).

The Article 29 Working Group has previously published guidelines on how to determine a legitimate purpose[905] and mentions as examples, *inter alia*, exercising the right to freedom of expression or information; unsolicited non-commercial messages, including for political campaigns or charitable fundraising; employee monitoring for safety or management purposes; processing for research purposes (including marketing research).[906] Recital 47 GDPR underlines the importance of taking the 'reasonable expectations' of the data subject into account when balancing the interests. With the adoption of the GDPR, public authorities are explicitly no longer allowed to use point f as a ground for processing.

---

899. Government Official Report SOU 1997:39, 305, 355 and 36.1.
900. Decision by the Data Protection Authority from 25 Jul. 2007, No. 1036–2006.
901. Decision by the Data Protection Authority from 6 Nov. 2007, No. 276–2007.
902. Decision by the Data Protection Authority from 10 Jul. 2006, No. 706–2006.
903. *See also* Recital 49 GDPR.
904. Swedish Data Protection Authority, 'Monitoring in working life', 22.
905. Article 29 Working Party, Opinion 06/2014 on the notion of legitimate interests of the data controller under Art. 7 of Directive 95/46/EC, 9 April 2014, WP 217, ec.europa.eu/justice/article-29/documentation/opinion-recommendation/files/2014/wp217_en.pdf.
906. *Ibid.*, 25.

A statement by an individual not to agree to data processing will not automatically exclude a balance of interest argument but has to be weighed accordingly and will therefore raise the bar for a legitimate interest of the controller or third party.[907]

414. When it comes to sensitive data,[908] the GDPR stipulates special requirements in addition to the general provisions of Articles 5 and 6. Article 9(1)[909] stipulates a general prohibition for processing of sensitive data. According to Article 9(2), however, controllers may process sensitive data if the individual has explicitly consented to it or if it is necessary for certain specific reasons.

A valid consent has to fulfil all the requirements stipulated in Article 4(11) and Article 6 as well as be explicit, according to Article 9(2)a,[910] which usually excludes acceptance by action alone.[911] Publication of the sensitive data by the individual also allows processing of that data, pursuant to Article 9(2)e.

Sensitive personal data may also be processed, according to Article 9(2),[912] if it is necessary, *inter alia*:

- due to obligations of the controller or of the data subject within employment, social security and social protection law (point b);
- to protect the vital interests of the data subject or another person where the data subject is not physically able to provide a consent (point c); or
- to establish, exercise or defend legal claims (point f).

Non-profit organizations may process sensitive data within their administration, pursuant to Article 9(2) point d.[913] Sensitive data may, furthermore, under certain conditions, be processed for healthcare, pursuant to point h or i,[914] as well as for research or statistical purposes according to point j.[915]

Article 10 deals specifically with personal data on criminal convictions and offences and only allows public authorities to process such data, unless otherwise stipulated by national law. The Swedish Data Protection Act (*dataskyddslag*) regulates the use of the Swedish personal number (national security number) in Chapter 3 section 10 and stipulates that the personal number may only be processed without consent if it is clearly necessary in order to identify a particular person.[916]

According to Article 35(3)b a data protection impact assessment is required in case large amounts of sensitive data are being processed.

907. Compare Art. 7(3) which allows individuals to revoke their consent. The provision is, however, not applicable if the processing is necessary. Also compare Art. 17(1)b which concerns the right to be forgotten in cases where the data subject withdraws consent.
908. For a definition *see* I B *supra* (para. 391).
909. Previously s. 13 Swedish Personal Data Act.
910. Section 15 in the previously in force Swedish Personal Data Act.
911. *See* Swedish Data Protection Authority, 'Samtycke enligt personuppgiftslagen', 10 Oct. 2007.
912. Section 16 of the previously in force Swedish Personal Data Act.
913. Section 17 of the previously in force Swedish Personal Data Act.
914. Previously s. 18 Swedish Personal Data Act.
915. Previously s. 19 Swedish Personal Data Act.
916. Compare s. 22 of the previously in force Swedish Personal Data Act.

IV. Rights of the Data Subject

415. Chapter III GDPR stipulates several rights of the data subject. The individual not only has a right to receive information about, *inter alia*, the controller and the purposes of the processing (Articles 13 and 14), but also:

- a right of access (Article 15);
- a right to rectification (Article 16);
- a right to erasure ('right to be forgotten') (Article 17);
- in certain cases a right to data portability (Article 20), and
- a right to object and not to be subject to automated individual decision-making (Articles 21 and 22).

V. Transfer to a Third Country

416. Chapter V GDPR[917] deals with transfers of personal data to third countries and stipulates specific rules for transfer of personal data to a country outside of the EU or the EEA, that is third country.

Article 44 GDPR[918] establishes a prohibition for transferring personal information to a third country unless certain conditions are met. In general, a transfer is allowed to third countries on the basis of an adequacy decision (Article 45), or if the transfer is subject to appropriate safeguards such as standard data protection clauses, approved codes of conduct (Article 46), or binding corporate rules (Article 47).

A judgment by the CJEU from 2003 provided some clarity in this regard.[919] Since this decision, typical publication of information on a website has not been considered a transfer to a third country, unless the organization hosting the website is established outside the EEA. In particular the Court of Justice held that:

> there is no transfer [of data] to a third country […] where an individual in a Member State loads personal data onto an Internet page which is stored with his hosting provider which is established in that State or in another Member State, thereby making those data accessible to anyone who connects to the Internet, including people in a third country.[920]

VI. Sanctions and Supervision

417. Chapter VIII GDPR regulates remedies, liability and penalties. In case the controller does not comply with the provisions of the GDPR, the individual shall be compensated for damages caused by the unlawful processing, according to Article

917. Previously ss 33–35 Personal Data Act, as well as Arts 25–26 Data Protection Directive.
918. Previously s. 33 Personal Data Act.
919. Case C-101/01 *Bodil Lindqvist* [2003] ECR I-12971.
920. *Ibid.*, point 71.

82 GDPR.[921] In 2013 the Swedish Supreme Court, applying the previously in force Swedish Personal Data Act, decided that the amount of damages should be awarded according to pre-defined amounts and considered SEK 5,000 to be the regular amount for infringement of privacy.[922] For minor intrusions, the amount should be set to SEK 3,000. In some cases Swedish courts have awarded higher damages.[923] These cases often concern criminal or health records, e.g., for publication of a criminal conviction on Facebook, the District Court of Umeå awarded SEK 10,000 in damages.[924]

The GDPR introduced stronger administrative fines in Article 83. Though the Swedish Data Inspection Authority did not often impose administrative fines based on the Swedish Personal Data Act, this might change with the GDPR. In December 2019, the authority issued a fine of EUR 35,000 against a website for infringement of the Credit Information Act and the GDPR.[925]

Chapter 6 sections 4–7 Swedish Data Protection Act complement Article 83, and the Swedish Data Inspection Authority issued guidelines on its competency regarding fines according to Article 58(2).[926] Regulating potential criminal liability[927] is left to the Member States according to Article 84. Sweden did, however, not introduce such provisions.[928]

418. The Swedish Data Protection Authority (*Datainspektionen*)[929] is the appointed supervisory authority for privacy-related issues.[930] It issues directives and guidelines and also carries out inspections and handles complaints. Article 57 GDPR specifies the task of the supervisory authority, while Article 58 details its investigative powers.

There is no longer a general duty to notify the Data Protection Authority of any processing of personal data (previously section 36 Personal Data Act). The GDPR does, however, introduce a duty to inform the supervisory authority of personal data breaches. A data breach is a breach of security that leads to any unauthorized access to or alteration of personal data (Article 4 point 12). In accordance with Article 33

921. Section 48 of the previously in force Swedish Personal Data Act.
922. Decision by the Supreme Court from 6 De. 2013, NJA 2013 s. 1046.
923. *See* for more examples Öman, *Dataskyddsförordningen (GDPR) m.m.*, Ch. VIII Art. 82.
924. Decision by the District Court of Umeå from 29 Aug. 2014, Case No. B 100-14.
925. Decision by the Swedish Data Protection Authority from 13 Dec. 2019, No. 2018–22737, www.datainspektionen.se/nyheter/administrative-fine-of-35-000-eur-imposed-on-the-swedish-website-mrkoll.se/.
926. Swedish Data Protection Authority, *Datainspektionens riktlinjer för korrigerande befogenheter enligt artikel 58.2 dataskyddsförordningen* from 19 Dec. 2018, No. 345–2018, www.datainspektionen.se/globalassets/dokument/ovrigt/riktlinjer-korrigerande-befogenheter---gdpr.pdf.
927. Previously regulated in s. 49 Swedish Personal Data Act: A person could be sentenced to a fine or imprisonment of up to six months in case of non-compliance with ss 13–21. Other acts leading to criminal liability included omission of notification under s. 36 para. 1 and transfer to personal data to a third country contrary to ss 33–35.
928. Government Bill (*Proposition*) 2017/18:105, ' Ny dataskyddslag', 143 et sequ.
929. www.datainspektionen.se.
930. Article 51 GDPR and s. 3 Swedish Data Protection Regulation (*Förordning (2018:219) med kompletterande bestämmelser till EU:s dataskyddsförordning*), previously s. 2 Personal Data Ordinance (*personuppgiftsförordning (1998:1191)*).

GDPR, the controller has to notify the breach to the Swedish Data Inspection Authority within seventy-two hours. Between 25 May and 31 December 2018, the Swedish Data Inspection Authority received 2,262 such reports;[931] almost half of the incidents were due to letters or e-mails, containing personal data, being sent to the wrong recipient, while 23% were due to unauthorized access to personal data. Sixty-one per cent of the incidents were caused by human errors, and only 14% were caused by direct attacks such as phishing or theft.

VII. Risk-Based Approach and Privacy by Design

419. The GDPR introduced new requirements with regards to security of processing, two of them being data protection by design and data protection by default in Article 25. The former, also called privacy by design, aims at implementing data protection principles directly on a technical and organizational level. An example mentioned in Article 25(1) is pseudonymization which facilitates, *inter alia*, data minimization. The EDPB has issued guidelines on the implementation of privacy by design.[932]

In addition, Chapter IV section 2 GDPR, and especially Article 32, deal with security of processing. The Article 32 provision is an example of a risk-based approach which is also expressed in, *inter alia*, Articles 24(1), 25(1) and 35. Article 32(1) stipulates that the controller and processor shall implement technical and organizational measures to ensure 'a level of security appropriate to the risk'. According to Article 32(2) the security assessment should particularly consider the risks of 'accidental or unlawful destruction, loss, alteration, unauthorised disclosure of, or access to personal data'.

§3. Other Legislation Dealing with Personal Data Protection

420. Besides the GDPR and the Data Protection Act, other EU and national legislation deal with privacy and data protection in certain circumstances. The new Data Protection Directive,[933] for example, regulates personal data processing by authorities dealing with the prevention and detection of crime.

931. Swedish Data Inspection Authority, *2 300 personuppgiftsincidenter rapporterades under 2018*, 4 Mar. 2019, www.datainspektionen.se/nyheter/2-300-personuppgiftsincidenter-rapporterades-under-2018/.

932. European Data Protection Board (EDPB), *Guidelines 4/2019 on Article 25 Data Protection by Design and by Default*, 13 Nov. 2019, edpb.europa.eu/our-work-tools/public-consultations-art-704/2019/guidelines-42019-article-25-data-protection-design_en.

933. Directive (EU) 2016/680 of the European Parliament and of the Council of 27 April 2016 on the protection of natural persons with regard to the processing of personal data by competent authorities for the purposes of the prevention, investigation, detection or prosecution of criminal offences or the execution of criminal penalties, and on the free movement of such data, and repealing Council Framework Decision 2008/977/JHA.

A Swedish example is the Camera Surveillance Act (*kamerabevakningslag (2018:1200)*)[934] that stipulates rules for the use of camera surveillance by private and public entities. Camera surveillance of private activities no longer requires a permit but organizations have to follow the GDPR. The EDPB published guidelines on the use of video surveillance in July 2019.[935] Public authorities in Sweden have to apply for a permit to use video surveillance according to the Camera Surveillance Act.

421. The majority of public authorities process personal data about citizens to some extent. In these cases, the Personal Data Act normally does not apply; instead, special statutes dealing with specific databases held by the different authorities are applicable. For example, the Patient Data Act (*patientdatalag (2008:355)*) deals with processing of personal information within the health sector,[936] the Act on the National Address Register (*lag (1998:527) om det statliga personadressregistret (SPAR)*) covers provisions on access to the national register of individuals' addresses,[937] the Criminal Data Act (*brottsdatalag (2018:1177)*)[938] regulates the processing of personal data by the Swedish law enforcement agencies, and the Act on Processing of Data by the Tax Agency for Taxation Purposes (*lag (2001:181) om behandling av uppgifter i Skatteverkets beskattningsverksamhet*) states rules on the use of data by the tax authorities.[939]

§4. Processing That Is Exempted from the Personal Data Act

I. Processing by Non-automated Means

422. As mentioned[940] processing of personal data which is not wholly or partly automated does not fall within the scope of the GDPR, according to Article 2(1). In other words, all manual processing is exempted from its application.

934. The 2018 Act replaced the previously in force Camera Surveillance Act (*kameraövervakningslag (2013:460)*) which in turn replaced the Act on Public Camera Surveillance (*lag (1998:150) om allmän kameraövervakning*).
935. European Data Protection Board (EDPB), *Guidelines 3/2019 on processing of personal data through video devices*, 12 Jul. 2019, edpb.europa.eu/our-work-tools/public-consultations/2019/guidelines-32019-processing-personal-data-through-video_en.
936. *See* for more information the website of the Swedish Data Inspection Authority: www.datainspektionen.se/other-lang/in-english/the-patient-data-act/, accessed 15 Jan. 2020.
937. *See also* the website www.statenspersonadressregister.se/ovre-meny/english-summary.html, accessed 15 Jan. 2020.
938. *See* for more information the website of the Swedish Data Inspection Authority: www.datainspektionen.se/other-lang/in-english/the-criminal-data-act/, accessed 15 Jan. 2020.
939. For more examples *see* Öman, *Implementing Data Protection*, 392.
940. *See* I C *supra* (paras 392–394).

II. Processing for Private Purposes

423. Article 2(2) point c GDPR[941] exempts processing for purely private purposes. Examples for private use of personal information include private address books, writing of texts by individuals, and diaries on a computer.

Publication of private data on a website can never be regarded as private purposes even if the website is operated as a hobby. The CJEU held in the *Lindqvist* judgment that the:

> exception must […] be interpreted as relating only to activities which are carried out in the course of private or family life of individuals, which is clearly not the case with the processing of personal data consisting in publication on the Internet so that those data are made accessible to an indefinite number of people.[942]

Recital 18 GDPR mentions as examples of household activities 'correspondence and the holding of addresses, or social networking and online activity undertaken within the context of such activities'.

III. Processing for Journalistic Purposes

424. According to Article 85(2) GDPR, Member States can provide exemptions from certain chapters in the GDPR for 'journalistic purposes or the purpose of academic, artistic or literary expression'. Chapter 1 section 7 Swedish Data Protection Act is an example of such an exemption. Pursuant to this section, Articles 5–30 and 35–50 GDPR as well as Chapters 2–5 Data Protection Act do not apply where personal data is processed for journalistic purposes or the purpose of academic, artistic or literary expression.

Journalistic purposes should be interpreted broadly[943] and have been described as activities whose purpose is 'the disclosure to the public of information, opinions or ideas, irrespective of the medium which is used to transmit them.'[944] The CJEU has held that search engine providers do not fall within the category of journalistic purposes.[945]

The Swedish Supreme Court has previously defined journalistic purposes as 'to inform, criticize or foster a debate on questions for society which are of interest for the general public'.[946] In other words, it is not necessary that the author of the publication is a journalist; the relevant factor is if the purpose of the processing, for example, publication of certain personal information on a website, is to inform the public or raise discussion on issues of society.

941. Previously s. 6 Personal Data Act and Art. 3(2) Data Protection Directive.
942. Case C-101/01 *Bodil Lindqvist* [2003] ECR I-12971, point 47.
943. Case C-345/17 *Buivids* [2019] ECLI:EU:C:2019:122, point 51; *see also* Case C-73/07 *Tietosuojavaltuutettu v. Satakunnan Markkinapörssi Oy and Satamedia Oy* [2008] ECR I-09831.
944. *Ibid.*, point 53.
945. Case C-131/12 *Google Spain* [2014] ECLI:EU:C:2014:317, point 85.
946. Decision by Supreme Court from 12 Jun. 2001, NJA 2001 s. 409.

IV. Processing Versus Freedom of the Press

425. According to Article 85(1) GDPR,[947] 'Member States shall by law reconcile' the right to privacy with the right to freedom of expression and information. Sweden has done this in Chapter 1 section 7 paragraph 1 Data Protection Act which exempts the use of personal information in the context of freedom of the press and freedom of expression from the application of the GDPR. In other words, newspapers and other protected media that fall within the scope of either the Freedom of the Press Act (*tryckfrihetsförordning (1949:105)*) or the Fundamental Law on Freedom of Expression (*yttrandefrihetsgrundlag (1991:1469)*) do not have to follow the data protection rules.

There are several possibilities for a publication to fall within the scope of the Freedom of the Press Act or the Fundamental Law on Freedom of Expression, *inter alia*:

- written matters in the printing press;[948]
- radio programmes which are directed to the general public;[949]
- technical recordings;[950]
- database rule for newspapers and other media;[951]
- certificate by the Swedish Press and Broadcasting Authority (*Myndigheten för press, radio och tv*).[952]

426. The *database rule* is especially important for publications on the Internet. Newspapers publishing their content on a website are covered by Chapter 1 section 9 Fundamental Law on Freedom of Expression.

A 'certificate of no legal impediment to publication' (*utgivningsbevis*) issued by the Swedish Press and Broadcasting Authority can be obtained by a website, under the following conditions:

- a legally responsible editor (*utgivare*) is appointed and the Radio and TV Authority is notified thereof;
- the website has a common presentation;
- the website is not interactive, that is, only the website owner can make changes to the content;
- the website is available to the public;
- there has to be a link to Sweden, for example, the editorial office is in Sweden; and
- the name of the website cannot be confused with another activity registered with the Swedish Press and Broadcasting Authority.

947. Previously s. 7 para. 1 Swedish Personal Data Act and Art. 9 Data Protection Directive 1995.
948. Chapter 1 Art. 5 Freedom of the Press Act.
949. Chapter 1 Art. 6 Fundamental Law on Freedom of Expression.
950. Chapter 1 Art. 10 Fundamental Law on Freedom of Expression.
951. Chapter 1 Art. 9 Fundamental Law on Freedom of Expression.
952. www.mprt.se/en/.

The certificate gives constitutional protection but also stipulates certain obligations for the website owner: The editor is solely criminally liable for the content of the publications. The published information has to be documented and archived for six months.

Unmoderated online discussion forums, guest books or blogs cannot receive a 'certificate of no legal impediment to publication', unless every comment or entry is approved by the editorial staff prior to publication on the website.[953]

427. In the past years many organizations and websites have obtained such a certificate[954] and are therefore exempted from the GDPR. An example is an online service that collected decisions of the lower courts and structured the data according to the address of the accused, in the original version with a map function. The site was met by a lot of criticism,[955] but the Swedish Data Protection Authority could not intervene as the site was exempted from the then in force Swedish Personal Data Act due to its 'certificate of no legal impediment to publication'. Even an investigation by the Chancellor of Justice (*Justitiekanslern*/JK)[956] looking into a possible prosecution for defamation did not lead to any charges.[957] This is just one example of the challenges with regards to a balance of interest between privacy and freedom of expression in Sweden and illuminates the risks connected with the wide application of exemptions. As a result of these challenges, the Fundamental Law on Freedom of Expression was amended in 2018 and now includes a possibility to prohibit publication of sensitive personal data in Chapter 1 section 20.

V. Processing Versus Freedom of Information

428. Sweden has a very strong principle of openness, which is enshrined in Chapter 2 Freedom of the Press Act. In general, all records held by authorities are public unless otherwise stated in the Public Access to Information and Secrecy Act (*offentlighets- och sekretesslag (2009:400)*).

Based on Article 86 GDPR, Chapter 1 section 7 Swedish Data Protection Act[958] exempts the data protection rules for any data processing by public authorities within the principle of openness. The Public Access to Information and Secrecy Act refers in Chapter 21 Article 7 back to the GDPR and the Data Protection Act, which in practice means that documents held by a public administration can be kept secret if the transfer of the personal data would violate either of these laws.

953. Chapter 1 s. 9 para. 1 point 1 Fundamental Law on Freedom of Expression.
954. According to the register of the Swedish Press and Broadcasting Authority, there are 1,456 (compared to 884 in 2014) companies in Sweden that have a certificate, *see* www.mprt.se/sokverktyg/#tab-2, accessed 2 Jan. 2020.
955. A short news report in English, published on 28 Jan. 2014, by the Swedish Public Radio Broadcaster is available at sverigesradio.se/sida/artikel.aspx?programid=2054&artikel=5768451.
956. JK is the responsible supervisory authority in cases of freedom of expression; *see* para. 10.
957. Read the decision in Swedish at jk.se/Beslut/Tryck-OchYttrandefrihetsarenden/699-14-31.aspx.
958. Previously s. 8 Swedish Personal Data Act.

Although Article 86 and Chapter 1 section 7 Data Protection Act lead to the non-applicability of the GDPR in cases of freedom of information, Chapter 21 Article 7 Public Access to Information and Secrecy Act does allow for privacy concerns to be taken into consideration.

Chapter 2. Protection of Telecommunications Privacy

§1. Legislative Framework

429. In 2002, the EU enacted Directive 2002/58/EC of the European Parliament and of the Council of 12 July 2002 concerning the Processing of Personal Data and the Protection of Privacy in the Electronic Communications Sector (hereinafter 'Directive on Privacy and Electronic Communications'). The Directive aimed to harmonize the provisions regarding privacy 'with respect to the processing of personal data in the electronic communication sector', according to Article 1.

Sweden transposed the Directive on Privacy and Electronic Communications, together with the other Directives concerning the regulatory framework for electronic communications[959] into Swedish national law in 2003 by enacting the Electronic Communications Act (*lag (2003:389) om elektronisk kommunikation*). The 2009 amendments[960] to the Directive were implemented into Swedish law in 2011.

Though the Electronic Communications Act is not applicable to the content being transmitted in electronic communication networks, it contains several provisions regarding privacy.[961] In particular, the Act stipulates several obligations for operators and rights for their subscribers in Chapter 6.

In addition, some provisions of the Swedish Penal Code (*brottsbalk (1962:700)*) can be applicable to protection of privacy in telecommunication, especially Chapter 4 section 8 dealing with breach of postal or telecommunication secrecy.

§2. Object of Protection

I. Content of a Message

430. Chapter 4 section 8 Swedish Penal Code protects the content of a message and stipulates:

> A person who unlawfully obtains access to a communication which a postal or telecommunications firm delivers or transmits in the form of mail or as a telecommunication, shall be sentenced for breach of postal or telecommunication secrecy to a fine or imprisonment for a maximum of two years.

The provision protects messages that are being transmitted. The term 'message' does not include books or newspapers, though packages containing a message fall

959. *See* Part I Ch. 1 §1 *supra* (paras 39 et seq.).
960. Directive 2009/136/EC of the European Parliament and of the Council of 25 November 2009 amending Directive 2002/22/EC on universal service and users' rights relating to electronic communications networks and services, Directive 2002/58/EC concerning the processing of personal data and the protection of privacy in the electronic communications sector and Regulation (EC) No. 2006/2004 on cooperation between national authorities responsible for the enforcement of consumer protection laws.
961. Government Bill (*Proposition*) 2002/03:110, 'Lag om elektronisk kommunikation, m.m.', 1.

within the scope. Typically, the definition would cover telephone conversations, as well as sound, text, images, or data transmitted through radio, light or electromagnetic waves.[962]

The sender or receiver does not have to be specified; even messages from anonymous addressors or to an undefined group of people are covered by Chapter 4 section 8. The message has to be in transit in order to be protected. Once the message has reached the sender, Chapter 4 section 8 Penal Code will therefore no longer apply. Other provisions in the Penal Code might, however, come into play.

431. Unlawful access implies that the offender does not have any authorization to open or read the message. Consent by the sender or receiver therefore prevents any criminal liability. The offender does, however, not necessarily have to read the message; already accessing it can lead to committing a 'breach of telecommunication secrecy'.

In addition to Chapter 4 section 8 (*brytande av post- eller telehemlighet*), several other provisions of the Penal Code can be of interest. In particular:[963]

- Chapter 4 section 9: intrusion into a safe depository (*intrång i förvar*), for example, unauthorized opening of a letter.[964]
- Chapter 4 section 9a: eavesdropping (*olovlig avlyssning*).[965]
- Chapter 4 section 9b: preparation of a breach of telecommunication secrecy or of eavesdropping.[966]
- Chapter 4 section 9c: breach of data secrecy (*dataintrång*).[967]

Chapter 4 section 8 Swedish Penal Code, as well as the other crimes just mentioned, do not stipulate any obligations for the postal or telecommunication companies. Instead, they criminalize unauthorized access to messages or data as such and state a punishment for the offender in this respect.

962. In accordance with the earlier definition of telemessage in the previously in force Tele Act (*telelag (1993:597)*).
963. *See* for more detail Part VII Ch. 2 §1 I A *infra* (paras 449 et seq.).
964. The provision is subsidiary to Ch. 4 s. 8 Penal Code.
965. Chapter 4 s. 9a Penal code: 'A person who, in a case other than as stated in s. 8, unlawfully and secretly listens to or records by technical means for sound reproduction, speech in a room, a conversation between others or discussions at a conference or other meeting to which the public is not admitted and in which he himself does not participate, or to which he has improperly obtained access, shall be sentenced for eavesdropping to a fine or imprisonment for a maximum of two years.'
966. Chapter 4 s. 9b Penal code: 'A person who employs technical means with the intention of committing a breach of telecommunication secrecy … or to commit a crime as defined in s. 9a, shall be sentenced for preparation of such a crime to a fine or imprisonment for a maximum of two years.'
967. Chapter 4 s. 9c Penal code: 'A person who … unlawfully obtains access to a recording for automatic data processing or unlawfully alters or erases or inserts such a recording in a register, shall be sentenced for breach of data secrecy to a fine or imprisonment for a maximum of two years.'

II. Other Data Concerning the Message

432. The Swedish Electronic Communications Act defines the terms 'electronic message' and 'traffic data'. According to Chapter 6 section 1, an electronic message is all information that is exchanged or transferred between a finite group in a public electronic network. Transmissions via radio or on TV are not covered unless the information can be linked to a specific user.

Traffic data is information that is processed in order to transmit an electronic message in an electronic communications network or in order to bill this message. Commonly, traffic data includes information on which numbers or addresses have been used for communication and the date and time of the message. Traffic data can also include location data, which indicates the geographical position of the terminal equipment, such as a mobile phone or computer, of a user.

Network operators traditionally also process information about a subscription, including the name and address of the subscriber.

§3. Obligations for Network Operators

I. Security of Communications

433. According to Chapter 6 section 3 and 3a Electronic Communications Act, the provider of a publicly available electronic communications service must take appropriate measures to protect the processed data. Having regard to the available technology and the costs of their implementation, these measures shall ensure a level of security appropriate to the risk of privacy intrusion.

These two provisions transpose Article 4(1) Directive on Privacy and Electronic Communications and are not to be confused with the operational reliability and security in the service stipulated by the Access Directive and the Universal Service Directive.

434. In accordance with the new Article 4(3) of the Directive on Privacy and Electronic Communications the Swedish Electronic Communications Act was amended to include the obligation to notify the supervisory authority in cases of personal data breaches. A personal data breach is defined as an 'event that leads to accidental or unlawful destruction, loss or alteration, or unauthorised disclosure of, or unauthorised access to, data processed in connection with the provision of a publicly available electronic communications service'.[968]

According to Chapter 6 section 4a network operators have to notify the supervisory authority, PTS, in case of a personal data breach (*integritetsincident*). In addition, according to Chapter 6 section 4b, network operators have to keep lists of such

968. Chapter 6 s. 1 point 3 Electronic Communications Act.

breaches. PTS has issued guidelines that specify more in detail how network operators should notify the authority.[969] The guidelines stipulate, for example, that the notification has to occur within twenty-four hours of the breach, and that it should, *inter alia*, describe the causes and consequences of the breach, the type and content of the data and the initiated measures to remedy the weakness and to avoid similar incidents in the future. In its guidelines, PTS explicitly refers to Commission Regulation (EU) No. 611/2013 of 24 June 2013 on the measures applicable to the notification of personal data breaches under Directive 2002/58/EC of the European Parliament and of the Council on privacy and electronic communications. As network operators fall within the Electronic Communications Act they have to report personal data breaches to PTS; only circumstances and breaches that are not covered by the Electronic Communications Act fall within the GDPR and have therefore to be reported to the Swedish Data Inspection Authority.[970]

II. Confidentiality of Communications

435. The providers of a publicly available electronic communications service are obliged to keep confidential personal information concerning a subscription or the content or other related data of an electronic message. Chapter 6 section 20 Electronic Communications Act, transposing Article 5 Directive on Privacy and Electronic Communications, stipulates a principle of confidentiality of communications. The principle does not apply to the subscribers themselves or any other party taking part in the message.

Confidentiality (*tystnadsplikt*) applies to:

- information about a subscription (name and address of the subscriber, telephone number, IP number);[971]
- the content of an electronic message; or
- any other data concerning a particular electronic message (traffic and location data, such as telephone number/IP address of the sender and receiver, the date and time of a communication, the identification number of the terminal equipment (IMEI-number)).

436. Chapter 6 sections 21–23 Electronic Communications Act stipulate several exemptions from the principle of confidentiality. Providers can, in certain cases,

969. Swedish Post and Telecom Agency (PTS), 'Vägledning om skyldigheten att rapportera integritetsincidenter', 26 Aug. 2013; a summary in Swedish is available at pts.se/sv/Bransch/Internet/Integritet/Regler/Rapportera-integritetsincidenter/.
970. The Swedish Post and Telecom Authority informed about the relation between the Electronic Communications Act and the GDPR on its website: pts.se/sv/bloggen/pts-bloggen/hur-paverkas-tolkningen-av-lek-av-gdpr/, accessed 3 Jan. 2020.
971. The information has to be directly or indirectly linked to a subscriber. Therefore the PUK-code, for example, though processed by the operator, does not fall within this category, which means that the principle of confidentiality (Ch. 6 s. 20) does not apply. In this case, however, the information cannot be released to the police either.

even be obliged to release personal data. For example, the police can request access to certain personal information in accordance with Chapter 6 section 22 Electronic Communications Act.

Operators are obliged to release personal data based on a court order for secret wiretapping (*hemlig avlyssning av elektronisk kommunikation*) or surveillance (*hemlig övervakning av elektronisk kommunikation*) in accordance with Chapter 27 section 18 or 19 Swedish Code of Judicial Procedure (*rättegångsbalk (1942:740)*). Secret wiretapping concerns the content of an electronic message and can only be ordered by the court for offences with a punishment of a minimum of two years imprisonment or if the crime is expected to lead to a two years imprisonment.[972] Secret surveillance regarding traffic data and location data can be ordered for offences with a minimum of six months imprisonment and also for data intrusion according to Chapter 4 section 9c Swedish Penal Code. Chapter 27 sections 18 and 19 Code of Judicial Procedure were amended in 2012 and according to the new paragraph 3 in section 18 an order for secret wiretapping now also gives the right for surveillance.

Apart from the provisions in the procedural Code, which concern pre-trial cases, the Act on Retrieval of Data on Electronic Communication by Law Enforcement Agencies (*lag (2012:278) om inhämtning av uppgifter om elektronisk kommunikation i de brottsbekämpande myndigheternas underrättelseverksamhet*) allows the police and customs to request traffic data, including location data, under certain circumstances with regards to their intelligence activities. Any such request has to be approved by a prosecutor at the Swedish Prosecution Authority (*Åklagarmyndigheten*)[973] and reported to a specific supervisory authority, the Swedish Commission on Security and Integrity Protection (*Säkerhets- och integritetsskyddsnämnden*).[974]

The supervisory authority for network operators, PTS, has published information about the obligations of network operators[975] and has issued a Regulation with regards to the compensation for operators.[976]

437. In addition, Chapter 6 section 17 Electronic Communications Act prohibits wiretapping and stipulates that anybody other than the user may not access or in any other way process information in an electronic message without the consent of the user. This provision not only applies to telecom operators but to any third party who accesses electronic messages.

---

972. Chapter 27 s. 18 Code of Judicial Procedure.
973. Section 3 Act on Retrieval of Data on Electronic Communication by Law Enforcement Agencies (amended in 2019 to include an approval).
974. The Commission on Security and Integrity Protection (www.sakint.se/) supervises the activities of crime-fighting agencies (e.g., secret surveillance) the processing of personal data by the Swedish Police, including the Swedish Security Service.
975. In Swedish at www.pts.se/sv/Bransch/Internet/Integritet/Regler/Utlamning-av-teleuppgifter/, accessed 6 Mar. 2020.
976. Swedish Post and Telecom Agency's Regulation on Compensation for Disclosure of Stored Data for Crime-Fighting Purposes (*PTSFS 2013:5 Post- och telestyrelsens föreskrifter om ersättning vid utlämnande av lagrade uppgifter för brottsbekämpande ändamål*), 11 Dec. 2013.

III. Processing of Data

A. Obligation to Delete Personal Data

438. Chapter 6 section 5 Electronic Communications Act stipulates an obligation for network operators to erase or anonymize traffic data. The provision transposes Article 6 Directive on Privacy and Electronic Communications and only allows telecom operators to process personal data to the extent this is necessary for the transmission of the message.

Providers of an electronic communication service may only process traffic data for billing purposes or with the consent of the subscriber.[977] Such processing is permissible only up to the end of the period during which the bill may lawfully be challenged or payment pursued.

Location data, which is not traffic data, may be processed with regards to value added services.[978] The data either has to be anonymized or may otherwise only be processed with the consent of the user to the extent and for the duration necessary for the provision of the value added service.

439. Chapter 6 section 7 Electronic Communications Act, transposing Article 6(5) Directive on Privacy and Electronic Communications, stipulates that only certain people may access personal data. The group includes employees given the task of billing, customer inquiries or marketing of electronic communication services.

The general principle to delete personal data does not apply if a court or the police need access to the information, or if messages are covered by a court order for surveillance of the communication.[979] The data should, however, never be stored for longer than one year, unless justified for a specific reason, such as police investigations or court proceedings.[980]

B. Obligation to Store Personal Data

440. In transposing Directive 2006/24/EC of the European Parliament and of the Council of 15 March 2006 on the retention of data generated or processed in connection with the provision of publicly available electronic communications services or of public communications networks and amending Directive 2002/58/EC (hereinafter 'Data Retention Directive') the Electronic Communications Act was amended to include an obligation to store personal data.[981]

977. Chapter 6 s. 6 Electronic Communications Act.
978. Chapter 6 s. 9 Electronic Communications Act.
979. Chapter 6 s. 8 Electronic Communications Act.
980. Government Bill (Proposition) 2002/03:110, 'Lag om elektronisk kommunikation', 392.
981. Sweden was late in transposing the Directive. The European Court of Justice ruled on 4 Feb. 2010 that Sweden failed to adopt, within the prescribed period, the provisions necessary to comply with the Data Retention Directive. Case C-185/09, *European Commission v. Kingdom of Sweden*, Judgment of the Court of 4 Feb. 2010.

The new section 16a–16f in Chapter 6 Electronic Communications Act introduced and specified network operators' obligation to store traffic data for crime-fighting purposes. According to Chapter 6 section 16a network operators had to retain data that is necessary to track and identify the source and the target for the communication, the date, time and duration, the type of communication, the equipment and the localization of the mobile communication equipment at the beginning and the end of the communication. The provisions were further specified by sections 37–44 Ordinance on Electronic Communication (*förordning (2003:396) om elektronisk kommunikation*). With regards to Internet access section 43 Ordinance on Electronic Communication specified, for example, that the following data has to be stored: IP address, information about the subscription, date and time for logging on and off from the Internet access, capacity that was used, information that identifies the equipment that was used. The supervisory authority, PTS, also issued guidelines on which data has to be retained.[982]

In 2014, the CJEU declared the Data Retention Directive invalid.[983] The Swedish government, however, deemed the existing legislation to be in line with the principles emphasized in the CJEU case.[984] This interpretation was questioned by several Swedish network operators and led to a court decision in 2017 that declared that Swedish rules not applicable.[985] In the aftermath of this decision,[986] the Swedish government introduced amendments that now require access to the retained data by the Police Authority, Security Service or Customs to be approved by a prosecutor at the Swedish Prosecution Authority (*Åklagarmyndigheten*). The obligation to retain data now only applies to mobile communications, and traffic data only includes data on who contacted whom (number and subscriber) and the time. IP addresses are not stored for telephony and messaging, but for Internet access.

The maximum retention periods are now divided between the types of data: location data for calls should be stored for two months, data on Internet access for ten months, other data six months (Chapter 6 section 16d Electronic Communications Act).[987] Chapter 6 section 16c states that processing of the retained data is only allowed for the purposes of releasing the data to certain authorities according to the previously stated legislation.[988]

441. The obligation to store data has led to a challenging balance of interest between protection of privacy and copyright regulation. As stated earlier, the 'order

982. Swedish Post and Telecom Agency (PTS), Uppgifter som ska lagras för brottsbekämpande ändamål – en vägledning, 23 May 2012.
983. Case C-293/12 *Digital Rights Ire*land [2014] ECLI:EU:C:2014:238.
984. Ministry Publications Series, *Datalagring, EU-rätten och svensk rätt*, Ds 2014:23, 2 Apr. 2015, www.regeringen.se/rattsliga-dokument/departementsserien-och-promemorior/2014/06/ds-201423/.
985. The Administrative Court of Appeal in Stockholm requested a preliminary ruling by the CJEU which resulted in: Case C-203/15 *Tele2 Sverige* [2016] ECLI:EU:C:2016:970.
986. For a short summary of the events in English, *see* Governmental report (SOU) 2017:75, Datalagring – brottsbekämpning och integritet, www.regeringen.se/rattsliga-dokument/statens-offentliga-utredningar/2017/10/sou-201775/, 31-47.
987. Compared to a general six months retention period for all types of data.
988. *See* §3 II *supra* (para. 436).

to provide information' (*informationsföreläggande*) according to the Swedish Copyright Act[989] can only force telecom operators to release personal data about their subscribers in the event this information is still stored in their systems. In a Supreme Court judgment from 2012[990] this argument was confirmed and the interest of the copyright holders was considered outweighing the interest of privacy of the subscribers. The Supreme Court also stated, however, that data that is being stored due to the network operators' data retention obligation (Chapter 6 section 16a–16f Electronic Communications Act) cannot fall under the 'order to provide information' and can therefore not be released to copyright holders.

C. *Cookies*

442. Chapter 6 section 18 Electronic Communications Act deals explicitly with cookies and transposes Article 5(3) Directive on Privacy and Electronic Communications. Electronic communication networks may be used to store or gain access to information stored in the terminal equipment of a subscriber or user only if the subscriber or user is provided with information about the purpose of the processing and has consented to the processing by the data controller.

The 2009 amendment to the Directive on Privacy and Electronic Communications was implemented into the Swedish Electronic Communications Act in 2011 and exchanged the earlier 'right to refuse' with the requirement of consent. The requirement was, however, not interpreted in a clear manner in practice to start with. The Swedish Interactive Advertising Bureau (IAB Sweden),[991] for example, together with some other industry organizations produced a Recommendation in 2011 for the use of cookies by market players.[992] IAB's recommendation built upon the OBA Framework (Online Behavioural Advertising) by IAB Europe. With regards to consent, the Recommendation states that certain browser settings can be regarded as consent by the user, which would entail no change in practice from the previous legal wording. With the adoption of the GDPR, however, the general view in the EU is that consent should have the same meaning for cookies as within the GDPR. The CJEU also ruled in October 2019 that valid consent for cookies requires an action on the part of the individual, which means, for example, that preselected ticks in a checkbox are not valid consent.[993]

The information and consent requirement does not apply in the event the storage or access is necessary in order to carry out the transmission of an electronic message over an electronic communication network,[994] or is otherwise required to provide an information society service explicitly requested by the subscriber or user. For example, if the user wishes to access a banking service that requires cookies to

989. *See* Part II Ch. 1 §8 *supra* (para. 179).
990. Decision by Supreme Court from 21 Dec. 2012, NJA 2012 s. 975.
991. iabsverige.se/.
992. The recommendation is available to the public at, www.minacookies.se.
993. Case C-673/17 *Planet49* [2019] ECLI:EU:C:2019:801, points 49–52.
994. The wording 'or facilitate' the transmission was deleted in the 2011 amendment of the section, thereby restricting the allowed use of cookies to cases where cookies are necessary for the transmission and not just facilitate it.

be stored or accessed on the user's computer, the data controller is allowed to employ cookies in the technical process. Caching necessary for transmission for technical reasons is also permitted according to Chapter 6 section 18 Electronic Communications Act.

443. Furthermore, the Electronic Communications Act stipulates specific provisions on criminal liability with regards to non-compliance with Chapter 6 section 18. Unless liability is not covered by the Swedish Penal Code, violation of Chapter 6 section 18, intentionally or with gross negligence, can lead to a fine.[995]

IV. Directories of Subscribers

444. Chapter 6 sections 15 and 16 Electronic Communications Act, transposing Article 12 Directive on Privacy and Electronic Communications, stipulate some requirements for operators with regard to data processing in relation to directories of subscribers. A subscriber who is a natural person shall receive information about the purposes of a printed or electronic directory, free of charge and before the personal data is included in the directory. With regards to electronic directories, the subscriber shall also be informed about the search possibilities in the service.[996]

Personal data may only be processed in these directories with the consent of the subscriber. In addition, the user has to be able to request verification, correction or deletion of the data.[997]

§4. Sanctions and Supervision

445. In accordance with Article 15(2) Directive on Privacy and Electronic Communications, Chapter 6 section 2 Electronic Communications Act refers to the Personal Data Act. In particular, questions of civil liability are to be answered according to the Personal Data Act.

Chapter 7 Electronic Communications Act contains provisions on criminal liability for, *inter alia*, breach of confidentiality.

446. According to section 2 Ordinance on Electronic Communications (*förordning (2003:396) om elektronisk kommunikation*), the PTS is the responsible supervisory authority for data protection within the electronic communications sector. PTS monitors providers of electronic communications networks and also ensures compliance with the privacy rules of the Electronic Communications Act. In its supervisory capacity PTS also published guidelines on data protection within electronic communications.

995. Chapter 7 s. 15 Electronic Communications Act.
996. Chapter 6 s. 15 Electronic Communications Act.
997. *Ibid.*

Part VII. Computer-Related Crime

Chapter 1. General Legal Development

447. Sweden's long history of criminalizing computer-specific crime stretches back to the Data Act (*datalag (1973:289)*) of 1973 which *inter alia* criminalized data intrusion. At the time, the legislature obviously did not have Internet-based hacking in mind, but intended instead to penalize persons who physically broke into offices housing computers (or terminals) in order to change information in registers. The Swedish Penal Code does not refer to 'computer-crimes' as a stand-alone category of crimes, but nevertheless criminalizes acts where computers and technology are involved. Most computer-related crimes were present in criminal law long before the advent of information technology and will have their names and places in the traditional criminal law structure. Computer-specific crimes, however, are unique in the sense that they do not have their offline equivalents, they have a shorter history and they have been attributed places in the criminal law structure that may appear to be tentative or even randomly chosen.

For want of a given structure for computer crimes and computer-related crimes in national law, this chapter will follow the structure of the European Council Convention on Cybercrime. Sweden signed the Treaty on 23 November 2001 in Budapest, but has not ratified it yet, although most provisions in the Convention are covered by Swedish law.[998] Following the structure of the Cybercrime Convention,[999] there are four main categories of computer-related crimes. The first includes the core of computer-based offences, that is offences against the confidentiality, integrity and availability of computer data, and systems as well as those 'where computer and telecommunication systems are used as a means to attack certain legal interests which mostly are protected already by criminal law against attacks using

998. A Government-appointed Public Inquiry presented its proposal SOU 2013:39 'Europarådets konvention om it-relaterad brottslighet' in May 2013, presenting the remaining legislative amendments necessary to permit ratification uf the convention and its additional protocol by Sweden. The Inquiry was also tasked with analysing the need and making proposals for the legislative amendments needed to implement the draft (not yet formally adopted). Directive of the European Parliament and of the Council on attacks against information systems, repealing Council Framework Decision 2005/222/JHA, as well as considering the need for tougher penalties for breaches of postal or telecommunication secrecy, or data security, in order to allow greater scope to take more nuanced account of the seriousness of large-scale attacks on information systems.

999. European Treaty Series (ETS) No. 185.

traditional means'.[1000] The second category relates to ordinary crimes that are frequently committed using a computer system, but its traditional scope was not broad enough to cover situations involving new technologies. The third covers content-related offences regarding child pornography, whereas the fourth category covers infringement of intellectual property rights.

448. The Swedish Penal Code (*brottsbalk (1962:700)*) entered into force on 21 December 1962, that is well before the advent of information technology, as we know it today. Although the code has been amended extensively, its main structure has remained intact. One of the crimes described in the code from the outset is *breach of postal or telecommunications secrecy*, Chapter 4 section 8.[1001] This has traditionally been seen as an infringement on the liberty and privacy of the individual, and consequently we find the provision in Chapter 4 of the Code, where crimes against the peace and freedom of the individual are gathered. The traditional place of this crime in the Penal Code is the main reason why more contemporary amendments that include hacking are located in conjunction with this provision. Thus, the Swedish legislature has used Chapter 4 section 9 of the Penal Code as the section to deal with computer/technology-based crimes. Chapter 4 section 9a deals with illicit eavesdropping (bugging) using electronic means, section 9b deals with the illicit accessing of messages through electronic means and section 9c deals with illicit data intrusion.

Other criminalized acts, that can be applicable to computer-related crimes, can be found in other sections of the Penal Code and in other laws.

1000. *See* Explanatory Report to ETS No. 185, para. 35.
1001. In its current form, since 2012 (SFS *2012:280*).

Chapter 2. Application of Substantive Criminal Law in the Area of ICT

§1. Offences Against the Confidentiality, Integrity, and Availability of Computer Data and Systems

I. Illegal Access and Illegal Interception

A. *Illegal Access*

449. 'Illegal access' as described by section 1 Article 2 Cybercrime Convention has its equivalent in Chapter 4 section 9c of the Swedish Penal Code. The provision in section 9c describes 'data intrusion' (*dataintrång*). This is an act, which the Cybercrime Convention would refer to as 'illegal access' and is the equivalent of 'hacking' in the vernacular. The crime itself consists of accessing information aimed to be processed through an automated process without permission. It also includes the illicit alteration, deletion or insertion of such data as well as the blocking or disruption of such data.

It is interesting to note that already back in the 1970s, when the act was first introduced, the Swedish legislature tried to implement a technologically neutral phrasing so that the law would keep up with future technical developments. So, instead of criminalizing illegal access to computer systems (which is the path chosen by the Cybercrime Convention and which may be conceptually easier to understand for the general public but more difficult to define and is constantly changing), the legislators criminalized illegal access to computer data. This is why section 9c is phrased as the illicit accessing of information (i.e., computer data). Although this may seem like a major difference at first, the reality is that the Swedish interpretation of the phrasing encompasses both illicit access to computer systems and illicit access to computer data. The way in which this is achieved is two-fold.

First, the definition of 'information' is interpreted in its widest form. Much like the definition of the term 'computer data' in the Convention, the Swedish interpretation of 'information' in section 9c defines *not only what* 'kind' of data is encompassed by section 9c, but also where the data can be in order for it to be encompassed by the section. Thus, the Swedish interpretation is such that the section encompasses all forms of data that can be processed by a computer. This includes data 'permanently' stored on a computer (a document or picture on the hard drive, for example), temporarily stored for processing (ones and zeros in the Random Access Memory of a computer) or actual programs/applications which process the previously mentioned forms of data along with data that is under transmission in wires.[1002]

Second, the phrasing of section 9c is such that it also includes situations where a perpetrator *may* be able to illicitly gain access to information even if she or he did in fact not do so. In other words, any illicit access to a computer device/system is

1002. If the data is part of an electronic message or transmitted through the air, then illicit accessing of it is covered through other sections of the Penal Code, such as Ch. 4 s. 8.

illegal because any such access would entail the possibility to also access data/information without permission. As a matter of fact, since there is no requirement for the illicit accessing to entail the circumvention of any security measures, the key factor becomes whether the person had 'authorization'[1003] to access the information or not.

In summary, by using a wide definition of data/information and setting the penalization point to the possibility of gaining access to unauthorized data/information, the Swedish Penal Code criminalizes both the illicit accessing of computer data and of computer systems.[1004]

450. The rules on data intrusion are subsidiary to the rules in Chapter 4 sections 8 and 9 Penal Code which define illicit *breaking of postal or telecommunications secrecy* and *intrusion into a safe depository* for such purposes, respectively. While section 9b deals with conspiracy to such crimes, section 9 criminalizes illicit wiretaps and will be discussed in the next section.

Anyone who unlawfully obtains access to a message that a postal or telecommunications company conveys may under section 8 be convicted of breaking the secrecy of the message to a fine or imprisonment for up to two years. The provision protects messages both in the traditional form and in the form of electronic messages, meaning messages conveyed through telecommunication. Messages conveyed by radio or data systems, however, fall outside the criminal area. The criminal law protection applies regardless of the format (e.g., audio, video, or text) of the content of the message (i.e., the contents of the envelope), from the time the message was delivered for transmission until it is received by the intended recipient.[1005]

Chapter 4 section 9 extends the reach of section 8, which only encompasses messages from the time they are sent/transmitted to the time they are received, thus protecting messages before and after they are sent/transmitted. Through section 9, illicitly opening a letter or telegram or illicitly accessing a message that is stored in a sealed manner, locked in or otherwise inaccessible is penalized as well.

Originally designed to protect postal delivery and storage of letters, the provision was later updated to cover telegrams, telephony and, more recently, other forms of telecommunication, including messages conveyed through information technology (through the previously discussed section 9c).[1006] The penalty for acts that fall under sections 8 and 9 is a fine or imprisonment for up to two years. Attempt and preparation for an intrusion, that if completed would not have been insignificant, is also punishable under section 10. Private transmission, that is, not relying on third parties for the transmission is, however, not protected by the criminal provision.

1003. It is worth noting that 'authorization' does not only refer to a technical access through a user account on a system, but to a generic concept of whether the person had consent to gain access to a specific information by someone who can be considered the 'owner' of the information or not. Thus, data intrusion can be committed on a completely unprotected system as long as the 'owner' of the system did not authorize entry. *See* Government Bill (*Proposition*) 2006/07:66, 'Angrepp mot informationssystem', 34 et seq.

1004. Government Bill (*Proposition*) 2006/07:66, 49–51.

1005. *Ibid.*

1006. *See* Government Bill (*Proposition*) 2006/07:66; and Government Bill (*Proposition*) 2017/18:105 'Ny dataskyddslag'.

While unsuccessful attempt in this case is not criminalized, preparation for the commission of the crime is through a specific provision in section 9b. Affixing a technical aid with the intent to break confidentiality in the manner described in section 8 is regarded as conspiracy to commit the offence, and the penalty is a fine or imprisonment for up to two years.

Under section 10, attempt, preparation and solicitation to commit data intrusion that, if successful, had not been considered minor and to commit serious data intrusion are punishable offences (in its current form, since 2018 (SFS 2018:601)).

B. Illegal Interception

451. As stated above, the illegal interception of communication during transmission or storage is covered by Chapter 4 sections 8, 9, 9b, and 9c. The provision in Chapter 4 section 9a covers the illegal interceptions or recordings of a private conversation, through any technical means, which neither the listener nor the public is meant to be privy to. In other words, this provision forbids illicit eavesdropping or bugging of a room to protect personal privacy as well as the privacy of boardrooms and the like.

The rule is subsidiary to the criminal provision on breach of postal or telecommunications secrecy (section 8). The punishment is a fine or imprisonment for up to two years. Attempt is not punishable, while preparations fall within an ancillary provision in section 9b.

In addition, if the criminal act causes injury, it may lead to criminal liability for damages, provided that the act caused injury to a physical object and that the damage was covered by the offender's criminal intent. If such harmful acts are directed against vital interests of society (critical infrastructure) liability under the criminal law provisions regarding sabotage and serious sabotage may come into play.[1007]

C. Common Provisions for Illegal Access and Illegal Interception, and the Confidentiality of Collected Traffic Data

452. Current Swedish legal provisions on confidentiality and disclosure of operators comply with the provisions of the Cybercrime Convention's Articles 20 and 21. These national provisions are not, however, found in the Penal Code. Rules on disclosure of telecommunications carriers and providers are found in the Electronic Communications Act (*lag (2003:389) om elektronisk kommunikation*), notably Chapter 6. According to Chapter 6 section 21 operators have to respect the

1007. In this context, it should be pointed out that serious criminal damage, sabotage and serious sabotage are punishable as terrorist offences, under the conditions set out in the Act on Sanctions for Terrorist Offences (*lag (2003:148) om straff för terroristbrott*).

confidentiality of the use of secret measures of compulsion, namely secret surveillance (bugging), covert remote surveillance and the detention of deliveries or shipments. Such secrecy also applies to the subscriber of services concerned.[1008] These measures ensure that service providers *inter alia* keep information about official police investigations carried out with their assistance and the result of these confidential.

453. The penalty for the criminal acts that the Convention refers to as 'illegal access' and 'illegal interception' – in Swedish law mainly constituting the singular crime data intrusion, Chapter 4 section 9c – is a fine or imprisonment for a maximum of two years. For damaging property and seriously damaging property, the penalties are a fine or imprisonment for a maximum of one year and four years respectively. The penalty for sabotage is imprisonment for a maximum of four years and for serious sabotage imprisonment for a minimum of two and a maximum of eighteen, or life imprisonment.

In its normal degree of gravity, a conviction for the crime of data intrusion carries the penalty of a fine or up to two years imprisonment. Where aggravating circumstances exist, the crime will be categorized as serious data intrusion, carrying a minimum penalty of six months imprisonment and a maximum of six years. The aggravating circumstances to be considered are whether the criminal act has caused serious damage, has encompassed a large quantity of data or if it in other ways has been of a particularly dangerous nature. Large scale Denial-of-Service (DOS) – and DDOS attacks are examples of intrusions that would be deemed as aggravating circumstances.[1009]

The provision was amended, following its introduction in 1998, as a result of adaptation to the EU Framework Decision on Attacks on Information Systems,[1010] and later to EU Directive 2013/40/EU on Attacks on Information Systems, that replaced the framework decision.[1011]

The penalty for attempt generally holds the same maximum as the completed form of the same crime[1012] and may not go below imprisonment if the minimum penalty for the completed crime is imprisonment for two years or more. For instigation and accessory crimes, the same penalties apply as for the main crime. Certain latitude exists for reduction concerning accessories to crime.[1013] Aggravating circumstances are described in Chapter 29 section 2 Penal Code, for example, if the crime forms part of criminal activities that have been carefully planned or carried out with a significant degree of organization in which the perpetrator has played a significant role.

Swedish provisions on penalties for legal persons, stipulated in Chapter 36 sections 7–10 Penal Code, make companies liable for crimes that have been carried out in the conduct of business. A condition for this is that the crime has constituted a

1008. The rules on disclosure, in the same Chapter of the Electronic Communications Act, meet the Convention requirements of Art. 20 para. 3 and Art. 21 para. 3.
1009. Government Bill (*Proposition*) 2006/07:66, 50 et seq.
1010. OJ L 69, 16.03.2005.
1011. The section is in its current form since 2014, SFS 2014:302.
1012. Chapter 23 s. 1 Penal Code.
1013. Chapter 23 s. 5 Penal Code.

serious disregard of the particular obligations that the business entails or that the crime is of a particularly serious kind. An additional requirement is that the company has been negligent, that is, not done what could reasonably have been expected of it, in order to prevent the crime. The calculation of the size of the fine follows from the provisions in Chapter 36 section 8 Penal Code, that is not less than SEK 5,000 and not more than SEK 10,000,000.

454. Computer data, as defined by Chapter 4 section 9c Penal Code, that is illicitly changed can be deemed as a forgery if it involves the changing of a document or a record. Forgery of computer data will be discussed in a later section.[1014] If, on the other hand, the change is made in a data process that does not qualify as such a record, the illegal changing of the data would fall under Chapter 4 section 9 c Penal Code. As mentioned above, the illicit changing, deleting, blocking or inserting into a register of computer data is considered as data intrusion. Thereby any alteration of computer data as defined and interpreted by Chapter 4 section 9c is considered to be 'hacking' if carried out without consent.

As stated above, Chapter 4 section 9c was amended in order to encompass DOS attacks.[1015] Following this amendment, any action that seriously disrupts or obstructs the use of computer data is also considered as data intrusion. It is important to note here that accidental or minor disruptions do not fall under the provision. The reasoning behind this follows Chapter II Article 4 paragraph 2 Cybercrime Convention whereby the Member States can reserve the right to only criminalize serious forms of interception. Thus, the Swedish legislation requires both intent and the occurrence of serious damage as a result of DOS attacks in order for these to be considered data intrusions.

Besides the section of the Penal Code that deals with computer-related offences, other sections of the Penal Code may also be applicable to DOS attacks and the like. To destroy or damage property, movable or immovable, to the detriment of another person's right to the property, falls under the criminal offence of *inflicting damage.*[1016] If the act entailed serious danger to someone's life or health – for example, if the act results in the malfunctioning of medical equipment – or if damage was inflicted on property of great cultural or economic significance or was otherwise serious, the act may be considered as *gross infliction of damage.*[1017] These provisions primarily refer to physical life situations, such as when a car or a house is damaged, but can also be applied to when computer data or computer systems are

1014. *See* §2 I *infra* (paras 459–460).

1015. Amendment of Ch. 4 s. 9c through Act 2007:213, proposed in Government Bill (*Proposition*) 2006/07:66, 49–51. DOS attacks as well as DDOS attacks (Distributed DOS attacks) are intentionally launched against a computer system in order to prevent the proper operation of the system, thereby denying users of its services. The most common attack type is saturation attacks, in which the system will use a scarce function or resource almost exclusively in order to manage data generated by the attack. For more information, *see*, e.g., www.crime-research.org/articles/network-security-dos-ddos-attacks, accessed 15 Mar. 2010.

1016. Chapter 12 s. 1 Penal Code.

1017. Chapter 12 s. 3 Penal Code.

damaged. Since the provisions are not limited to physical damages, damage originating from 'cyber attacks' (i.e., data intrusion) also falls under the provision, for example, when a DOS attack results in economic damages for the victim of the attack.

The destruction or damaging of property that has considerable significance for national defence, public security, justice or the administration or for maintaining public order and security, or by other measures that seriously interferes with or prevents the use of such property may be considered as sabotage.[1018] This also applies if a person through criminal damage or other acts seriously interferes with or prevents public intercourse or use of telegraph, telephone, radio or similar public facilities *inter alia* for the supply of water, light, heat or power. If danger has been caused to national security, to several human lives or to property of particular importance by the offence, the perpetrator may be sentenced for aggravated sabotage.[1019]

Once again, these provisions do not require the source of the damage to be physical and they do not even require the result of the damage to be physical. For example, the hacking or DOS attack on the systems controlling traffic lights would fall under the provisions of Chapter 13 section 4.

II. Data Interference and System Interference

455. Although these acts are described in the Cybercrime Convention as separate acts from illegal access and illegal interception, they are not separately criminalized under Swedish law. Data and system interferences are subsumed under the hacking offence data intrusion described above.

III. Misuse of Devices

456. The Cybercrime Convention has a specific provision on 'misuse of devices', a concept borrowed from US Federal criminal law that finds few equivalents in European law.[1020] The Convention thus calls not only for the criminalization of using devices for committing crimes under the Convention but also for the criminalization of possession and 'the production, sale, procurement for use, import, distribution or otherwise making available of'[1021] such devices. For Sweden and several other signatories to the Convention, there are no specific provisions or offences for these forms of 'preparatory' acts/measures. They are, instead, subsumed under general rules on attempt and preparation of crimes. Using this technique, current legislation complies in all substantial aspects with the requirements of the Convention on criminal liability for non-independent forms of crime – all steps taken in preparing the execution of the crimes concerned are covered –

1018. Chapter 13 s. 4 Penal Code.
1019. Chapter 13 s. 5 Penal Code.
1020. Compare Title 18 Part I Ch. 47 s. 1029 US Code on 'Fraud and related activity in connection with access devices'.
1021. Chapter II Art. 6 para. 1a Cybercrime Convention.

although attempted ancillary forms of petty offences are not always punishable. The rules regarding preparation to commit crime do, therefore, make specific criminal provisions on abuse of tools or devices superfluous.

The general rule on criminal attempts specifies that if anyone has commenced the execution of a crime, the person shall, in cases where there is a specific provision to that effect linked to the crime in question, be sentenced for attempt to commit the offence.[1022] A prerequisite for liability is, however, that there was clear danger of completion of the crime or that this danger was excluded only due to accidental circumstances. No liability will exist if the offender voluntarily suspended the act, before reaching the point of completion. The penalty for attempt will be determined on the same basis as the completed crime.[1023]

457. Chapter 23 section 2 Penal Code stipulates criminal responsibility for preparation to commit a crime, for any person who:

(1) receives or gives money or other items as payment for a crime or to cover the costs of carrying out a crime; or
(2) acquires, manufactures, supplies, receives, stores, transports, prepares or procures something particularly designed or well-adapted to be used as an aid in a crime.

When these conditions are met, the person shall be charged for the preparation of the offence in question whether it was completed or not.

For certain explicitly specified crimes in the Penal Code, the act of conspiracy can also result in criminal liability, covering situations where a person, in consultation with other persons, agrees to carry out a criminal act or otherwise conspires to bring it about. Criminal responsibility for preparation is excluded if the prospects for success of the attempt were small.

The rules on preparation were amended in 2001, when criminal responsibility was extended, and the provision on preparation of crimes was given its current, more general phrasing.[1024] The introduction of a reference to procuring 'something particularly designed … to be used as an aid in crime' in Chapter 23 section 2 was motivated by necessary modernization, as such aids could be physical items but also more arbitrary items such as computer viruses and other software produced solely for hacking purposes or other types of criminal activities such as counterfeiting.[1025]

1022. Chapter 23 s. 1 Penal Code.

1023. In relation to the obligations under the Convention, non-independent liability exists in Swedish law for crimes under Arts 3 (illegal interception), 4 (data interference), 5 (system disturbance), 7 (data falsification) 8 (computer fraud) and 9 (child pornography). From pre-IT case law, it is worth noting that a person caught with a main key to a residence or hotel, or with keys to premises or housing to which the person has no connection, can incur responsibility for preparation of theft. *See*, e.g., Decision by Supreme Court from 18 Oct. 1960, NJA 1960 s. 442.

1024. *See* SFS 2001:348. The rules have since been amended in other aspects, most recently in 2016, (SFS 2016:508).

1025. *See* Government Bill (Proposition) 2000/01:85, 'Förberedelse till brott m.m.', 41.

The penalty for preparing or conspiring cannot be higher than the highest level of penalty for the offence itself but may be lower than the lowest level of penalty for the offence.[1026]

According to Chapter 23 section 4 Penal Code, criminal liability shall be imposed not only on anyone who carries out a prohibited act but also on other persons who have given advice or assisted in the criminal act. This responsibility includes all crimes in the penal code and penal provisions of other laws and regulations, provided that imprisonment is within the range of penalties for the offence.

458. Using devices or programs that gain unauthorized access to closed services or to telecommunication equipment can be punishable as fraud.[1027]

§2. Other Computer-Related Offences

I. Computer-Related Forgery

459. Chapter 14 section 1 Penal Code stipulates that a person who by writing another person's – real or fictitious – name, or by deceit obtains another person's signature, or by other means produces a false document of proof or fraudulently alters or adds to a genuine document, shall be deemed guilty of forgery or falsification of a document, which is the term reserved for this crime in Swedish law. A condition for such an act to be punishable is that the measure jeopardizes the verification or proof value of the document.[1028]

The vast majority of electronic documents, however, such as saved documents of a word processor, would not meet the fundamental requirement for forgery. Before the contents have been compiled and materialized into a physical document, any manipulation of the information in question may meet the requirements for criminal

1026. Article 6 of the Convention requires the extensive criminalization of functions with different types of tools, from technical tools and software that are particularly suited for use in the crimes covered by the Convention to computer passwords, access codes and similar information. The latter are intended to only have a legal purpose, but may, if they come into the wrong hands, be used to commit crimes. As far as tools of the former kind are concerned, the amendment in 2001 was intended to include them and make the provision more technologically neutral. It is at first more doubtful whether passwords, access codes and the like can be seen as particularly likely or designed to be used as a tool in crime. Because they are part of the security arrangements around the computer facility or computer system, they have a very important role and can best be compared with keys. The possession of illicitly obtained keys can, on the other hand, constitute a typical step-in the preparation of a crime.

1027. *See* II *infra* (para. 461).

1028. From the original Act introducing the Penal Code 1962:700. *See* for extensive reasoning Government Official Report SOU 2007:92, 'Urkunden i tiden – en straffrättslig anpassning'. A decision from Svea Court of Appeal (Svea Hovrätt) states that documents that only exist in a format created by a word processor are more like transcripts or copies and thus lack the level of originality that is required under Ch. 14 Penal Code; Decision by Svea Court of Appeal from 31 May 2002, No. B 5358–01, 67.

liability for data intrusion (if there is a case of illicit access), but would not constitute forgery as the information is not (yet) part of an object that can be forged. For the same reason the rules on counterfeiting can rarely be applied to information in electronic form.

The penalty for falsification of a document is prison up to two years. For *gross falsification of a document* the penalty is prison of not less than six months and not more than six years.[1029] In considering whether the crime is serious or not, particular regard needs to be given to whether the forgery pertains to documents archived by public authorities or documents of proof of particular importance in general commerce, such as bonds, stocks or instruments of real estate mortgage.[1030] Another reason for considering an act serious can be that the act has been of a particularly dangerous nature. If the act of forgery is considered to be of minor gravity, the sentence may concern alteration of documents of proof and amount to a fine or prison up to six months.[1031]

As of 2016, the use of another person's identification data without permission is criminalized as unauthorized use of identification and carries a penalty of a fine or up to two years imprisonment, according to Chapter 4 section 6b. The unauthorized use is an offence when it has created damages for the victim or an inconvenience.[1032] Identification data is described as data that is normally used to identify or specify a certain physical person. Apart from name and civic registration number, this may include date of birth, email address, photographs, aliases, etc.

460. Attempt and preparation of forgery and aggravated forgery are also punishable.[1033] This does not apply if the crime, had it been completed, would have been considered to be minor, in which case it would be labelled rendering a document of proof inaccurate.

The sections about forgery and counterfeiting only encompass situations where a perpetrator changes a genuine document. A closely related offence occurs when a person destroys, renders useless or disposes of a genuine document without permission. A person found guilty of such an act will be convicted for the suppression of a document.[1034] The penalty is imprisonment for up to two years. If the offence is minor, the penalty is a fine or imprisonment of up to six months. If aggravating circumstances are demonstrated, the penalty is imprisonment of between six months and a maximum of four years. Attempt and preparation for the suppression of documents are punishable.[1035] This does not apply if the crime, had it been completed, would have been considered to be minor.

1029. Chapter 14 s. 3 Penal Code.
1030. From the original Act introducing the Penal Code, 1962:700.
1031. Chapter 14 s. 2 Penal Code.
1032. SFS 2016:485. *See* Government Bill (*Proposition*) 2015/16:150.
1033. Chapter 14 s. 2 Penal Code.
1034. Chapter 14 s. 4 Penal Code.
1035. Chapter 14 s. 12 Penal Code.

II. Computer-Related Fraud

461. Under Swedish criminal law, fraud is regulated in a general manner, Chapter 9 section 1 (with a petty form of the crime described in Chapter 9 section 2, and an aggravated form in Chapter 9 section 3) covering all situations where a person 'by deception induces someone to commit or omit to commit some act which involves gain for the accused and loss for the deceived or someone represented by the latter'. The same applies for 'a person who, by delivering incorrect or incomplete information, or by making alterations to a programme or recording or by other means, unlawfully affects the result of automatic data processing or any other similar automatic process so that gain accrues to the offender and loss is entailed by any other person'. The penalty for fraud is imprisonment for at most two years. Should the gain/loss be negligible, the minor form of the crime would be applicable, Chapter 9 section 2. If no gain or loss results from the act, but the victim nevertheless is harmed, Chapter 9 section 8 holds liability for dishonest conduct when a person acts dishonestly by misleading someone and inducing her or him to do or omit to do something, thereby harming her or him or someone she or he represents.

Liability for fraud, as defined in the above-mentioned provision, also follows from the act of providing inaccurate or incomplete information, for example, by altering a computer program or recording, or otherwise illicitly affects the outcome of an automated information process or a similar automated process, so that the offender benefits to the detriment of someone else. This provision thus encompasses computer system or data manipulation which is done for financial profit such as 'hacking' ATM's or the copying of the magnetic stripes on credit cards ('skimming'). The provision would, however, also encompass 'phishing' attacks where, for example, copies of banks' web pages would be set up in order to steal the bank customers' login details.[1036]

Under aggravating circumstances, the offender may be sentenced for serious fraud to imprisonment of not less than six months and a maximum of six years.[1037] In determining the seriousness of the offence, consideration will be given to whether the offender has misused public confidence or used a forged document or misleading accounting or if the act otherwise was of a particularly dangerous nature, pertained to a substantial value or entailed considerable damage.

If the crime, in view of the extent of damage and other circumstances, is considered to be of a minor nature – for instance, with regard to the amounts involved – the sentence may refer to fraudulent behaviour instead of fraud, and the penalty set to a fine or imprisonment of up to six months.[1038]

1036. This section was added to the Penal Code in 1986 through SFS 1986:123, and although the expression 'the outcome of an automated information process' may seem alien today, it is the result of the earliest attempts to create a wide and technology-neutral definition for digitized data stored on various mediums, such as magnetic tapes. For developments in the EU related to credit card fraud, *see* www.ec.europa.eu/internal_market/payments/fraud/index_en.htm, accessed 15 Mar. 2010. For links to articles and research on this topic, *see*, e.g., www.crime-research.org/articles/1562, accessed 15 Mar. 2010.

1037. Chapter 9 s. 3 Penal Code.

1038. Chapter 9 s. 2 Penal Code.

Section 3a was introduced in its current wording in 2017 in order to capture the specific and almost exclusively computer-related type of fraud, consisting of sending requests for payment under false pretences to a large number of recipients, amounting to considerable amounts. A person convicted of doing so shall be sentenced for serious payment fraud to a penalty of a minimum of six months and a maximum of six years.[1039]

Attempt and conspiracy to commit fraud and serious fraud is a criminal offence, according to Chapter 9 section 11 Penal Code, while petty offences are not punishable at these preliminary stages.

§3. CONTENT-RELATED OFFENCES

462. The Act on Child Pornography[1040] came into force on 1 January 1999, as Criminal Code Chapter 16 section 10a. According to this section, all forms of handling child pornography are prohibited. It is thus prohibited to depict children in pornographic images, to transfer or make available images of child pornography, to broker contacts between buyers and sellers of child pornography, etc. Images in electronic form are covered by the provision. The responsibility is not limited to photos where children are involved in acts which clearly have a sexual meaning. Pornographic images involving children that occur in conjunction with one or more adults engaged in sexual acts are also subject to criminalization. Any person who through commercial activities or otherwise for gain negligently distributes child pornographic images may also be sentenced for child pornography crimes. The law does not, however, prohibit the viewing of child pornography on the Internet, although the Act is currently under review, *inter alia* in this respect.

463. Current criminal responsibility for child pornography in Swedish law is in many respects more stringent than required by the Convention. In principle, any handling of child pornographic material is prohibited.

A person found guilty of child pornography-related crimes may be sentenced to imprisonment for up to two years. If the crime is considered to be a minor offence, the applicable penalty is a fine or imprisonment for up to six months. Under aggravating circumstances, child pornography-related crimes may result in penalties between six months and six years of imprisonment. Aggravating circumstances include situations where the crime is committed professionally or for profit, as a part of criminal activities perpetrated systematically or on a large scale. Further aggravating circumstances are situations where a particularly large number of images are used or situations where the images depict children exposed to particularly ruthless treatment.

Criminal responsibility includes attempt and preparation of the crime, provided that it would not, if completed, have been considered minor.[1041]

1039. SFS 2017:442.
1040. SFS 2005:90.
1041. Chapter 16 s. 17 Penal Code.

As of 2017 a new content-related crime is described in Chapter 4 section 6c, namely illegal breach of integrity. The crime is committed through violating a person's integrity through the dissemination of:

(1) a picture of or other data about a person's sexual life;
(2) a picture of or other data about a person's state of health;
(3) a picture of or other data about a person's exposure to a crime against his or her person;
(4) a picture of a person in an exposed situation, or
(5) a picture of a person's wholly or partially naked body.

In addition, it is required that the dissemination is intended to inflict serious harm to the person concerned, in which case the perpetrator shall be convicted of illegal breach of integrity to a fine or imprisonment of up to two years, unless the act, considering its intended purpose and other circumstances, is deemed defendable.[1042]

§4. Offences Related to Infringements of Copyright and Related Rights

464. Swedish copyright rules include both criminal penalties and other sanctions for crimes infringing on intellectual property. According to section 53 Act on Copyright in Literary and Artistic Work (lag *(1960:729) om upphovsrätt till litterära och konstnärliga verk*; hereinafter 'Copyright Act') liability applies to anyone who, with intent or negligence, commits an act that infringes on the copyrights of literary or artistic works.

Section 26g and h Copyright Act regulate the use of software and computer programs. A person who has obtained the right to use a computer program (i.e., bought it) can copy it and even modify it in order to ensure that it functions as intended. To this end, the rightful owner of a program may even correct errors in the program itself to ensure that it works as intended. The rightful owner may also create security backups of the program if this is necessary for the intended use of the program. These copies may, however, not be used once the owner no longer has the right to use the original program (e.g., if the original CD with the program on it was sold to a third party).

Decompilation of a computer program is allowed in situations where the computer program is being examined with the intent to make it compatible with another computer program. Such decompilation is only allowed if it is carried out by a person who has a right to use the program being decompiled, if the information is not readily available elsewhere and if only the relevant sections of the program are decompiled. The information thus gained cannot be used for purposes other than to make the program compatible with another program. Nor can it be handed over to third parties unless the purpose of the handover is to ensure the compatibility measures in question.

1042. SFS 2017:1136. *See* Government Bill (*Proposition*) 2016/17:222 p. 97.

Copying computer programs for private use is allowed as long as the copy is not used in business or public activities and the perpetrator does not make use of the copies for anything other than personal use.[1043]

Penalties for copyright infringement are a fine or imprisonment for up to two years. Attempt and preparations for copyright infringement lead to the same penalties, section 53 paragraph 5 Copyright Act. A restriction in the general prosecution principle applies for this crime to the extent that a copyright violation may only be prosecuted by the prosecutor if the plaintiff brings charges to that effect, or if prosecution is warranted from a general point of view.[1044]

According to section 5 Act on Responsibility for Electronic Bulletin Boards (*lag (1998:112) om ansvar för elektroniska anslagstavlor*; hereinafter 'BBS Act'), the owner of the BBS[1045] or a similar forum is obliged to delete or otherwise prevent the circulation of certain messages, including messages whereby a user of the BBS is obviously committing copyright violations. The liability provision in the Act on Liability for Electronic Bulletin Boards is subsidiary to the rules of the Copyright Act, according to section 7.

1043. Section 53 para. 2 Copyright Act.
1044. Section 59 Copyright Act.
1045. Section 1 BBS Act defines BBS as a service for the electronic conveying of messages.

Chapter 3. Application of the Criminal Procedure Law in the Area of ICT

§1. Search and Seizure of Stored Computer Data

465. Search and seizure are criminal procedural measures of coercion – in some jurisdictions appearing jointly, in others separately – through which law enforcement authorities, investigating a suspected crime, may search a property (search), belonging to one or more persons, and confiscate (seizure) objects that could be relevant to the investigation, and later serve as evidence to the crime. Seizure may, according to Chapter 27 section 1 Swedish Code of Judicial Procedure (*rättegångsbalk (1942:740)*), include objects, which could reasonably be expected to have significance for the investigation of a crime or that could be the product of criminal activity. Seizure does therefore not require a suspect or a crime of a certain degree of gravity, with some exceptions. Seizures can be decided following any type of crime and against both suspects and others, pursuant to Chapter 27 section 1 Code of Judicial Procedure. Seizure may be ordered only if the reasons for the action outweigh the interference and personal interests of the suspect. Seizures often include written documents[1046] and through the development of case law, electronic documents (i.e., a separate compilation of electronic data) are equated with written documents.[1047]

For seizure of electronic data, it is crucial that the data has been transferred to a physical medium – the Code of Judicial Procedure assumes physical form and would not permit seizing intangible objects, should such objects be possible to seize.[1048] It is uncertain whether data in electronic form, which has not been compiled, can be considered equivalent to a written document and therefore possible to seize. The log files demonstrating the albeit temporal existence of such data do, however, qualify as objects that can be searched and 'seized' in the sense, that for example, an ISP may be coerced, using the same or similar mechanisms, to provide printouts of relevant log files. Data stored with a telephone operator may not be seized as a substitute measure for covert remote surveillance, an instrument defining exclusive possibilities for obliging a telecom operator through coercive powers in order to obtain information on telecommunications and other electronic communications. There are, however, other provisions in the Electronic Communications Act with obligations for telecommunications carriers to provide certain information to law enforcement authorities.[1049]

1046. Chapter 27 s. 2 Code of Judicial Procedure.

1047. *See*, e.g., Government Bill (*Proposition*) 1998/99:11, 'Ny skyddsåtgärd vid immaterialrättsintrång', 54 et seq., Ministry Publications Series (Ds) 2003:29, 'FORMEL – Formkrav och elektronisk kommunikation', 95 et seq., as well as Government Official Report SOU 1992:110, 'Datastraffrättsutredningen'.

1048. *See* Ministry Publications Series (Ds) 2005:6, 'Brott och brottsutredning i IT-miljö, Europarådets konvention om IT-relaterad brottslighet med tilläggsprotokoll', 126 et seq.

1049. *See* Directive 2006/24/EC of the European Parliament and of the Council of 15 March 2006 on the retention of data generated or processed in connection with the provision of publicly available electronic communications services or of public communications networks and amending Directive 2002/58/EC.

466. A search warrant gives authorities a legal title to search premises for objects that may be seized. The preconditions for a search warrant, however, are stricter than the conditions for seizure – Chapter 28 section 1 Code of Judicial Procedure provides a positive permission for searches in the premises of the suspect of a crime, but defines the scope for searches in other premises more negatively. An electronic message, transferred to paper or materialized in another physical form is, with the exceptions listed below, accessible to seizure under the normal rules. Similarly, an electronic message that is stored in a computer by someone other than a telecom operator, for example, by the subscriber, may be seized, if the conditions are otherwise satisfied.[1050]

Searches may be carried out, if there are grounds for assuming that a criminal offence, for which imprisonment may follow, has been committed. Searches may be carried out in houses, rooms or enclosed storage facilities, either to search for objects that are subject to seizure or to determine other factors that may have importance for the investigation of the offence, pursuant to Chapter 28 section 1 Code of Judicial Procedure.

467. A search of the premises or property of a suspect requires that he or she is reasonably suspected of a crime, pursuant to Chapter 28 section 1 Code of Judicial Procedure. Searches may still be carried out, at lower levels of suspicion, but only when there is strong reason to believe that the search will produce objects to be seized or that other investigative advantages can be won. Search of the property of other persons than the suspect may be undertaken if the premises were the scene of the crime or the scene of arrest of the suspect. A search (in this context, reference is made to a so-called real search, that is, pertaining to objects, rather than personal search, pertaining to anything related to a specific individual) may, according to Chapter 28 section 1 Code of Judicial Procedure, be undertaken in order to search for items that may later be subject to seizure – a decision to seize an object can only be made once the object has been found – or to discover evidence that may be relevant to the investigation of a crime. Using a search warrant for the detection of crimes is not consistent with these requirements. Nor may the purpose of the search be to provide information on other crimes than the crime, the investigation of which was the basis for issuing the search warrant, or in order to ascertain whether the suspect may have committed crimes to a greater extent (i.e., in greater volumes or frequency) than expected initially.[1051]

The conditions for searches follow the same general restriction as seizure, namely that the search can be permitted only if the grounds of the measure outweigh the interference.[1052] There are no specific rules concerning the examination of computers in relation to searches and seizures. When a search warrant is issued in order to gain access to digitally stored information, the object of the search can be either the data carrier (usually a computer) or data stored in the data carrier or the code (the

1050. *See* Ministry Publications Series (Ds) 2005:6, 278 et seq. *See also* Gunnel Lindberg, *Straffprocessuella tvångsmedel – När och hur får de användas*, 2nd edn (Stockholm: Thomson Förlag, 2005).

1051. *See* Government Bill (*Proposition*) to the original Code of Judicial Procedure, published in NJA II 1933, 97 et seq., as well as the Decision by the Parliamentary Ombudsman JO 1988/89 53.

1052. Chapter 28 s. 3a Code of Judicial Procedure.

pattern of ones and zeros, not linked to specific data) that represents the stored information. If the carrier is the object for the action, the specific rules restricting later seizure of written documents in Chapter 27 Code of Judicial Procedure are not applicable, although the carrier may contain sensitive material and vice versa.[1053]

468. Searches can be carried out without any limitations on the type of premises to be searched, and can therefore, if conditions in Chapter 28 Code of Judicial Procedure are met, be made wherever there is a computer or other equipment likely to have been used in a crime. The prohibition of seizures in Chapter 27 section 2 Code of Judicial Procedure may however be indirectly relevant here. If there are legal obstacles to the seizure of an object, then a search for the same object is not permissible.[1054]

Facilities open to the public may be searched for the purpose stated above, even if there is no suspect.[1055] This includes shops, restaurants, cafes, theatres, cinemas, and – arguably – Internet cafés open to the public. Facilities usually used by persons likely to engage in criminal activity may also be searched for these purposes and under the same conditions.[1056]

The 2012 Act on Data Retrieval grants law enforcement agencies the right to retrieve traffic data retained by telecommunication service providers, in accordance with Act on Electronic Communications. Traffic data is defined as data about messages that have been transferred in an electronic communications network, about what pieces of equipment that have been present inside a certain geographical area, and data concerning in which geographical area certain electronic communication equipment is or has been located.

The EU legal act, underlying the obligation to retain traffic data – the 2006 Directive on the Retention of Data[1057] – was declared invalid in 2014 by the Court of Justice of the EU,[1058] as its provisions were deemed to violate the EU Charter of Fundamental Rights, in particular the right of privacy. This led to the Swedish legislation being challenged in a preliminary ruling by the Court of Justice of the EU in 2016.[1059] The CJEU ruled that a general obligation to retain traffic data violates EU law, which in its turn has prompted a need to revise the Swedish legislation on this point.

1053. *See* Government Official Report SOU 1992:110, 344 and 350.
1054. *See* Decision by Supreme Court from 28 Jun. 1977, NJA 1977 s. 403.
1055. Chapter 28 s. 3 first paragraph Code of Judicial Procedure.
1056. For an interesting contribution to the discourse related to this issue, and useful references to relevant case law, *see* Henrik Bengtsson & Emil Dicksved, 'Dataintrång', *Ny Juridik* 4 (2009).
1057. Directive 2006/24/EC of the European Parliament and of the Council of 15 March 2006 on the retention of data generated or processed in connection with the provision of publicly available electronic communications services or of public communications networks and amending Directive 2002/58/EC.
1058. Case C-293/12.
1059. Tele2 Sverige AB.

§2. INTERCEPTION

469. Communication between computers may be intercepted under the rules in Chapter 27 Code of Judicial Procedure, which also regulate secret telecommunications interception. This measure means that messages sent to or from a telecommunication address may be secretly intercepted and listened in on in real time or recorded by technical means in order to reproduce the content of a message at a later time. The term 'telecommunication' in this context is defined in Chapter 6 section 19 paragraph 3 Act on Electronic Communications as sound, text, images, data or other forms of information conveyed by means of radio or light or electromagnetic oscillations.[1060]

Secret telecommunications interception may be used in investigations concerning offences with a lower penalty threshold of two years imprisonment. It may also be used in situations dealing with attempt, preparation or conspiracy to commit such crimes, if these independent forms of crime are specifically criminalized.[1061]

Covert remote surveillance is a different instrument that may not be used to obtain the content of messages but only the traffic that conveys the message, its source and destination. Covert remote surveillance may be used in the investigation concerning criminal offences for which the minimum penalty is six months in prison, as well as for two specific crimes: hacking and child pornography crimes.[1062]

§3. JURISDICTION

470. Chapter 2 section 1 Penal Code establishes Swedish jurisdiction over all crimes committed on Swedish territory, as well as over offences believed to have been committed on Swedish territory. Jurisdiction also extends to all Swedish citizens and foreigners resident in Sweden, and for crimes committed abroad, under the dual criminality condition.[1063] Exceptions in the latter case are made for crimes committed on territory not belonging to any state, and for crimes that do not carry more than fines as a penalty under Swedish law.

471. For purposes of determining criminal jurisdiction, a crime is considered to have been committed where the criminal act was carried out, where the commission of the crime was completed or, concerning attempts, where it would have been completed.[1064] In addition to this, Swedish courts also have formal jurisdiction over

1060. *See* Government Bill (*Proposition*) 2002/03:110, 'Lag om elektronisk kommunikation, m.m.'

1061. Chapter 27 s. 18 Code of Judicial Procedure. This threshold was established by amendments proposed in Government Bill (*Proposition*) 2002/03:74, 'Hemliga tvångsmedel – offentliga ombud och en mer ändamålsenlig reglering'.

1062. These provisions in the Code of Judicial Procedure were introduced through SFS 2003:1146, resulting from Government Bill (*Proposition*) 2002/03:74.

1063. Chapter 2 s. 2 Penal Code.

1064. Chapter 2 s. 4 Penal Code.

crimes committed abroad, *inter alia* for crimes committed against Sweden, a Swedish municipality or other constituency, or against a Swedish public facility. Moreover, Swedish courts have formal jurisdiction over crimes that carry a minimum penalty of four years imprisonment[1065] even if they were committed outside of Swedish territory and even if the actions are not criminalized in the country where they were committed. In order to launch prosecution of crimes committed abroad, however, Chapter 2 section 5 Penal Code requires the prosecution service to obtain a government authorization to prosecute (*åtalsförordnande*), as a restraining measure on the exercise of universal jurisdiction.[1066]

§4. Extradiction and Judicial Cooperation

472. Following the Act on Surrendering of Persons from Sweden in Accordance with a European Arrest Warrant (*lag (2003:1156) om överlämnande från Sverige enligt en europeisk arresteringsorder*), surrendering may not be denied on the sole ground that the subject of the warrant is a citizen of the requested state. The Act, implementing an EU Framework Decision,[1067] is applied in relation to other EU Member States instead of extradition procedures.

473. Swedish law contains several mechanisms to ensure proper cooperation between different jurisdictions, based upon international treaties, conventions and agreements. The central instruments that outline Sweden's obligations in this regard are the European Convention on Mutual Assistance in Criminal Matters ratified by Sweden on 1 February 1968, the Convention Implementing the Schengen Agreement, signed on 19 June 1990, as well as the EUROPOL and EUROJUST systems established under the EU for cooperation between police authorities and prosecution services respectively.[1068]

§5. Electronic Evidence

474. The Swedish criminal procedure is mainly oral and there is considerable freedom for the court to accept any type of evidence. The Code of Judicial Procedure contains no definition of or any specific provisions concerning evidence in digital form. This is a consequence of the fact that Swedish procedural law does not distinguish between different types of evidence that may be presented before a court. Chapter 35 section 1 stipulates that the court shall try everything that has been

1065. Chapter 2 s. 3 Penal Code.

1066. *See also* Government Official Report SOU 2002:98, 'Internationella brott och svensk jurisdiktion'.

1067. Council Framework Decision of 13 Jun. 2002 on the European arrest warrant and the surrender procedures between Member States (2002/584/JHA), amended by Council Framework Decision 2009/299/JHA of 26 Feb. 2009 amending Framework Decisions 2002/584/JHA, 2005/214/JHA, 2006/783/JHA, 2008/909/JHA and 2008/947/JHA.

1068. For more information on the cooperation of these agencies *see* www.europol.europa.eu/ and www.eurojust.europa.eu.

presented in the case before it and then decide what has been proven, a procedural principle of free trial of evidence in the sense that any evidence may be presented and the court given wide latitude in evaluating the evidence presented.[1069] Taking this principle into the digital environment, electronic evidence may consist of any kind of information derived from digital technology environments, as well as information processed and presented by means of electronic equipment.[1070]

Aggregated presentations covering all relevant evidence – seized computers, individual files, log files from service providers, results from covert account monitoring, etc. – are frequently made by the prosecution, in order to make technically complex operations judicially manageable. Indirect transcriptions are therefore the norm rather than an exception, when it comes to technical evidence. The possibility of introducing evidence through witnesses, such as the authorities or law enforcement agents that had access to the evidence, is frequently used.[1071]

1069. Naturally, there *are* certain limitations, cf. Chs 35 s. 14 and 36 s. 3 Code of Judicial Procedure.
1070. *See* Jonas Ekfeldt, *Om informationstekniskt bevis*, Stockholm 2016, and Stefan Kronkvist, *Brott och digitala bevis – En handledning*, 2nd edn (Stockholm: Norstedts Juridik, 2007), 15 et seq.
1071. *Ibid.*

Part VIII. Conclusions

475. Various areas of cyber law have been harmonized within the EU in recent years. Sweden has transposed Directives and Regulations in the fields of intellectual property law, data protection and telecommunications. Contract and procedural law have remained in the sovereignty of the national states, which may lead to minor legal differences in the various countries.

Though both the Swedish Contracts Act (*lag (1915:218) om avtal och andra rättshandlingar på förmögenhetsrättens område*) and the Swedish Code of Judicial Procedure (*rättegångsbalk (1942:740)*) are not specifically adapted to any technological development, the principles of freedom of contract and the non-existence of any exclusionary rules regarding evidence have opened up for a technology-neutral interpretation of the provisions. The Acts have proven to be flexible enough to allow electronic means in contracting and electronic messages as evidence in court.

In general, Swedish law is well prepared to deal with new developments in ICT to the extent that the laws are kept technology neutral. The tendency to amend legislation to suit specific technologies can, however, be noticed in a few areas, even within the fields that are harmonized within the EU, which has led to difficulties regarding interpretation of the existing law on a few occasions.

Selected Bibliography

Books

English

Carlson, Laura. *The Fundamentals of Swedish Law*. Lund: Studentlitteratur, 2019.

Seipel, Peter (ed.). *Law and Information Technology: Swedish Views (SOU 2002:112)*. Stockholm: IT Law Observatory, 2002.

Wahlgren, Peter (ed.). *IT Law*. Scandinavian Studies in Law, Vol. 47. Stockholm: Stockholm Institute for Scandinavian Law, 2004.

Wolk, Sanna (ed.). *Ownership of the Copyright in Works and the Patent Right in Inventions Created by Employees in Finland, Sweden, Germany, Austria, the United Kingdom, Estonia and Argentina, Gröna Serien, No. 120*. Stockholm: Institute of Intellectual Property Law and Marketing Law: Institutet för Immaterialrätt och Marknadsrätt (IFIM), 2002.

Swedish

Hultmark, Christina. *Elektronisk handel och avtalsrätt*. Stockholm: Norstedts Juridik, 1998.

Levin, Marianne & Åsa Hellstadius. *Lärobok i immaterialrätt*. 12th edn. Stockholm: Norstedts Juridik, 2019.

Kronqvist, Stefan. *Brott och digitala bevis: En handledning*. 3nd edn. Stockholm: Norstedts Juridik, 2013.

Lindberg, Agne, Johan Kahn & Björn Krouthén. *IT-avtal: Särskilt om outsourcing*. Stockholm: Norstedts Juridik, 2009.

Olsson, Henry & Jan Rosén. *Upphovsrättslagstiftningen: En kommentar*. 2nd edn. Stockholm: Norstedts Juridik, 2016.

Öman, Sören. *Dataskyddsförordningen (GDPR) m.m.: en kommentar*. Stockholm: Norstedts Juridik, 2019.

Ramberg, Jan & Christina Ramberg. *Allmän avtalsrätt*. 11th edn. Stockholm: Nordstedts Juridik, 2019.

Seipel, Peter. *Juridik och IT: Introduktion till Rättsinformatiken*. 8th edn. Stockholm: Nordstedts Juridik, 2004.

Storr, Pam & Christine Storr. *Medierätt: juridiska perspektiv på praktiska frågeställningar*. Stockholm: LGG Publishing, 2020.

Selected Bibliography

Articles

English

Chamberlain, Johanna, & Jane Reichel. 'The Swedish Understanding of Privacy as a Fundamental Right in a Comparative Perspective–Overview and Possibilities.' In *Comparative Perspectives on Privacy in an Internet Era*, Russell L. Weaver, Jane Reichel, Steven I. Friedland, Durham (eds), NC: Carolina Academic Press (2019): 85–112.

Edstrom, Jerker & Henrik Nillson. 'The Pirate Bay Verdict: Predictable, and Yet ... '. *European Intellectual Property Review* 31(9) (2009): 483–487.

Öman, Sören. 'Implementing Data Protection in Law: Scandinavian Studies in Law', Vol. 47 (IT Law). Stockholm: Stockholm Institute for Scandinavian Law, 2004.

Öman, Sören. 'Protection of Personal Data: But How?'. In *Law and Information Technology-Swedish Views (SOU 2002:112)*, Peter Seipel (ed.), Stockholm: IT Law Observatory (2002).

Ramberg, Christina Hultmark. 'The E-commerce Directive and Formation of Contract in a Comparative Perspective'. *European Law Review* 26(5) (2001): 429–450.

Wennerström, Erik. *EU-Legislation and Cybercrime: A Decade of European Legal Developments*. Scandinavian Studies in Law Vol. 47 (IT Law). Stockholm: Stockholm Institute for Scandinavian Law, 2004.

Wistam, Henrik & Therese Andersson. 'The Pirate Bay Trial'. *Computer and Telecommunications Law Review* 15(6) (2009): 129–130.

Swedish

Bengtsson, Henrik. 'Marknadsföring med hjälp av elektroniska meddelanden'. *Ny Juridik* 3 (2009): 35–51.

Bengtsson, Henrik. 'Svenska domännamnstvister: Praxis enligt den s.k. II-stiftelsens systems för alternativ tvistelösning'. *Nordiskt Immateriellt Rättskydd* 3 (2005): 256–277.

Bengtsson, Henrik & Emil Dicksved. 'Dataintrång'. *Ny Juridik* 4 (2009): 40–61.

Hübner, Johan. 'Analog tillämpning av lagen om handelsagentur på återförsäljare av datorprogram'. *Lov & Data* 93 (2008): 14–15.

Online Publications

English

Agency for Digital Government (DIGG). 'Compulsory e-invoicing in the public sector', www.digg.se/about-us/compulsory-e-invoicing-in-the-public-sector.

Swedish Data Protection Authority, 'The Credit Information Act', www.datainspektionen.se/other-lang/in-english/the-credit-information-act.

Swedish Data Protection Authority, 'The General Data Protection Regulation (GDPR)', www.datainspektionen.se/other-lang/in-english/the-general-data-protection-regulation-gdpr.

Swedish

All decisions and reports by the Swedish Data Protection Authority are available at www.datainspektionen.se.

All decisions and reports by the Swedish Post and Telecom Agency (PTS) are available at www.pts.se.

All Government Bills (Proposition), Government Official Reports (SOU) and Ministry Publications Series (Ds) can be searched by their number at www.regeringen.se.

Selected Bibliography

Index

The numbers here refer to paragraph numbers.

Index

Index

www.ingramcontent.com/pod-product-compliance
Lightning Source LLC
Chambersburg PA
CBHW071432230926
51846CB00001B/199